# Constitutional Structure
and Purposes

# Constitutional Structure and Purposes

## Critical Commentary

Michael Conant

Contributions in Legal Studies, Number 98

GREENWOOD PRESS
Westport, Connecticut • London

**Library of Congress Cataloging-in-Publication Data**

Conant, Michael.
   Constitutional structure and purposes : critical commentary / Michael Conant.
      p. cm.—(Contributions in legal studies, ISSN 0147–1074 ; no. 98)
   Includes bibliographical references and index.
   ISBN 0–313–31669–4 (alk. paper)
   1. United States. Supreme Court—Decision making.   2. Constitutional law—United
States.   3. Legal certainty.   I. Title.   II. Series

   KF8748.C56   2001
   347.73'26—dc21

                                                                    00–033123

British Library Cataloguing in Publication Data is available.



Library of Congress Catalog Card Number: 00–033123
ISBN: 0–313–31669–4
ISSN: 0147–1074

First published in 2001

Greenwood Press, 88 Post Road West, Westport, CT 06881
An imprint of Greenwood Publishing Group, Inc.
www.greenwood.com

Printed in the United States of America

The paper used in this book complies with the
Permanent Paper Standard issued by the National
Information Standards Organization (Z39.48–1984).

10 9 8 7 6 5 4 3 2 1

**Copyright Acknowledgment**

The author and publisher gratefully acknowledge permission to reprint from the following source:

Excerpts from Michael Conant, *The Constitution and the Economy: Objective Theory and Critical Commentary* (Norman: University of Oklahoma Press, 1991) are reprinted here with permission from University of Oklahoma Press.

# Contents

# Introduction

This study of constitutional structure and purposes is an epistemological critique of judicial reasoning. The central question is to what extent can opinions of the Supreme Court of the United States in constitutional controversies produce reliable knowledge of law. In other words, what is the level of uncertainty in constitutional law? There are at least two separate and distinct elements to the answer. First, the Supreme Court must have the power to correct errors in its past constitutional opinions by overruling them, because the people do not stand ready to amend the Constitution in order to correct judicial errors. But the second element is more significant and concerns the quality of reasoning in Court opinions. The common failure of the Court to write opinions based on the underlying principles that are incorporated in constitutional language and constitutional topology, the primary interrelations between the clauses, means the justices have essentially assumed great discretion in decision-making. Consequently, Alexander Bickel described a large group of Court opinions in the twentieth century as a "web of subjectivity."[1] Bickel quotes Justice Oliver Wendell Holmes's private notes, describing another impediment to principled constitutional opinions. Holmes described a 1914 case in which he was writing the majority opinion, and in order to keep a majority, he had to delete the principled reasoning that was in his draft of the opinion. Holmes said privately that he believed the other justices' reasons for insisting on the omissions were extralegal.[2]

The chapters here are complementary to my earlier volume, *The Constitution and the Economy: Objective Theory and Critical Commentary.*[3] The studies relate to the Commerce Clause and to the constitutional limitations, mainly the First and Fourteenth Amendments. Chapter 3, on racial caste systems, is an expanded and explanatory revision of the first half of the chapter on equal protection in my earlier volume. Chapters 4 and 5 comment on judicial interpretations of the Commerce Clause that were not covered in the earlier volume. Chapters 6 and 7 criticize Supreme Court opinions construing the First Amendment, a topic not covered in the earlier volume.

The thesis here is that the origin of the Constitution in the ratification by the people requires an interpretation based on original meanings of constitutional language. Textual exegesis may only require finding the plain meaning of language at the time of adoption. But most constitutional language may not have plain meanings. The total historical context of words and phrases may require substantial study of historical usages in English law to understand the eighteenth-century scope of the legal terms. Even common words of English, such as "commerce," had more than one meaning in 1787, so that interpretive decisions had to be made on which definition was correct in comprehensive fundamental law.

The originalist methodology, based on separation of governmental powers, is the method that most justices assert that they utilize.[4] This method rejects the view of some modern scholars and judges that the duty of the Supreme Court is to reinterpret constitutional language to fit modern times. The crucial issue is when does judicial expansion or contraction of a constitutional clause invade the amending power. Since judicial self-restraint is a political theory, some critics argue that constitutional language should be manipulated to meet a justice's personal view of modern basic law. The approach here is that such a view is based on a misunderstanding of the original great breadth and scope of constitutional language. The legislative powers in Article I, for example, are plenary powers unless expressly limited in the Constitution. The same breadth applies to the constitutional limitations. The Fourth Amendment protection against unreasonable searches thus applies to telephone lines going into one's house even though there were no telephones in 1791.

The critical studies here center on the failure of the Court to emphasize constitutional structure and purposes in an effort to reach principled decisions and opinions. Constitutional structure first requires treating the Constitution as a unified whole. The Committee on Stile at the constitutional convention was assigned the duty to create a consistent, integrated document. The substantive powers of Congress in Article I are clearly distinguished from the procedural allocations to the judiciary in Article III, so that no court should attempt to find substantive powers implied by Article III. The interrelated clauses relating the slave trade to the Commerce Clause and to eminent domain are treated in chapter 2 to show that while the Constitution recognized slavery, the commerce power was adequate for Congress to terminate all transactions in slaves after 1808.

Constitutional purposes is a concept completely different from the subjective intent of the framers and ratifiers, which is totally indeterminate. Constitutional purpose is concerned with determining the meaning of language by exploring the social problems and issues that led to the adoption of each clause. It asks what objective evidence is available to describe the total circumstances provoking the framers to adopt the particular language in each clause. In chapter 3, on racial segregation, the caste system of slavery and the postwar attempts of southern states to continue the caste system by enacting Black Codes are thus crucial in determining the meaning of the Equal Protection Clause of the Fourteenth Amendment. Chapter 4, on baseball and antitrust, illustrates the error of the extreme application of precedent to statutory reasoning and the necessity for Congress to overrule such judicial opinions. Chapter 5, on gun possession in or near schools, explains the scope of national power to regulate local actions in a federal system of delegated powers. The flag salute cases of chapter 6 demonstrate the relation of the Bill of Rights to state regulatory power and the importance of overruling to establish principled reasoning on the higher status of civil rights. In chapter 7, on the flag desecration cases, the first and foremost interest is why the first Congress chose the phrase "freedom of speech" in the First Amendment rather than "freedom of expression." This raises the issue of to what extent five members of the Court have valid constitutional power to convert the word "speech" to include physical acts.

The epistemic task of finding true knowledge in constitutional opinions is one of searching constitutional language, structure, and purposes for principles that are sustainable over time. This search must be made with constant recognition that the amending power is reserved to the people. In the complex, difficult constitutional case, a final resort to pragmatic reasoning should occur only if established constitutional principles are demonstrated to be in conflict and if no search for purposes shows that one of the principles should take a higher status than the other. Such a principled method requires the wholesale rejection of established constitutional concepts that have only mistaken judicial origin and no real constitutional foundation. As noted in chapter 1, substantive due process is the most prominent of these fallacious concepts.

The author is grateful for critical comments on the manuscript by professors Jesse Choper and William Muir and Judge William Fletcher of the United States Court of Appeals. All errors that remain must be assigned to the author. Word processing was ably completed by Joseph Chytry and Cynthia Lee.

## NOTES

1. Alexander M. Bickel, *The Supreme Court and the Idea of Progress* 45–100 (New York: Harper & Row, 1970).
2. *Id.* at 46–47, citing *Pipe Line Cases*, 234 U.S. 548 (1914).
3. (Norman: University of Oklahoma Press, 1991).
4. See the extended search for original meanings in historical materials by Chief Justice William Rehnquist in *Seminole Tribe of Florida v. Florida*, 517 U.S. 44 (1996), overruling, *Pennsylvania v. Union Gas Co.*, 491 U.S. 1 (1989).

# 1

# Constitutional Structure and Purposes: Epistemological Critique of Judicial Reasoning

The constitutional opinions of the Supreme Court of the United States are supposed to inform all lower courts and all interested citizens of the meaning of constitutional clauses as applied to the facts of contested cases. The epistemological issue is to what extent judges, lawyers and other careful readers can gain reliable knowledge of constitutional law from majority opinions of the Court. Epistemic indeterminacy treats the question of whether the law can be known.[1] Five-to-four opinions of the Court are the strongest example of unsettled law, and it can be argued that in constitutional cases there is no such thing as settled law because all such opinions may be overruled.[2] The likelihood of overruling increases when a new justice is appointed. Even unanimous opinions of the Court, as in the school segregation cases, may be reached by compromise and may not express the precise views of any of the justices on the scope or breadth of a constitutional clause.[3] Failure to overrule a previous inconsistent decision may leave the legal community in doubt about the meaning of an opinion with wide social impact.[4]

This chapter begins with a general review of the epistemological problems in law. The foundation requirement is a summary explanation of objective epistemology, the view that specialized knowledge in any field of learning is not subjective to the individual but is collective understanding. It becomes objective knowledge by publication so that it is subject to critique by other specialists in the field.[5] The epistemology of science is evolutionary in the sense that each generation builds on the tested and accepted findings of fact and methods of analysis of all previous generations.[6] Thus, we speak of the accumulation of objective knowledge as the very essence of scientific progress. As to any single step in the growth of knowledge, Karl Popper describes it as one of conjecture and criticism. He summarizes the schema in its simplest form as follows:[7]

$$P_1 \rightarrow TT \rightarrow EE \rightarrow P_2,$$

where $P_1$ is the problem to be solved; TT, the tentative theory or hypothesis, is the imaginative conjectural solution first reached; EE or error elimination is a severe critical examination of the conjecture based on evidence and comparative evolution of competing conjectures; and $P_2$ is either a solution or the new problem situation as it emerges from the first critical attempt to solve the original problem.

This study of the theory of knowledge underlying legal reasoning is concerned with the causes of uncertainty and consequent unpredictability in constitutional law. One objective is to show that the progress characteristic of the natural and physical sciences in the last 100 years could not occur in legal reasoning, because of its epistemic inadequacies. One finds in legal scholarship very little discussion and hence little consensus on the meaning of basic terms and primary relationships that is necessary for one generation of scholars to build on the published learning of previous generations.

Another impediment of scientific advance in the law is the fact that in the cases when academic studies of law are generally accepted by scholars, they may be ignored by some or all of the courts. In contrast, advances in the physical sciences, when tested and accepted by scientists, are generally adopted by engineers and put into practice. In the law, consensus among scholars is almost impossible to attain and acceptance by judges is problematic. Roscoe Pound, for example, one founder of sociological jurisprudence, demonstrated that legal rules and principles must be analyzed in their total social contexts.[8] Legal norms are not abstractions to be viewed in isolation but generalizations about social control of human behavior that must be viewed in social context. These advances in learning were largely ignored by the courts of the time.

Ernest Nagel summarizes the epistemic requirements for adequate explanations of phenomena in two stages.[9] The first is that in deductive explanation the premises must be true. If the premises are merely definitions, they must be generally accepted means of communication. In legal writings this requirement is often not met. Writers on legal theory have differing definitions of such fundamental concepts as legal positivism.[10]

An equally important difficulty is the fact that in legal writings and especially in appellate opinions, major premises are often assumed but not articulated. Justice Oliver Wendell Holmes pointed out that legal rules, whether common-law or statutory, are designed to carry out social policies that usually are unstated.[11] When an appellate court hears a difficult, novel controversy, the case is likely to present a conflict between legal principles that is in effect a conflict between social policies. Justice Holmes deplored the common failure of courts as follows:

> I think that the judges themselves have failed adequately to recognize their duty of weighing considerations of social advantage. The duty is inevitable, and the result of the often proclaimed judicial aversion to deal with such considerations is simply to leave the very ground and foundation inarticulate and often unconscious.[12]

A second epistemic requirement is that premises be compatible with established empirical facts and in addition be supported by evidence other than the observational data upon which the solution to the current problem is based. This is designed to exclude ad hoc premises, for which there is no evidence. In legal analysis, this would require scholars and appellate courts to discuss the factors upon which legal principles are founded. For example, the legal principle that public grants of monopoly, such as patents, trademarks, copyrights, and utility franchises shall be strictly construed is based on the principle of the Anglo-American common law that favors market competition over grants of monopoly.[13] The antitrust statutes reinforce this legal principle.[14] In decisions of cases concerning governmental grants of monopoly, statement of principle alone leaves it without scientific foundation. Citation of economic treatises that demonstrate that competition results in more efficient allocation of resources and a distribution of income more closely responsive to productivity would meet the epistemic requirement of separate evidence to support the premises adopted for decision.

The Supreme Court opinion in *Sony Corp. of America v. Universal City Studios, Inc.*[15] illustrates the issue. Universal and other owners of copyrights of filmed television programs that were telecast on the public airwaves sued Sony and other manufacturers of videotape recorders for contributory infringement of copyrights. Plaintiffs alleged that purchasers of videotape recorders had used them to record for personal use at a later time copyrighted films that had been exhibited on commercially sponsored television. The Supreme Court upheld a district court finding of fact that there was not substantial evidence that the practice impaired the commercial value of the copyrights. Consequently, sale of the videotape recorders to members of the general public who did not use them commercially did not constitute contributory infringement. The contest centered on interpretation of the ambiguous national copyright statute, which did not expressly deal with the issue of video recording for home use. The Court correctly resorted to the general principle that the limited monopoly granted to copyright holders was a secondary consideration. The primary social purpose of conferring the monopoly was compensation to stimulate artistic creativity for the public good. The express exemption in the copyright act for "fair use" was held to extend to home video recording because the consumer was merely shifting time at which he or she would view the telecast. Since the videotape recorders were capable of significant noninfringing uses, the manufacture and sale of the machines was not contributory infringement.

From an epistemological point of view, given the strong legal presumption in favor of trial court findings of fact, the question is how the four dissenting justices could reject the majority reasoning and vote to resolve statutory ambiguity in favor of extension of governmental grants of monopoly.[16]

## NATURE OF DEFINITIONS: MINIMIZING AMBIGUITY

Definitions are not right or wrong. They are more useful, less useful, or useless. They are the primary explanations of the signs by which human beings communicate.[17] In any field of endeavor in which over time the specialists have created a technical vocabulary, the need for rigor and general consensus in definitions is the ideal objective, which in practice cannot be reached. While total efficiency in communication is an unattainable ideal, articulation of definitions in order to reassure other parties in negotiations that there is agreement on meanings is useful. In law, the scope of key definitions may determine the scope or breadth of the contested legal rules, either restricting or enlarging the application of the law to actual cases.

A first step in the effort to reduce ambiguity in definitions is to recognize that technical meanings of legal terms will likely have narrower meanings than the same terms have in ordinary English. Trespass to person or property as a technical term of the law with definable elements is not equivalent trespass in other English usages. The technical terms are elements of a system of legal classification. The scope of the law, like medicine or the other sciences, is so extensive that ideas must be divided into classes before specialists can begin to communicate. For example, title to property is one field of law, but trespass to property is one of the torts, another field of the law. A particular field of law may be thought of as comparable to a *genus* and a particular legal rule as a *species*. It is important not to define any field of law in terms of another. A bailment cannot be defined as a type of contract because some types of bailments have no consideration, a requirement for a contract.

The law student must be warned that language changes over time, though usually quite slowly. In an adversary legal system, however, lawyers may engage in word magic, redefining legal terms and phrases so that they lead to the creation of legal rules that support the lawyer's side of the litigation. The opponent must be alert to point out that redefining legal concepts in order to expand or contract the scope of legal rules is a mere device and not sound legal argument.

In constitutional law, one must be especially alert about changing definitions over time. The national Constitution was written in eighteenth-century English. The appropriate definitions of constitutional terms are found in eighteenth-century dictionaries and documents that illustrated those terms.[18] Since the amending power is strictly defined in Article V, the changing use of the language should not be allowed to amend the constitution. An example to be explained later is the word "process" in the Fifth Amendment. There is overwhelming evidence that "process" in 1791 was a synonym for "procedure." Consequently, the Due Process Clause is solely a procedural immunity, "procedural due process" is redundant, and there is no constitutional basis for the oxymoron "substantive due process."[19]

## DEFINING LAW AND LEGAL PROCESS

Law and the legal process are two coordinate and complementary terms. It is most useful to define law as would a social scientist standing on the margin of society and observing law as one subset of the social norms. It is most useful to define the legal process, the structure and functioning of legal institutions and personnel, in technical legal terms.[20] The elements of the legal process, court systems, judges, lawyers, and the methods of legal reasoning can be defined only by legal specialists.

Social control and its subset law can only be defined in terms of norms. A norm is a usual behavior pattern in a society to which the great majority of persons both adhere and consider the correct way to behave.[21] The necessary physical acts of eating, sleeping, and walking are not norms, but eating most cooked foods in Western societies with a knife and fork or spoon is a norm.

Social control is defined as all the methods a society uses to guide and enforce conformity to its norms.[22] Social scientists classify social control as either informal or formal. Informal social controls are those that do not require formal institutions for enforcement. In both primitive (nonliterate) societies and modern societies, symbols, ceremonies, rites, and rituals cause conformity to some norms. Other common informal social controls include public opinion, discharge from employment, ostracism by former friends, and similar sanctions. Formal social controls, such as religion and law, are those that use organized institutions for enforcement.

Law is defined as those norms that, if necessary, will be enforced by the physical force of organized society.[23] In modern societies, the organized society is government. Consequently, it is most useful to define law as the aggregate of those norms that, if necessary, will be enforced by the physical force of government.[24] Relatively few of the norms of modern society are considered important enough to be selected for legal enforcement. Constitutional law primarily concerns the structure of government and the civil rights of individuals against government. It is basic and superior law because it is ratified by the people. Most law is either derived from customary norms that the courts adopt as common law or is statutory law passed by elected legislatures.

The social scientist's positive, descriptive definition of law as norms that will be enforced by the government can easily be reconciled with Justice Holmes' statement of a practicing lawyer's definition of law. Holmes wrote that law is nothing more pretentious than "prophecies of what the courts will do in fact."[25] This pragmatic definition is based on the fact that the exact scope or breadth of legal rules to be applied to a novel set of facts is unknown. A lawyer counseling a client about his novel plan of behavior can only predict the marginal expansion or contraction of the existing rules that may or may not be applied by a judge to his case. Since the lawyer recognizes the uncertainties of the fuzzy borders of legal rules, he can only predict the scope of the enforceable norms that government, through its courts and sheriffs, will enforce.

The knowledge that the ultimate coercion of law is physical force causes most persons to conform to law, and force by government agents becomes unnecessary. Only a small percentage of persons violate the criminal law and are arrested. Losing defendants in civil actions almost always pay the damages ordered by the court rather than wait for a sheriff to arrive and seize their property. In any society without corruption in government, law is strictly enforced, which fosters a cultural attitude of obedience to law. When automatic obedience to law by government officials and the public is a prominent cultural trait, there exists a social equilibrium where long-term investment in plant and equipment is secure and economic development takes place. The long-run effect is continuously rising per capita real income.

It is essential to understand that law is a descriptive term of norms enforced by government in power.[26] There can be both good law and bad law as any person in any nation evaluates elements of the operating legal system. Where there is representative government, the essentials of legal coercion are general social acceptance of the application of physical power, in threat or in fact, by an authorized agent of government, for a known legal cause, using known legal methods, and at a time established by law. In contrast, a totalitarian government may adopt the most oppressive legal norms, including slavery, torture, and even genocide. Slavery in the Confederate States and the Holocaust in Germany were carried on pursuant to statutory rules.

The legal process is the complementary part of a legal system to the legal norms. Legal process is defined as the structure and functioning of legal institutions. It includes the courts, judges, and lawyers and all their functions. The laws creating courts, laws for appointment or election of judges, and the entire law of procedure are part of the legal process. While the definition of law is retrospective as it describes existing legal norms and their history, the legal process is currently operative and describes how law courts function to hear and decide controversies. This includes all the reporting and publishing of court opinions and all the techniques of legal reasoning of judges in applying law to the facts of controversies and in deciding appeals.

## LEGAL RULES AND PRINCIPLES

It is useful to divide legal norms into two classes, legal rules and legal principles. In some areas of law the difference between specific rules and broader principles may be only a matter of degree. But in others, such as the maxims of equity and canons of documentary construction, principles seem to be a distinct type of norm.

Legal rules are the narrower norms and are defined as norms that create enforceable right-duty relationships. Legal rights are expectations that another person or persons will behave in a certain way, which expectation the law will enforce.[27] Legal duties are the corollaries of legal rights and are the expectation that one must behave in a certain way, which expectation the law will enforce. Thus, the definition of right-duty relationships enforceable in the courts is derived from the definition of law. Right-duty relationships in tort arise when one party causes injury to another's person, property, reputation, or business relations. Right-duty relationships arise in contract when parties make promises that fulfill the technical requisites for enforceable contract. In property law, the owner has a right of possession and use against all other persons.

Legal principles are broad, general standards of behavior such as those in constitutions and statutes that create the structure of government and of legislative powers.[28] Another key group of principles are found in judicial opinions that define basic fairness in legal method. Principles are usually too general in nature to create enforceable right-duty relationships. Thus the constitutional separation of government into legislative, executive, and judicial branches is a principle that is executed by a large number of statutory rules. The duty of judges to follow established legal principles and the rules that enforce them can be traced ultimately to the ratification of the Constitution and its amendments by the people of the nation.

Principles of fairness in legal method may originate over time by induction from a diverse set of legal rules. Once established as a principle of law, it takes a higher status than legal rules. In a dynamic legal system such as the common law, newly developed legal rules must be tested against and conform to the legal principles applicable to the controversy. In most litigation, issues of legal principles may not arise. If there is one legal principle found by the judge to be applicable to a given controversy, it will likely determine the outcome. But the more difficult cases on appeal present conflicts between applicable principles and require judges to weigh the social importance of the principles in deciding which will prevail.

*Riggs v. Palmer*[29] is one of the most noted cases that presented conflicting legal principles. At a time when there was no statute in New York regulating the topic, the beneficiary in a will murdered his grandfather, the testator of the will who named him as beneficiary. The New York statute regulating wills contained legal rules requiring that a valid will must be given full effect, which would give the legacy to the murderer. This legal rule is exemplary of the general principle, based on constitutional allocations of legislative and judicial power, that statutes must be given full application to the facts of controversies within the scope of the statutory language. But the court noted the conflicting principle of the legal system: "No one shall be permitted to profit by his own wrong, or to take advantage of his own wrong, or to found any claim upon his own iniquity, or to acquire property by his own crime."[30] The court gave controlling weight to the second principle and denied recovery by the murderer.

Judge Richard A. Posner notes that means-end rationality would support the

*Riggs* decision.[31] Any rational person who had considered the possibility of being murdered by his legatee would have disinherited the legatee. The court's adoption of the second principle effectuates what would have been rational behavior of an informed testator. The decision corrects for the asymmetric information of the parties at the time the legatee decided to murder the testator. Another key aspect of the *Riggs* case illustrates the epistemic weakness of the law. Two justices dissented in the case.

The maxims of the law are a set of principles created to maximize justice in the Anglo-American legal system. While most of the maxims were generalizations created by courts of equity, it is clear these principles were also adopted by common-law courts in order to mitigate the injustices of formalistic application of legal rules. Some three hundred legal maxims were compiled by Sir Francis Bacon at the beginning of the seventeenth century, but only twenty-five survived to be published in 1630, after his death.[32]

Bacon explained that maxims are not binding legal rules. A maxim "points at the law but does not settle it."[33] By inductive reasoning, these generalizations are made by inference from any number of legal rules found in past cases or statutes in different areas of the law. Bacon asserts that uncertainty of law, the principal and most just challenge to the English legal system, would be somewhat more settled and corrected by judicial application of maxims.[34] The function of maxims in helping to decide doubtful cases, reinforcing legal argument, and correcting unprofitable subtleties and vulgar errors would in some measure change the very nature and complexion of the whole law.[35] Citing a great civilian, Bacon labels maxims *legum leges*, "laws of laws."[36]

Herbert Broom cites a key legal maxim that is founded on the relation of the citizen to the state. *Salus Populi est suprema Lex* indicates that public welfare is the highest law.[37] Defense of the nation or fighting urban fires may require private rights be sacrificed for the public good. Issues relating to taxation and regulation are usually resolved based on presumptions favoring public welfare.

Another group of maxims are labeled fundamental legal principles. The first is that there is no wrong without a remedy.[38] If a person can persuade a court that he or she has a legal right, then anyone who has invaded that right has committed a legal wrong. The court must award the injured party a remedy. This maxim led to the creation of the legal proceeding called an action on the case. As social and technological environments change, new wrongs are recognized and new causes of action are created, for which courts create remedies.

Broom has collected some hundreds of legal maxims in his treatise. Classic opinions containing major dilemmas of justice, such as *Riggs v. Palmer*, could not present ample justification without resort to legal maxims. Justice Earl in *Riggs* reminds us that Aristotle recorded the maxim requiring equitable construction of statutes. *Aequitas est correctio legis generaliter latae, qua parte deficit* (Equity is the correction for law that is stated in general terms and for that reason is considered, in part, deficient).[39] *Riggs* was written in the nineteenth century. It is questionable whether law students today receive adequate education about legal maxims to remember to use them when, as lawyers, they are writing appellate briefs.

The canons of documentary construction are another large set of legal principles. They are most often met as the canons of statutory construction.[40] But these principles apply to the interpretation of all written documents. Some of the earliest examples relate to wills and contracts.[41] In the United States, the canons are of special significance in constitutional interpretation.

As principles, the canons of construction are generalized propositions of normative behavior, tools that are available for judges to resolve interpretive issues. Each canon gives judges the benefit of knowledge of how similar issues were decided by prior judges. But since they are tools, any single canon of construction may be accepted and used or rejected by the judge or appeal justices deciding an interpretive issue in any particular case. A judge may find that the application of a canon in a past case with facts very similar to his current case was in conflict with the obvious meaning of the statute, and he will reject its application to the current case.

One of the most difficult issues in using canons of construction is that their level of generality means that some of the canons will state exceptions to other more general ones. Many scholars note the famous article of Karl Llewellyn in which he sets up columns of canons next to those which appear contrary.[42] In this review of some of those canons, it will be shown that in most cases Llewellyn has merely listed broad canons and their necessary exceptions under special factual circumstances. This illustrates again the functional nature of canons of construction as tools whose usefulness must be a matter of judicial judgment in each specific factual instance.

In order to illustrate the argument that most canons have special exceptions rather than contradictory opposing canons, I shall present a few of those posed by Llewellyn with their "contrary" stated. Statutes in derogation of the common law will be strictly construed, except that remedial statutes will be liberally construed.[43] Statutes affirming a common-law rule are to be construed in accordance with the common law, but a statute whose language is inconsistent with the common law and is designed to replace common law acts to supercede it.[44] Statutes *in pari materia* must be construed together except when the legislative language indicates a design to depart from the general purposes of previous enactments.[45] Definitions and rules of construction contained in an interpretation clause are part of the law and binding, but they will not be extended beyond their necessary import.[46] If language is plain and unambiguous, it must be given effect, but not when this would lead to absurd or mischievous consequences.[47]

Constitutions are another example where many of the key clauses are stated as general principles.[48] But, unlike maxims and canons of construction, the principles enunciated in a written constitution are binding law on the judiciary. Those clauses of a constitution that create the basic structure of government are clearly general principles, but most require legislative action to become law. The Constitution of the United States vests the legislative power in the Congress, but this does not preclude the executive from issuing secondary rules that explain the detailed application of a set of statutes.[49] Such rules, as for example those issued by the Internal Revenue Service, are subject to ultimate test in the judiciary to determine that they do conform to the controlling statute.

The enunciation of specific legislative powers of Congress in Article I, Section 8, of the Constitution is clearly a statement of principles. If the national government was to function, these powers had to be construed as plenary powers and their application liberally construed. The necessary-and-proper clause was added to Section 8 to insure broad construction.[50] Subject to express limitations in the Constitution, enumerated powers such as the war power, the taxing power, and the commerce power were primary essentials to a functioning government. The eighteenth-century canon of documentary interpretation that treated preambles as directory elements of documents reinforced this view.[51] A constitution that would "insure domestic Tranquility, provide for the common defense, and promote the general Welfare" had to be one whose enumerated powers were construed as broad principles.

The constitutional limitations guaranteeing the civil rights of persons against government are also general principles. Thus the provisions of the Fifth and Fourteenth Amendments and many state constitutions that "no person shall be deprived of life, liberty or property without due process of law" is a generalized procedural protection whose origins can be traced in part to Magna Carta.[52] In the Bill of Rights, this very general principle is partially redundant to the specific procedural protections in amendments four through eight. The first Congress clearly wished to specify these in detail in case there were any gaps or ambiguities in the received protections of the English constitution. The full and fair hearing before impartial judges and juries that constitutes the due procedure of the law applies to both criminal and civil actions. This concept of required or appropriate procedure would apply both to rules of procedure adopted by courts and to later procedure statutes enacted by legislatures.

A key canon of interpretation is *noscitur a sociis*, the meaning of a doubtful word may be ascertained by reference to the meaning of words associated with it.[53] The coupling of words together shows that they are to be understood in the same sense.[54] Thus, the meaning of a word in a constitution or statute must be ascertained by reference to the context and by considering whether the word in question and the surrounding words are in fact referable to the same subject matter. This rule is reinforced by an explanatory canon, *nemo enim aliquam partem recte intelligere possit antequam totum iterum atque iterum perlegerit.*[55] The sense and meaning of the law can be collected only by comparing one part with another and by viewing all parts together as one whole, and not one part only by itself.

Justice Joseph Story's famous chapter on Rules of Interpretation[56] adopts these principles of phrase structure and context as he found them in the main writing on interpretation available to the framers of the Constitution, that of Thomas Rutherforth.[57] As to the context of the constitutional language, Story noted, "The antecedent situations of the country and its institutions, the existence and operations of the State governments, the powers and operations of the confederation, in short, all the circumstances which had a tendency to produce or obstruct its formation and ratification, deserve a careful attention."[58] He concluded that "the safest rule of interpretation after all will be found to be to look to the nature and objects of the particular powers, duties, and rights, with all the lights and aids of contemporary history, and to give to the words of each just such operation and force, consistent with their legitimate meaning, as many fairly secure and attain the ends proposed."[59]

As noted, what many commentators have called the most egregious violation of the canons of documentary interpretation of the Constitution took place in the series of Supreme Court opinions adopting substantive due process.[60] The prohibitions of the Fifth and Fourteenth Amendments against depriving a person of life, liberty, or property without due process of law must be read as an integrated whole. Once the word "process" is shown to be a synonym for "procedure," no substantive regulation can be valid. Life, liberty, and property are the list of elements whose deprivation can legally occur only after the full hearing and fair procedure that the courts rule is due process.[61]

The most offensive distortion of the Due Process Clause was the Supreme Court's lifting the word "liberty" from the clause and its unwarranted substantive creation of liberty of contract.[62] Charles Shattuck's famous article of 1891 had reminded the legal community that the word "liberty" in the Due Process Clause had only one meaning in the state constitutions from which the First Congress borrowed it. That was solely a criminal law concept, "freedom from physical restraint of the person."[63] Nonetheless, in 1905 the Court majority essentially usurped the amending power by a vote of 5 to 4 and, in spite of the strong dissent of Justice Holmes, gave foundational support to constitutional "liberty of contract" in *Lochner v. New York.*[64] In the field of labor relations, *Lochner* and subsequent opinions wrote laissez-faire economics into the Constitution.[65]

## DISSENTING OPINIONS AS EPISTEMIC DEFICIENCIES

The separation of governmental powers in the Constitution was designed to create two political branches, the legislature and the executive. Public pressure for change in law was to center in these two political branches. The judiciary, an appointed elite not responsible to the voters, was to be a different type of governmental institution, a nonpolitical branch designed to interpret law as it heard and settled disputes. But there was significant legal fiction about the high level of certainty in law that enabled citizens to plan their behavior in order to conform to established law. While large parts of the common law and statutory law are specific enough for reasonable reliance by the public, the general principles of constitutions are less determinate. The few constitutional controversies that are granted certiorari by the Supreme Court are novel cases where the application of general principles must be defined and delimited. In such cases, one is likely to find a high level of dissenting opinions. Consequently, the Court, when rendering multiple opinions in constitutional cases, does not appear to the public to be an impartial judicial institution. This appointed body seems to have political divisions as it meets highly contested public-law issues.[66] The media labels for justices such as William Brennan as liberals and for justices such as Antonin Scalia as conservatives foster the view that the Court in key cases closely resembles a political institution. One of the most notable opinions of the last fifty years was *Roe v. Wade,*[67] which took the issue of abortion out of the political arena of the state legislatures and into the judiciary. Some groups who opposed the decision picketed in front of the Supreme Court building when later abortion cases were heard, acting as if they could influence what they felt was a political decision.

The background to the American views on dissenting opinions was the British practice of appeals courts delivering seriatim opinions. But the context of this practice was that, under the system of parliamentary supremacy, the highest appeals courts, the House of Lords and the Privy Council, were part of the legislature.[68] Since the judiciary was not regarded as a distinct department of government, no one considered an institutional need for judicial consensus. During the first ten years of the U.S. Supreme Court, the justices followed the English practice in the lower appellate courts of King's Bench and issued seriatim opinions.[69]

When John Marshall became Chief Justice in 1801, he adopted the radically changed method of a single opinion for the majority of the Court.[70] In the first case that was decided after he became Chief Justice, the report began "Marshall, C. J., delivered the opinion of the Court."[71] Thus Marshall brought to the Court a view of the judiciary under separated powers as a distinct institution whose position and influences in the nation depended on consensus of the justices. During his first four years as Chief Justice, Marshall delivered all but two of the twenty-six opinions of the Court. In Marshall's absence, the two opinions were read by the senior justice present.[72] Both Marshall and Story were so concerned to present to the public the consensus of the Court as an institution that, when in the minority, they refrained from published dissent and submitted in silence to the judgment of the Court.[73] And Justice William Johnson wrote in 1822 that Chief Justice Marshall in some instances delivered opinions of the Court "even when contrary to his own Judgement and Vote."[74]

Marshall's pressures for consensus on the Court displeased President Thomas Jefferson, who felt the national character of the Chief Justice's opinions took power from state governments.[75] The Jefferson appointees to the Court, beginning with Justice Johnson, did dissent when they felt they could not follow Marshall's leadership.[76] But Marshall established a tradition, and the method of the opinion of the Court written by one justice became standard. This is a majority opinion in which justices writing concurring opinions may or may not join. Marshall himself filed fewer than ten dissents in thirty-four years on the Court, and only one was in a constitutional case. In *Ogden v. Saunders,*[77] the Court upheld prospective state bankruptcy laws by a vote of 4 to 3 in spite of the exclusive grant in the Constitution delegating bankruptcy powers to Congress. This offense to the original language of the Constitution provoked Marshall to deviate from his usual silence and explain his dissent.

Judge Learned Hand commented on how hard it was for the Supreme Court to achieve unanimity about the borders of the legislative power delegated to Congress in the Constitution. "On such issues experience has over and over again shown the difficulty of securing unanimity. This is disastrous because disunity cancels the impact of monolithic solidarity on which authority of a bench of judges so largely depends."[78] Judge Hand does not cite cases, but one can hypothesize that one key issue of his times about which he may have been concerned was the Commerce Clause. The erroneous 5-to-4 decision in *Hammer v. Dagenhart*[79] was not followed in the 5-to-4 decision in *National Labor Relations Board v. Jones & Laughlin Steel Corp.*[80] and was subsequently overruled in the unanimous decision in *United States v. Darby.*[81] *Hammer v. Dagenhart* was a prime example of the majority's failure to analyze the issues in terms of original constitutional structure and purposes. Structural analysis demonstrates that the language in Article I, Section 8, was designed to delegate to Congress a set of plenary powers so that the nation could be governed successfully.[82] The purpose of the Commerce Clause was to give Congress a plenary power to regulate transactions, both domestic and foreign. *United States v. Darby* was clearly correct interpretation based on an originalist analysis of constitutional language and its context.

The extent to which dissenting opinions on the Supreme Court have increased is in contest. Collective data on all types of cases before the Court show that before 1940 both dissents and concurrences in most years occurred in less than 20 percent of the cases.[83] Starting with the appointment of Chief Justice Harlan Fiske Stone in 1941, the cases with dissents rose to 80 percent and have mostly stayed over 80 percent. One study concludes that the new policy of permitting or even encouraging the free expression of views by Chief Justice Stone led to the sharp rise of dissents and concurrences that has continued to this day.[84] This is highly unlikely. As to constitutional cases, it is more likely that the proportion of cases concerning civil liberties in which certiorari has been granted is a primary factor provoking dissent. As the caseload in terms of numbers of petitions for certiorari has increased, the percentage of such petitions granting full hearing has had to drop. Only the most difficult cases of constitutional and statutory interpretation are argued and decided.

Judge Frank Easterbrook did a detailed study of separate and dissenting opinions and concluded that in the forty years since 1943 the level of actual disagreement on the Court was stable.[85] While 80 percent of the constitutional opinions in 1933 were unanimous, in the postwar years of his sample about 25 to 30 percent of constitutional opinions were unanimous. When cases with one dissent are added to the unanimous total, the figure is fairly stable at 30 to 40 percent. He suggests that in constitutional cases the broad general language plus the philosophical differences of justices account for the higher level of dissent than in statutory cases.[86] The philosophical differences of justices can be of several kinds. One is whether the Court is under a duty to search for the original meaning of constitutional language or may interpret the clauses in terms of changed modern language. Another is that each of the justices may draw on his or her philosophical view on the extent to which government in any particular situation should regulate the behavior of citizens. In cases concerning freedom of speech under the First Amendment, as explained in chapter 7, justices adhering to the original meaning of language would not convert the word "speech" to the word "expression" in order to protect expressive physical acts such as flag burning. Other justices, with a philosophical view to expand the First Amendment, would convert some physical acts into "symbolic speech" and vote to protect such behavior.

Dissenting justices in constitutional cases are not bound to follow the rejected majority opinion in later similar cases.[87] This derives from the fact that the Supreme Court is not bound by *stare decisis* when making a constitutional interpretation. The implications of this canon of interpretation have led to much confusion among commentators. They are well aware that only the Constitution was ratified by the people and that no earlier Supreme Court opinion was so ratified. And they are aware that the extreme difficulties of amendment means that the Court must be free to correct its past errors in constitutional cases by overruling them. Yet many commentators and some justices speak of a limited form of *stare decisis* in constitutional cases. They use the term "precedent" not as a binding past judicial ruling, as it is used in the common law and as applied to statutory interpretation. Rather, they use constitutional precedent as binding only on lower courts but merely as a synonym for a past similar case when referring to the Supreme Court.

The confusion of Supreme Court justices over the weight to be given past constitutional opinions of the Court derives from a conflict between two philosophically conservative policies. The first and clearly correct policy is that justices, being under oath to treat only the Constitution as superior law, should adhere to their dissenting views in later similar cases unless convinced that the first dissent was error.[88] The second, incorrect policy, violating their oath to treat only the Constitution as superior law, is to adopt the common law reasoning of *stare decisis* and abandon their prior dissent in later similar cases, thus joining later majority opinions that they consider erroneous.

One of the most strikingly unfortunate failures to adhere to a prior well-reasoned dissent in later similar cases was that of Justice Potter Stewart in *Roe v. Wade*.[89] In the earlier case of *Griswold v. Connecticut*,[90] the majority held that a disused state statute making it a crime to use artificial birth control was unconstitutional. The Court created a constitutional civil right of privacy. While the Court could not find privacy in the Constitution, it held that "penumbras formed by emanations" from the First, Third, Fourth, Fifth, and Ninth Amendments resulted in a general guarantee of privacy. Justice Stewart dissented and joined in a longer dissent of Justice Hugo L. Black, criticizing this as a revival of the totally discredited doctrine of substantive due process.[91]

In *Roe*, the majority invalidated a Texas law making it a crime to secure an abortion and expressly revived substantive due process as it extended the constitutional right to privacy. Justice Stewart surprised most commentators when he abandoned his strong dissent in *Griswold* and concurred in the Court's decision, stating:

> [I]t was clear to me then, and it is equally clear to me now, that the Griswold deci-
> sion can be rationally understood only as a holding that the Connecticut statute
> substantively invaded the "liberty" that is protected by the Due Process Clause of
> the Fourteenth Amendment. As so understood Griswold stands as one in a long line
> of pre-Skrupa cases decided under the doctrine of substantive due process, and I
> now accept it as such.[92]

Justice Stewart agreed to follow what he considered erroneous constitutional law because the most recent precedent was contrary to his considered views. He did not repudiate his *Griswold* dissent when he adopted *stare decisis* as his governing method. Constitutional supremacy should have provoked him to join the *Roe* dissents of Justice Byron White and William Rehnquist, as the commentators demonstrated.[93] Instead, he elected to follow *stare decisis* and joined later cases where the Court applied substantive due process.[94]

It has been demonstrated that the epistemic reliability of constitutional law is low, which is another way of stating the high uncertainty level in this area of law. It can be argued that concurring and dissenting opinions may be a cause of uncertainty to counsel attempting to advise a client on the scope of a given clause. On the other hand, it is uncertainty about the scope of clauses that fosters dissent by justices on appeals courts. As has been noted, the prime example is the oxymoron of substantive due process, which is undefinable because the key element was the unwarranted lifting of the word "liberty" from a procedural clause and the judicial expansion of it to a substantive protection. Out of this conception, the Court created the civil right of privacy. A recent example is *Bowers v. Hardwick*,[95] in which the Supreme Court majority held that the Constitution does not forbid a state to make sodomy between consenting homosexual adults a crime. The dissenting opinion centered on the scope of the right of privacy as found in *Roe v. Wade*[96] and subsequent cases. Since the majority opinion had not attacked the underlying fallacy of the civil right to privacy, the dissenters were not burdened to defend the jurisprudence of substantive due process.[97]

The thesis here is that if courts will give the greatest weight to briefs and arguments that center on the structure and purposes of the clause in contest in a constitutional case, it will greatly reduce the level of uncertainty in constitutional law. If, as in *Bowers*, the majority and the dissenters on the Court base their arguments on precedents rather than on the meaning of the language in the Constitution, they are likely to perpetuate error. This was the teaching of Justice Hugo Black, and the majority of the Court have yet to learn the lesson.

## STRUCTURE AND PURPOSES: ANALYSIS
## TO REDUCE UNCERTAINTY

The studies in this volume are based on the view that the original structure of the Constitution and the purposes for the adoption of each clause are often neglected elements in constitutional opinions. As key interacting elements of an originalist interpretation of the Constitution, structure and purpose explain the power allocations of constitutional language and resolve conflicts over the meaning of language. This method rejects all natural-law approaches to constitutional interpretation as being in direct conflict with the positive-law character of the document. Leading historians and legal scholars have concluded that the founding fathers rejected natural law as a judicial decision tool.[98] As early as 1798, Justice James Iredell objected to one of the few instances when another justice used natural law as one of the bases of decision.[99] This issue is significant because the Supreme Court majority in effect used natural-law method in *Griswold* and *Roe* to create a constitutional right of privacy based in substantive due process.

The structure of the Constitution concerns firstly the separation of powers between the legislative, executive, and judiciary in order to create a system of checks and balances.[100] The second issue is federalism, the division of governing power between the national and state governments.[101] In the national government, the Supreme Court may have to resolve head-on conflicts between two or more constitutional clauses, such as whether every international agreement entered by the president is limited by the Treaty Clause. Another set of conflicts arises between national legislative powers and one or more constitutional limitations, such as the effects of particular clauses of the Bill of Rights on congressional or executive power. Similarly, there are contests between state legislative powers and the constitutional limitations, such as the extent to which the Bill of Rights is a constraint on state action.

Professor Laurence Tribe points out that structural analysis is necessary to avoid basic error of constitutional topology. "To understand the Constitution as a legal text, it is essential to recognize the sort of text it is: a *constitutive* text that purports, in the name of the People of the United States of America, to bring into being a number of distinct but interrelated institutions and practices, at once legal and political, and to define the rules governing those institutions and practices."[102]

The Constitution must be read as a unified whole because the governing powers in the three branches are interrelated in many ways. In Article I, Section 8, for example, the Congress is delegated the exclusive power to regulate international commerce, but if the Congress does not legislate on some class of private transactions, the judiciary, under its maritime jurisdiction in Article III, may adopt principles from the international law merchant to decide cases.[103] Each of the first three articles that delegate governing power contains cross-references to the other two, demonstrating the interdependence in the governmental structure. In the "sweeping" last clause of Article I, Section 8, Congress may make all law necessary and proper for the functioning of all three branches of government. Consequently, Congress may set the salaries of executive and judicial officers and regulate the judiciary with codes of civil and criminal procedure. As Tribe notes, the integrated whole of the Constitution is greater than the sum of its parts. "To take the structure as well as the text seriously, one must attend to the 'topology' of the edifice—those fundamental features that define how its components interlock and that identify the basic geometry of their interconnected composition."[104]

Charles Black has presented many instances to illustrate that inference from constitutional structure is a neglected method of construing the document.[105] The Supreme Court has preferred textual exegesis of particular clauses as opposed to inferences from structure. The expected impact of federalism and the separation of governmental powers is not spelled out in the Constitution. Even without reference to the Supremacy Clause of Article VI, Clause 2, it is fundamental that state statutes may not impair the functioning of the national government. Professor Black's foremost example is *McCulloch v. Maryland.*[106] The first issue was whether Congress might validly exercise its fiscal powers to create a corporation, the Bank of the United States. Chief Justice Marshall did not rely on the necessary-and-proper clause. Rather, the federal structure of the Constitution meant that the delegated powers in Article I, Section 8, were plenary and that Congress had authority to select the best method of execution of each of them. The second issue was whether a state could tax the Bank, an agency of the national government. The negative conclusion was essentially structural. The national government, in the execution of one of its plenary powers, may not be impaired by a state tax law. National supremacy is derived from the very structure of the powers delegated to Congress and not from the meaning of any single power.

While Professor Black points to key cases where he views structural analysis as superior to textual exegesis, he notes that in most cases there is a close interaction of the two methods.[107] The Bill of Rights, for example, was adopted and ratified to protect all persons in the nation in their civil rights against government. As a group, these civil rights, most of which had been created by the English charters, statutes, or judiciary, were considered by the First Congress to be fundamental privileges and immunities of Americans as they were added to the structure of the Constitution.[108] Eighteenth-century rules of documentary interpretation would require the language of the Second through Eighth Amendments (except the appeals clause of the Seventh Amendment) be applied to both the national government and the states.[109] The Sixth Amendment, for example, begins, "In *All* criminal prosecutions, the accused shall enjoy the right to a speedy and public trial, by an impartial jury of the State and district wherein the crime shall have been committed,"[110] But in the eminent domain case of *Barron v. Baltimore,*[111] Chief Justice Marshall in obiter dictum indicated that none of the Bill of Rights applied to state governments. Later Supreme Court opinions, failing to analyze constitutional structure and purposes, have erroneously cited the dictum of Marshall in *Barron* as if it were the rule of the case and binding precedent on future justices of the Supreme Court.

The historical deprivation of all civil rights to slaves and the speeches of the Republican drafters of the Fourteenth Amendment demonstrate their objective to overrule *Barron v. Baltimore.*[112] But, after the ratification of the Fourteenth Amendment, the Supreme Court majority, by a severely contested 5-to-4 vote, ignored the history and held that the "privileges or immunities of citizens of the United

States" did not include the Bill of Rights.[113] In spite of the efforts of Justice Hugo Black and others, the Court has refused to overrule the earlier opinions denying that the Fourteenth Amendment incorporated the Bill of Rights as effective against state government.[114] Instead, the Court has engaged in selective incorporation of most elements, making them enforceable against the states.[115]

The second element to assist resolving possible constitutional ambiguity is the search for purpose or function.[116] Unlike intent, purpose or function is not a subjective concept. It is concerned with the social issues, problems, or conflicts that caused the adoption of the particular clause. Language without context usually lacks meaning, so that a valid generalization is that language must be read in the light of some assumed purpose.[117] "A judge or scholar should begin by expounding his view of the theory and purpose behind the constitutional provision in question."[118] Purpose derived from social behavior and the community need to change or limit behavior not only helps fill in the content of constitutional language beyond the literal meaning of the words, but purpose also helps determine the perspective from which meaning should be examined.[119]

National regulation under the Commerce Clause of state transactions is exemplary. The key contextual factor was the absence of a national commerce power in the Articles of Confederation, so that state barriers to interstate transactions by individuals or firms initiated a drift toward anarchy and commercial warfare between the states.[120] The primary purpose that led to the Constitutional Convention was to end state economic autarchy. Consequently, exclusive national control of interstate and international commerce was the first purpose of the Commerce Clause. The very generality of the clause indicates that the second purpose was to give Congress a plenary power to regulate all commerce in the nation.[121] But the context of the adoption of the Commerce Clause was governmental regulation of private transactions, so that there is a presumption against national regulation of transactions by state governments to carry out governmental functions.[122] But, when a state agency undertook proprietary services such as local transit, the Supreme Court, in a 5-to-4 decision, held its transactions subject to federal regulation.[123] Justice Harry Blackmun, for the majority, held that "traditional governmental functions" was not a workable standard. He rejected any such rule of state immunity as "unsound in principle and unworkable in practice."

The studies in this volume emphasize constitutional structure and purposes, an originalist interpretation based on total rejection of *stare decisis* in Supreme Court constitutional adjudication. This approach is based on the fact that only the Constitution and its amendments are controlling law derived from ratification by the people. The necessary power in the Court to correct its earlier errors in constitutional cases by overruling them means that there is no such thing as settled constitutional law. Thus, epistemic uncertainty is necessarily higher in constitutional law than in common law or statutory law. An originalist interpretation necessarily reduces uncertainty in constitutional law because differences of legal opinion center only on meaning of original language structure and purposes.[124] This is a fraction of the extreme uncertainty that exists if justices assert authority to adopt new social policies by changing constitutional meaning to keep up with social change.[125]

Constitutional interpretation based on the taxonomy of the document and the original meaning of language that is found by a search for purposes is a specialized type of reasoning.[126] Structural analysis requires a high level of skill in mastering the original functions of the constitutional clauses and the interconnections between them. Language analysis requires rejection of the favorite method of some scholars, a search for the intent of the framers even though the subjective thoughts of fifty-five men cannot be derived from evidence of the expressions of a few.[127] The Convention of 1787 was deliberately closed to all outsiders, and no official report was made of the speeches in order to bar the influence of those who spoke in later interpretations of the final document. This was later emphasized by James Madison: "As a guide in expounding and applying the provisions of the Constitution, the debates and incidental decisions of the Convention can have no authoritative character."[128] No records of the proceedings of the framers was sent to the ratifying conventions that turned the proposed Constitution into law. The ratifiers voted for the language in the text, not the unknown subjective thoughts of the framers. The methodology adopted here is an objective theory of interpretation, as explained by Justice Holmes.[129] In order to resolve ambiguities in the general clauses of the Constitution, Justice Story explained in his famous chapter on interpretation that one may have to search for purposes, the institutional context in which the language was used.[130]

An outstanding example of judicial conflict over constitutional meaning is *Marsh v. Chambers*.[131] The majority, by a vote of 6 to 3, upheld Nebraska law providing compensation for a chaplain to open each legislative session with a prayer and state payment for publishing the prayers in book form. Chambers, a member of the Nebraska Legislature, had brought this action to enjoin the prayers and compensation as a violation of the Establishment Clause[132] of the First Amendment as made effective against the states by the Fourteenth Amendment. The First Amendment was a limitation on Congress, and the Supreme Court did not hold its religion clauses to be incorporated in the Fourteenth Amendment and thereby effective against the states until 1940.[133] Consequently, until 1940 states were free to establish and subsidize religion if that was consistent with limitations in their state constitutions.[134]

Chief Justice Warren Burger centered his approval of the Nebraska law on the long history of paid chaplains in the Congress. In 1789 both houses of Congress elected chaplains, and on September 22 a statute was enacted providing a payment of $500 per year to each chaplain.[135] Three days later the Senate and the House passed the proposed Bill of Rights containing the Establishment Clause and sent it to the state legislatures to consider for ratification.[136] Burger disclaimed exclusive reliance on the long history of legislative prayer. But he concluded, "This unique history leads us to accept the interpretation of the First Amendment draftsmen who saw no real threat to the Establishment Clause arising from a practice of prayer similar to that now challenged."[137] This implies that busy members of

Congress, working to understand bills as complex as the proposed Judiciary Act,[138] gave reflective thought to interpreting the scope of the broad principle of the Establishment Clause and reached a conclusion that it did not negate paid chaplains. There was no recorded evidence that any member of Congress gave thought to possible conflict between the chaplain statute and the proposed amendment, which was two years away from ratification as primary law. Even if some congressmen had reflected that some conflict might be raised about the chaplain law after the Establishment Clause was ratified, they would very likely have concluded that this was an issue for the judiciary to decide in some future year.

Justice Brennan, in dissent, asserted that the majority were using their version of historical behavior in the First Congress to carve out an exception to the Establishment Clause.[139] He cited with approval the statutory elements for the effective separation of church and state, as required by the Establishment Clause, in the three-part explanation of the Court in earlier cases. "First, the statute [at issue] must have a secular legislative purpose; second, its principle or primary effect must be one that neither advances nor inhibits religions; finally, the statute must not foster an excessive government entanglement with religion."[140] Brennan then explained how all three of these standards were violated by the Nebraska chaplain statute.

Brennan then presented a functional analysis of the underlying purposes of the religion clauses in the First Amendment. Citing the adoption of the words of Jefferson in many Establishment Clause opinions of the Supreme Court, he stated that the principles of "separation" and "neutrality" were the foundation for four purposes.[141] The first purpose was to guarantee the individual right to conscience. The second was to keep the state from interfering in the essential autonomy of religious life, either by taking upon itself the decision of religious issues or by unduly involving itself in the supervision of religious institutions or officials. The third was to prevent the trivialization and degradation of religion by too close an attachment to organs of government. The fourth was to assure that essentially religious issues do not become the occasion for battle in the political arena. That this excellent analysis of constitutional purposes should appear only in the dissenting opinion is striking evidence of epistemic weakness in the law.

The studies in this volume demonstrate that an emphasis on the structure and purposes of the Constitution would have enabled the Supreme Court to avoid some of its greatest errors. The structure of the Constitution creates a set of rebuttable presumptions on the relationships between national legislative powers, state legislative powers, and the civil rights of persons known as the constitutional limitations. The presumptions of the priority of one group of constitutional clauses over another are abstract structural principles. They create a framework of relationships that point toward solutions of hard, complex cases unless some sound, reasoned social policies rebut the presumptions. One fundamental example, based on the fight for individual rights that led to the American Revolution and the Declaration of Independence, is that, when in conflict, constitution limitations are presumed to have a higher status than national or state legislative powers. Since the sole purpose of civil rights of persons is to limit legislative power and protect individual liberty, civil rights can be effective only if given the initial presumption of higher legal status.

A number of the studies in this volume begin with the structural presumption in favor of civil rights. In chapter 3, the original meaning of the Equal Protection Clause of the Fourteenth Amendment is shown to be a general antidiscrimination clause, designed to replace such a clause dropped from the proposed Civil Rights Act of 1866 because the Thirteenth Amendment was not a sufficient foundation for such a clause. Evidence that the purpose of this clause was to prevent the racism in the society from being extended into state regulatory statutes establishes that *Plessy v. Ferguson*[142] and all its progeny were error. Chapter 5 is concerned with the structural issue of federalism, whether mere possession of a gun near a school can be regulated by Congress as commerce. Similarly, chapter 6 begins as a structural analysis of the relation of state police power to the Bill of Rights in order to criticize the school flag salute cases. While most of the chapters treat constitutional structure, all of them are concerned with the historical search of social context for constitutional purposes.

## NOTES

1. Ken Kress, *A Preface to Epistemological Indeterminacy,* 85 Northwestern U.L. Rev. 134, 138 (1990). One leading study begins with a chapter entitled "Stubborn Indeterminacy." Steven J. Burton, *Judging in Good Faith* 3–34 (New York: Cambridge University Press, 1992).

2. See Albert R. Blaustein and Andrew H. Field, *Overruling Opinions in the Supreme Court,* 57 Mich. L. Rev. 151 (1958).

3. *Brown v. Board of Education,* 347 U.S. 483 (1954).

4. See *Adkins v. Children's Hospital,* 261 U.S. 525, 548–49 (1923), citing as authority *Lochner v. New York,* 198 U.S. 45 (1905), a case most authorities thought was impliedly overruled in *Bunting v. Oregon,* 243 U.S. 426 (1917). See Thomas R. Powell, *The Logic and Rhetoric of Constitutional Law,* 15 J. Phil., Psych. & Scientific Method 654 (1918).

5. Karl R. Popper, *Objective Knowledge: An Evolutionary Approach* 1–31 (Oxford: Clarendon Press, 1972).

6. *Id.* at 67–70.

7. *Id.* at 119, 164.

8. Roscoe Pound, *Mechanical Jurisprudence,* 8 Colum. L. Rev. 605 (1908); Roscoe Pound, *The Need of a Sociological Jurisprudence,* 19 Green Bag 607 (1907); Roscoe Pound, *The Scope and Purpose of Sociological Jurisprudence,* 24 Harv. L. Rev. 591 (1911), 25 Harv. L. Rev. 140, 409 (1911–12).

9. Ernest Nagel, *The Structure of Science* 42–46 (New York: Harcourt, Brace & World, 1961).

10. Some scholars suggest that legal positivism includes analytical jurisprudence, while others suggest it does not. Compare H.L.A. Hart, *The Concept of Law* 7, 18–19 (Oxford: Claredon Press, 1961), with Samuel I. Shuman, *Legal Positivism: Its Scope and Limitations* 11–18 (Detroit: Wayne State University Press, 1963).

11. Oliver W. Holmes, *The Path of the Law,* 10 Harv. L. Rev. 457 (1897), reprinted in *Collected Legal Papers* 167 (New York: Harcourt, Brace, 1920).

12. *Id.* at 184.

13. See Michael Conant, *Antimonopoly Tradition Under the Ninth and Fourteenth Amendments: Slaughter-House Cases Re-Examined,* 31 Emory L.J. 785, 797–801 (1982).

14. *United States v. Paramount Pictures,* 334 U.S. 131, 157 (1948). Justice Thurgood Marshall explained the quasi-constitutional status of the antitrust laws:

Antitrust laws in general, and the Sherman Act in particular, are the Magna Carta of free enterprise. They are as important to the preservation of economic freedom and our free-enterprise system as the Bill of Rights is to the protection of our fundamental personal freedoms. And the freedom guaranteed each and every business, no matter how small, is the freedom to compete—to assert with vigor, imagination, devotion, and ingenuity whatever economic muscle it can muster. Implicit in such freedom is the notion that it cannot be foreclosed with respect to one sector of the economy because certain private citizens or groups believe that such foreclosure might promote greater competition in a more important sector of the economy.

*United States v. Topco Associates, Inc.,* 405 U.S. 596, 601 (1972).

15. 464 U.S. 417 (1984).

16. *Id.* at 457.

17. See Francis Lieber, *Legal and Political Hermeneutics* 303–5 (3d ed., St. Louis: F. H. Thomas and Co., 1880) (Appendix note L by William G. Hammond).

18. William W. Crosskey, 1 *Politics and the Constitution in the History of the United States* 3–14 (Chicago: University of Chicago Press, 1953).

19. See Crosskey, 2 *Politics and the Constitution, supra* note 18 at 1103–15; John H. Ely, *Democracy and Distrust: A Theory of Judicial Review* 18–20 (Cambridge: Harvard University Press, 1980); Michael Conant, *The Constitution and the Economy: Objective Theory and Critical Commentary* 224–27 (Norman: University of Oklahoma Press, 1991).

20. See Henry M. Hart, Jr., and Albert Sacks, *The Legal Process: Basic Problems in the Making and Application of Law* (tentative ed. 1958).

21. See Tamotsu Shibutani, *Social Processes* 149–73 (Berkeley: University of California Press, 1986). For a more theoretical analysis, see Edna Ullmann-Margalit, *The Emergence of Norms* (Oxford: Clarendon Press, 1977).

22. Edward A. Ross, *Social Control and the Foundations of Sociology* 3–38, E. F. Borgatta and H. J. Meyer, eds. (Boston: Beacon Press, 1959).

23. E. Adamson Hoebel, *The Law of Primitive Man* 3–28 (Cambridge: Harvard University Press, 1954); Karl N. Llewellyn and E. Adamson Hoebel, *The Cheyenne Way* 41–63 (Norman: University of Oklahoma Press, 1941).

24. Kantorowicz defines law as "a body of rules prescribing external conduct and considered justiciable." Hermann Kantorowicz, *The Definition of Law* 21 (Cambridge: Cambridge University Press, 1958).

25. Oliver W. Holmes, *The Path of the Law*, 10 Harv. L. Rev. 457, 461 (1897). Justice Scalia emphasizes predictability as a general principle of decision, noting that uncertainty has long been regarded as incompatible with the Rule of Law. Antonin Scalia, *The Rule of Law as a Law of Rules*, 56 U. of Chi. L. Rev. 1175, 1179 (1989). See Catherine Wells Hantzis, *Legal Innovation Within the Wider Intellectual Tradition:*

*The Pragmatism of Oliver Wendell Holmes, Jr.*, 82 Northwestern U. L. Rev. 541, 564–67 (1988); Thomas C. Grey, *Holmes and Legal Pragmatism*, 41 Stan. L. Rev. 787 (1989).

26. Justice Holmes observed that a positive, descriptive definition of law meant that it was useless and confusing to use the term "natural law." Oliver W. Holmes, *Natural Law*, 32 Harv. L. Rev. 40 (1918). See notes 98 and 99, *infra*, and accompanying text.

27. See Jonathan Cohen and H.L.A. Hart, *Symposium: Theory and Definition in Jurisprudence*, 29 Proceedings of the Aristotelian Society, supp., 213, 217 (1955).

28. See Ronald Dworkin, "The Model of Rules," 35 *University of Chicago Law Review* 39 (1967); Ronald Dworkin, *A Matter of Principle* 72–103 (Cambridge: Harvard University Press, 1985); Joseph Raz, *Legal Principles and the Limits of Law*, 81 Yale Law Journal 827 (1972).

29. 115 N.Y. 506, 22 N.E. 188 (1889).

30. 115 N.Y. at 511, 22 N.E. at 190.

31. Richard A. Posner, *The Problems of Jurisprudence* 106 (Cambridge: Harvard University Press, 1990).

32. James Spedding, Robert Ellis, and Douglas Heath, eds., 7 *Works of Francis Bacon* 309 (London: Longmans & Co., 1879) (hereinafter cited as "Spedding").

33. Paul H. Kocher, *Francis Bacon on the Science of Jurisprudence*, 18 J. of the History of Ideas 3, 6 (1957).

34. *Spedding,* 319.

35. *Id.* at 320.

36. *Id.*

37. Herbert Broom, *A Selection of Legal Maxims* 1, 10th ed., R.H. Kersley, ed. (London: Sweat & Maxwell, 1939).

38. *Id.* at 118.

39. *Riggs*, 22 N.E. at 189.

40. Norman J. Singer, *Statutes and Statutory Construction* (5th ed., Deerfield, Ill.: Clark, Boardman, Callaghan, 1992).

41. Broom, *Legal Maxims, supra* note 37 at 470–622.

42. Karl N. Llewellyn, *Remarks on the Theory of Appellate Decision and the Rules or Canons About How Statutes Are to Be Construed,* 3 Vand. L. Rev. 395 (1950).

43. Karl N. Llewellyn, *The Common Law Tradition: Deciding Appeals* 522 (Boston: Little, Brown, 1960).

44. *Id.*

45. *Id.* at 523.

46. *Id.*

47. *Id.* at 524.

48. *McCulloch v. Maryland*, 17 U.S. (4 Wheat.) 316 (1819). See Charles Black, *Structure and Relationship in Constitutional Law* 14 (Baton Rouge: Louisiana State University Press, 1969).

49. See Michael Conant, *In Defense of Administrative Regulation,* 39 Ind. L. J. 29 (1963).

50. U.S. Const., Art. 1, §8, cl. 18.

51. See Crosskey, 1 *Politics and the Constitution, supra,* note 18 at 374–79; Joseph Story, 1 *Commentaries on the Constitution of the United States* §457–§517 (5th ed., Boston: Little, Brown, 1891).

52. See Crosskey, 2 *Politics and the Constitution, supra,* note 18, at 1103–15.

53. Broom, *Legal Maxims, supra* note 37 at 396.

54. *Id.*

55. *Id.* at 400.

56. Story, 1 *Commentaries on the Constitution of the United States, supra,* note 51 at §397–§456.

57. Thomas Rutherforth, 2 *Institutes of Natural Law,* ch. 7 (Cambridge: J. Bentham, 1756).

58. Story, 1 *Commentaries on the Constitution of the United States, supra,* note 51 at §405.

59. *Id.* at §405a.

60. See Conant, *The Constitution and the Economy, supra,* note 19 at 227–35.

61. *Murray's Lessee v. Hoboken Land and Improvement Company,* 59 U.S. (18 How.) 272, 276–77 (1855).

62. See Owen N. Fiss, *Troubled Beginnings of the Modern State 1888–1910,* Vol. 8 of the *History of the Supreme Court of the United States,* ch. 6 (1993); Roscoe Pound, *Liberty of Contract,* 18 Yale L. J. 454 (1909); Charles Warren, *The New "Liberty" Under the Fourteenth Amendment,* 39 Harv. L. Rev. 431 (1926).

63. Charles E. Shattuck, *The True Meaning of the Term "Liberty" in those Clauses in the Federal and State Constitutions which Protect "Life, Liberty, and Property,"* 4 Harv. L. Rev. 365 (1891).

64. 198 U.S. 45 (1905).

65. See Howard Gillman, *The Constitution Besieged: The Rise and Demise of Lochner Era Police Power Jurisprudence* (Durham: Duke University Press, 1993); Stephen A. Siegel, Lochner *Era Jurisprudence and the American Constitutional Tradition,* 70 N.C.L. Rev. 1 (1991).

66. "The people see the Supreme Court as an institution in the normal context of American politics. They view the Court as Republicans and Democrats, and they judge it in the same offhand way as they do their acknowledged politicians during elections." Kenneth M. Dolbeare and Phillip E. Hammond, *The Political Party Basis of Attitudes Toward the Supreme Court,* 32 Public Opinion Quarterly 16, 30 (1968). See Stephen M. Griffin, *What Is Constitutional Theory? The Newer Theory and the Decline of the Learned Tradition,* 62 S. Cal. L. Rev. 493, 506–29 (1989).

67. 410 U.S. 113 (1973).

68. A. V. Dicey, *Law of the Constitution* 152 (London: Macmillan, 7th ed., 1908).

69. See Karl M. ZoBell, *Division of Opinion in the Supreme Court: A History of Judicial Disintegration,* 44 Cornell L. Quarterly 186, 192 (1959).

70. See Albert J. Beveridge, 3 *The Life of John Marshall* 18 (Boston: Houghton Mifflin Co., 1919).

71. *Talbot v. Seaman,* 5 U.S. (1 Cranch) 1 (1801).

72. *Stuart v. Laird,* 5 U.S. (1 Cranch) 299 (1803); *Ogden v. Blackledge,* 6 U.S. (1 Cranch) 272 (1804).

73. *Bank of the United States v. Dandridge,* 25 U.S. (12 Wheat.) 64, 90 (1827) (Marshall); *Cary v. Curtis,* 44 U.S. (3 How.) 236, 252 (1845) (Story).

74. Letter of Justice Johnson to Jefferson, December 10, 1822, quoted in Donald G. Morgan, *Justice William Johnson: The First Dissenter* 181–82 (Columbia: University of South Carolina Press, 1954).

75. Letter, Thomas Jefferson to Thomas Ritchie, Dec. 25, 1820, in Paul L. Ford, 12 *Works of Thomas Jefferson* 175 (New York: G. P. Putnam's Sons, 1905).

76. See, e.g., *Huidekoper's Lessee v. Douglass,* 7 U.S. (3 Cranch) 1, 72 (1805) (Johnson, concurring).

77. 25 U.S. (12 Wheat.) 213 (1827). See Beveridge, 4 *Life of John Marshall, supra* note 70, at 480–82.

78. Learned Hand, *The Bill of Rights* 72 (Cambridge: Harvard University Press, 1958).

79. 247 U.S. 251 (1918). The dissenters were Justices Holmes, Brandeis, Clarke, and McKenna.

80. 301 U.S. 1 (1937).

81. 312 U.S. 100 (1941).

82. See Crosskey, 1 *Politics and the Constitution, supra*, note 18 at 3–186.

83. Thomas G. Walker, Lee Epstein, and William J. Dixon, *On the Mysterious Demise of Consensual Norms in the United States Supreme Court,* 50 J. Politics 361, 363 (1950).

84. *Id.* at 384.

85. Frank H. Easterbrook, *Agreement Among the Justices: An Empirical Note,* 1984 Sup. Court Rev. 389.

86. *Id.* at 391.

87. For a detailed survey of judicial behavior relating to dissent, see Maurice Kelman, *The Forked Path of Dissent,* 1985 Supreme Court Rev. 227.

88. See dissents of Justice Holmes to substantive due process: *Lochner v. New York,* 198 U.S. 45, 75–76 (1905); *Adair v. United States,* 208 U.S. 161, 191 (1908); *Coppage v. Kansas,* 236 U.S. 1, 40 (1915); *Adkins v. Childrens Hospital,* 261 U.S. 525, 568–70 (1923). Justice Holmes's dissents in those cases were demonstrations of his humility and pleas to the erring Court majority to end their usurpations of the amending power. Dissenting in *Baldwin v. Missouri,* 281 U.S. 586, 595 (1930), he wrote:

As the decisions now stand, I see hardly any limit but the sky to the invalidating of those rights if they happen to strike a majority of this Court as for any reason undesirable. I cannot believe that the [Fourteenth] amendment was intended to give us carte blanche to embody our economic or moral beliefs in its prohibitions. . . . Of course the words "due process of law," if taken in their literal meaning, have no application to this case.

89. 410 U.S. 113 (1973).

90. 381 U.S. 479 (1965).

91. *Id.* at 529 (Black dissenting); *Id.* at 540 (Stewart, dissenting).

92. *Roe v. Wade,* 410 U.S. at 167–68.

93. See Archibald Cox, *The Role of the Supreme Court in American Government* 113 (New York: Oxford University Press, 1976); John H. Ely, *The Wages of Crying Wolf: A Comment on Roe v. Wade,* 83 Yale L. J. 920 (1973); Richard A. Epstein, *Substantive Due Process By Any Other Name: The Abortion Cases,* 1973 Supreme Court Rev. 159.

94. *Carey v. Population Services International,* 431 U.S. 678 (1977) (Stewart joins majority opinion holding restrictions on distribution of contraceptives to minors to violate due process); *Zablocki v. Redhail,* 434 U.S. 374, 391 (1978) (Stewart concurs separately, applying due process to right to remarry).

95. 478 U.S. 186 (1986).

96. 410 U.S. 113 (1973).

97. See Posner, *The Problems of Jurisprudence, supra,* note 31 at 55–56.

98. Robert M. Cover, *Justice Accused: Antislavery and the Judicial Process* 26–27 (New Haven: Yale University Press, 1975); Clinton Rossiter, *Seedtime of the Republic: The Origin of the American Tradition of Political Liberty* 270 (New York: Harcourt, Brace and Co., 1953); Zechariah Chafee, *How Human Rights Got into the Constitution 13*

(Boston: Boston University Press, 1952); John P. Reid, *In the Taught Tradition: The Meaning of Law in Massachusetts-Bay Two Hundred Years Ago*, 14 Suffolk U.L. Rev. 931 (1980).

99.

> [I]t has been the policy of all the *American* states, which have, individually, framed their state constitutions since the revolution, and of the people of the *United States,* when they framed the Federal Constitution, to define with precision the objects of the legislative power, and to restrain its exercise within marked and settled boundaries. If any act of Congress, or of the Legislature of a state, violates those constitutional provisions, it is unquestionably void; through I admit, that as the authority to declare it void is of a delicate and awful nature, the Court will never resort to that authority, but in a clear and urgent case. If, on the other hand, the Legislature of the Union, or the Legislature of any member of the Union, shall pass a law, within the general scope of their constitutional power, the Court cannot pronounce it to be void, merely because it is, in their judgment, contrary to the principles of natural justice. The ideas of natural justice are regulated by no fixed standard: the ablest and the purest men have differed upon the subject; and all that the Court could properly say, in such an event, would be, that the Legislature (possessed of an equal right of opinion) and passed an act which, in the opinion of the judges, was inconsistent with the abstract principles of natural justice.

> *Calder v. Bull*, 3 U.S. (3 Dall.) 386 (1798).

100. See Frank H. Easterbrook, *Formalism, Functionalism, Ignorance, Judges*, 22 Harv. J. L. & Pub. Policy 13 (1998); William N. Eskridge, Jr., *Relationship Between Formalism and Functionalism in Separation of Powers Cases*, 22 Harv. J. L. & Pub. Policy 21 (1998); Suzanna Sherry, *Separation of Powers: Asking a Different Question*, 30 Wm. & Mary L. Rev. 287 (1989); Peter L. Strauss, *Formal and Functional Approaches to Separation-of-Powers Questions—A Foolish Inconsistency?*, 72 Cornell L. Rev. 488 (1987).

101. See chapter 5 concerning federalism under the Commerce Clause; Michael Conant, *Federalism, The Mann Act, and the Imperative to Decriminalize Prostitution*, 5 Cornell J. L. & Pub. Policy 99 (1996).

102. Laurence H. Tribe, *Taking Text and Structure Seriously: Reflections on Free-Form Method in Constitutional Interpretation*, 108 Harv. L. Rev. 1221, 1235 (1995).

103. *Brown v. Van Braam*, 3 U.S. (3 Dallas) 334 (1797). See Conant, *The Constitution and the Economy, supra*, note 19 at 133–38.

104. Tribe, *Taking Text and Structure Seriously, supra*, note 102 at 1236.

105. Charles L. Black, *Structure and Relationship in Constitutional Law* (Baton Rouge: Louisiana State University Press, 1969).

106. 17 U.S. (4 Wheat.) 316 (1819).

107. Black, *supra,* note 105, at 31.

108. Richard L. Perry, ed., *Sources of Our Liberties: Documentary Origins of Individual Liberties in the United States Constitution and the Bill of Rights* (Chicago: American Bar Foundation, 1952). On the origins of the language "privileges and immunities" in colonial charters and Declarations of Rights in the colonies, see Michael Conant,

*Antimonopoly Tradition Under the Ninth and Fourteenth Amendments: Slaughter-House Cases Re-examined*, 31 Emory L.J. 786 (1982).

109. Crosskey, 2 *Politics and the Constitution in the History of the United States, supra*, note 18 at 1056–82.

110. U.S. Const., Amend. VI (emphasis added).

111. 32 U.S. (7 Pet.) 243 (1833).

112. See Crosskey, 2 *Politics and the Constitution in the History of the United States, supra*, note 18 at 1089–95; Horace Flack, *The Adoption of the Fourteenth Amendment* 233 (Baltimore: Johns Hopkins Universary Press, 1908); Howard J. Graham, *Our "Declaratory" Fourteenth Amendment*, 7 Stanford L. Rev. 3–39 (1954).

113. *Slaughter-House Cases*, 83 U.S. (16 Wall.) 36 (1873).

114. *Adamson v. California*, 332 U.S. 46, 68–123 (1947) (Black, dissenting); Hugo L. Black, *A Constitutional Faith* 34–40 (New York: Alfred A. Knopf, 1968).

115. *Duncan v. Louisiana*, 391 U.S. 145 (1968). The state cases concerning criminal procedure can best be argued as incorporated under the Due Process Clause of the Fourteenth Amendment because "process" was originally and still is a synonym for procedure.

116. See Michael Conant, *Systems Analysis in the Appellate Decisionmaking Process*, 24 Rutgers L. Rev. 293 (1970).

117. Karl Llewellyn, *The Common Law Tradition* 374 (Boston: Little, Brown, 1960). See Frank H. Easterbrook, *Textualism and the Dead Hand*, 66 Geo. Wash. L. Rev. 1119 (1998); Michael W. McConnell, *Textualism and the Dead Hand of the Past*, 66 Geo. Wash. L. Rev. 1127 (1998).

118. J. Skelly Wright, *Professor Bickel, the Scholarly Tradition, and the Supreme Court*, 84 Harv. L. Rev. 769, 785–86 (1971).

119. Kent Greenwalt, *How Law Can Be Determinate*, 38 U.C.L.A. L. Rev. 1, 15 (1990).

120. Statement of Justice Jackson in *Hood & Sons v. DuMond*, 336 U.S. 525, 533 (1949), citing U.S. Cong., *Documents, Formation of the Union*, 38 (1927). See Walton H. Hamilton and Douglass Adair, *The Power to Govern*, ch. 5 (New York: W. W. Norton, 1937); Forrest McDonald, *Novus Ordo Seclorum*, ch. 4 (Lawrence: University of Kansas Press, 1985).

121. See Crosskey, 1 *Politics and the Constitution in the History of the United States, supra*, note 18 at 17–186.

122. *National League of Cities v. Usery*, 426 U.S. 833 (1976). See Conant, *The Constitution and the Economy, supra*, note 19 at 121–23.

123. *Garcia v. San Antonio Metro Transit Auth.*, 469 U.S. 528 (1985), overruling *National League of Cities v. Usery*, 426 U.S. 833 (1976).

124. See Robert H. Bork, *Neutral Principles and Some First Amendment Problems*, 47 Indiana L.J. 1 (1971).

125. See, e.g., William Brennan, *Constitutional Adjudication and the Death Penalty: A View from the Court*, 100 Harv. L. Rev. 313 (1986).

126. See Posner, *Problems of Jurisprudence, supra*, note 31 at 105–08. This study disagrees with Posner's conclusion that legal reasoning is merely a type of practical reasoning. See Jeffrey Rosen, *Overcoming Posner*, 105 Yale L.J. 581 (1995).

127. See Raoul Berger, *Government by Judiciary: The Transformation of the Fourteenth Amendment* (Cambridge: Harvard University Press, 1977), attempting to pursue the intent of the framers.

128. See letter: James Madison to Thomas Ritchie, Sept. 15, 1821, in Max Farrand, ed.,
     3 *Records of the Federal Convention of 1787*, 447 (New Haven: Yale University Press,
     1911).
129. Oliver W. Holmes, *The Theory of Legal Interpretation*, 12 Harv. L. Rev. 417 (1899),
     reprinted in *Collected Legal Papers* 203 (New York, Harcourt, Brace and Co., 1920).
130. Joseph Story, 1 *Commentaries on the Constitution of the United States* 404 (Boston:
     Hilliard, Gray, 1833). See Conant, *Systems Analysis in the Appellate Decisionmaking
     Process, supra* note 116, at 317.
131. 463 U.S. 783 (1983).
132. U.S. Const., Amend 1. The clause states, "Congress shall make no law respecting an
     establishment of religion."
133. *Cantwell v. Connecticut*, 310 U.S. 296 (1940).
134. On the states with established religions in 1789, see Akhil Reed Amar, *The Bill of
     Rights: Creation and Reconstruction* 32–42 (New Haven: Yale University Press, 1998).
135. 1 Stat. 71 (1789).
136. 1 Stat. 97–98 (1789).
137. 463 U.S. at 791.
138. 1 Stat. 92 (1789).
139. 463 U.S. at 796.
140. *Id.* at 797, citing *Lemon v. Kurtzman*, 403 U.S. 602, 612–13 (1971).
141. 463 U.S. at 803 to 805, citing *Everson v. Board of Education*, 330 U.S. 1 (1947);
     *Reynolds v. United States*, 98 U.S. 145 (1879).
142. 163 U.S. 537 (1896).

# 2

# The Slave Trade at the Constitutional Convention: The Commerce Clause and the Limited Political Horizon of Delegates

At the Constitutional Convention of 1787, the delegated power in Congress to regulate foreign commerce and commerce among the several states was subject to an express constitutional limitation barring national prohibition of the slave trade until 1808 but allowing a small federal tax on such importation.[1] The compromise by the majority of eight states that wanted an immediate prohibition on the slave trade occurred because the South Carolina and Georgia delegates asserted that their states would not join the Union unless the slave trade was continued. But the language of the limitation conceded the obvious breadth of Article I, Section 8: the broad power in Congress to regulate, including to forbid, foreign and domestic transactions in slaves and the power to tax those transactions that were not forbidden.

The Southern states conceded the broad national power over the slave trade after 1807 first because it was no threat to slavery. The Fugitive Slave Clause in the Constitution expressly recognized slavery as an established social institution based in the state law of property.[2] While unmentioned at the Constitutional Convention, the additional protection against the abolition of slavery by Congress was the law of eminent domain. This was the right to compensation for property taken by government grounded in the historical constitutional rights by Englishmen. It was confirmed by incorporation in the Fifth Amendment in 1791.[3]

The issue that has not been adequately explored by historians is why the slave states would accept a compromise that could possibly lead after 1807 to a prohibition on foreign trade and regulation of domestic trade in slaves or an unknown amount of tax on transactions in slaves. Such claims could materially impair the value of masters' property rights in slaves. The thesis of this study is that within the limited political horizon of the framers, the period of time over which they could reasonably foresee change in national political power, the Southerners felt secure. They presumed that their voting bloc in the House of Representatives could prevent onerous regulation or taxation of the domestic slave trade, but their ultimate protection was their bargaining power as a bloc in the Senate. As part of the convention compromises, Article V not only guaranteed no revision before 1808 of the slave trade clause or of the clause that prevented specific taxes on slaves but also absolutely guaranteed the states equal suffrage in the Senate.[4]

One thesis of this study is that the key compromises of the convention demonstrated the interdependence of the scope of the Commerce Clause with the demand of the Southerners that slaves be counted for representation in the lower house of Congress. They wanted enough votes to be able to bargain to block burdensome statutes regulating transactions in slaves.[5] For this reason, the study begins with a review of the recent historical writing that examines the original meaning of the language of the Commerce Clause.[6] This is followed by an analysis of the political factors leading to the constitutional limitation on national statutes barring the end of the slave trade until 1808. The section on the Fugitive Slave Clause demonstrates the great bargaining ability of the Southerners to bring enforcement of their peculiar institution into the North. The Southerners were able to have slaves considered persons (though of a lower caste) for the purpose of partial representation in the lower house of Congress. But the Fugitive Slave Clause recognized the Southerners' property interest in slaves. The lifetime service obligaton of slaves, who could be bought and sold, was not based on contract but on the law of property.[7]


## THE COMMERCE CLAUSE

The Supreme Court has recently reached the opinion on the scope of the Commerce Clause that historians argue was the original meaning: Congress was delegated a plenary power to regulate commerce, all transactions, both foreign and domestic.[8] The original meaning of the language of the Commerce Clause, as supported by massive evidence of common usage in 1787, is the basis of this conclusion.[9] Only key elements of this evidence can be summarized here. While "commerce" had a number of narrow meanings in 1787, such as trade in goods or international trade, its broadest meaning, which one would expect to be adopted in fundamental law for the nation, comprehended all transactions for money and in barter.[10] Tench Coxe, noted economist, wrote, "The commerce of America, including our exports, imports, shipping, manufactures and fisheries, may properly be considered as forming one interest."[11]

Chief Justice John Marshall noted in *Gibbons v. Ogden* that in the eighteenth century the verb "to regulate" was a synonym for the verb "to govern."[12] Regulation could include both promotion through subsidy and any type of limitation, including total prohibition.

In the eighteenth century, the preposition "among" also had more than one meaning. In a few contexts, it was used as a synonym for "between."[13] But in most contexts the terms were not synonyms. At the Constitutional Convention, the committee of style would surely have adopted the words "between states" if they had meant from one territory to another.[14] "Among" would not have been used in an interterritorial sense when territories were contiguous because it would not have been idiomatic English. The most common use of "among" in eighteenth-century English was "intermingled with" or "in the midst of."[15] Such usage made idiomatic sense when applied to groups of persons, but not when applied to contiguous territories. Chief Justice Marshall noted in *Gibbons* that "among" in the Commerce Clause meant "intermingled with."[16] The Commerce Clause seems easier to understand when one uses the definition "in the midst of."

The crucial issue is which of the three main uses of the word "state" in the eighteenth century made idiomatic sense with the word "among."[17] As just noted, the territorial sense does not fit. Second, "state" meaning "government" does not make sense in the Commerce Clause because the clause is not concerned with intergovernmental transactions.

The third and most common use of "state" in the eighteenth century, like the word "nation" in the same clause, was a group of people with a common government.[18] This collective use of the noun "state" is the only one that makes idiomatic sense in the context of "commerce." Another example of the collective use is found in Article I, Section 2: "Representatives and direct taxes shall be apportioned *among the several States* . . . according to *their respective Numbers*."[19] This usage is reinforced by the evidence that the phrase "several states" was a collective term used to refer to the peoples or states as a unified group.[20] Commerce in the midst of the several groups of peoples forming the United States meant all commerce in which they engaged. The conclusion is that by ratifying this clause, the people vested in Congress a plenary power to regulate all commercial transactions, both interstate and intrastate. Thus it is not surprising that Tench Coxe spoke of one of the measures of the convention of 1787 as "the establishment of a national legislature with complete powers over commerce and navigation."[21]

In light of this evidence on the language of 1787, it would seem that Madison's condemnation of the slave trade could possibly refer to both foreign and domestic commerce:

> It were doubtless to be wished, that the power of prohibiting the importation of slaves had not been postponed until the year 1808, or rather that it had been suffered to have *immediate* operation. But it is not difficult to account, either for this restriction

on the general government, or for the manner in which the whole clause is expressed. It ought to be considered as a great point gained in favor of humanity, that a period of twenty years may terminate forever, *within these States*, a traffic which has so long and so loudly upbraided the barbarism of modern policy.[22]


## LIMITING THE SLAVE TRADE

The express constitutional limitations on the national government in Article I, Section 9, begin as follows: "The Migration or Importation of Such Persons as any of the States now existing shall think proper to admit, shall not be prohibited by the Congress prior to the Year one thousand eight hundred and eight, but a Tax or duty may be imposed on such Importation, not exceeding ten dollars for each Person."

The issue of the slave trade is first noted in the records of the Constitutional Convention on August 6, 1787, in the Report of the Committee of Detail.[23] Article VII, Section 1, of the draft delegated to the Legislature the power "to regulate commerce with foreign nations and among the several states."[24] Sections 4 and 6 were express limitations on the commerce power. Section 4 read as follows: "No tax or duty shall be laid by the Legislature on articles exported from any State; nor on the migration or importation of such persons as the several States shall think proper to admit; nor shall such migration or importation be prohibited."[25]

Section 6 read: "No navigation act shall be passed without the assent of two-thirds of the members present in each House."[26]

The debate on the importation of slaves led to impasse. Rufus King of Massachusetts and Gouverneur Morris of Pennsylvania argued against continued importation, especially since this would be counted in part for representation in the House.[27] This was echoed by George Mason of Virginia, who stated that "this infernal traffic originated in the avarice of British Merchants."[28] The response of Charles Pinkney of South Carolina was that South Carolina and Georgia would not join the Union if they could not continue to import slaves.[29] Hugh Williamson of North Carolina reiterated this view, but his view was not general in that state.[30] Gouverneur Morris ended the debate by proposing that all the issues in Sections 4 and 6 be referred to a committee. "These things may form a bargain among the Northern and Southern States."[31] The proposal carried.

The Committee of Eleven, composed of one person from each state present, reported on August 24. Under the compromise, the Eastern states gained by a recommendation that the sixth section, requiring a two-thirds vote for navigation acts, would be stricken. In exchange, the Southern states gained limited importation as follows: "The migration or importation of such persons as the several States now existing shall think proper to admit, shall not be prohibited by the Legislature prior to the year 1800—but a Tax or Duty may be imposed on such migration or importation at a rate not exceeding the average of the Duties laid on Imports."[32] On August 25, the prohibition on legislative termination of the slave trade was extended to 1808, and the maximum tax per person so imported was agreed at ten dollars.[33]

The accepted view at the convention was that the Commerce Clause delegated to Congress a general superintendency of trade, and that Article I, Section 9, was a temporary exception from that delegated power.[34] But the meaning of "migration" as opposed to "importation" led to some differences in view of the framers.[35] While the clause was adopted in order to preserve the importation of slaves, the framers adopted the euphemism "such persons."[36] They also added the word "migration," which had the same origin as "immigrants" and "emigrants" and in common parlance of the times had a voluntary connotation. Therefore "migration" could not apply to slaves.[37] In an effort to disguise their real objective, they included language that would apply to nonslaves, knowing full well that there was no move in Congress to limit the migration of such persons. This is confirmed by the language of the clause that permits Congress to impose a tax not exceeding ten dollars per person, which applied only to importation and not to migration.

The word "importation" had a special usage in the former colonies. Since the Articles of Confederation gave Congress few national powers, the commercial functions of the states were like those of separate nations from 1776 to 1789. Consequently, it was common usage to speak of importing goods from other states.[38] Even in 1822, the interstate meaning was still found in a Mississippi statute: "Slaves born and resident in the United States, and not criminals, may be imported."[39] This usage has been long forgotten because of the Supreme Court's misconstruction of the Imports and Exports Clause.[40] If its common usage in 1787 is applied to Article I, Section 9, Congress was barred until 1808 from limiting the entry of slaves in both international and interstate commerce to the states then existing. The interstate implications of the word "importation" were not discussed at the convention.

The opponents of the slave trade bargained for one antislavery aspect in the protection of the trade in Article I, Section 9. The privilege of importing slaves was made available only to "the states now existing." New states and territories could be barred from importation at any time. Congress acted in 1798 to bar importation of slaves in foreign commerce into Mississippi territory, but there was no limit on interstate importation.[41] In 1804, Congress barred importation of slaves into Southern Louisiana if they had been imported into the United States after May 1, 1798, except those brought by settlers who were bona fide owners of the slaves.[42] The majority in Congress thus exercised their power under Article IV, Section 3, to govern the territories. But at the time of the convention, the states of Virginia, North Carolina and Georgia claimed lands from the Eastern sea coast to the Mississippi river.[43] Their delegates could not have had foresight concerning how the phrase "the states now existing" would affect their right to import slaves until 1808. They probably did not consider the clause to be a significant concession.

The revolutionary spirit of the Declaration of Independence and petitions of the Quakers raised public awareness of the barbarous cruelty of kidnapping Africans and transporting them to America.[44] Consequently, the campaign in the Continental Congress against trade with England included a campaign against the British slave trade to America. While the Articles of Confederation[45] said nothing about the slave trade, two resolves of the Continental Congress called for its termination.[46] In fact, the slave trade did decrease markedly during the Revolutionary War since British ships could not land in America.[47] The resolves of the Congress, however, had no enforcement, so that some slave trade by carriers that were not British continued.

The effect of the campaign in the states against the slave trade had dramatic results in the North and in Virginia, Maryland, and Delaware. By the time the Constitution was ratified, eight states had enacted criminal statutes prohibiting the importation of slaves.[48] Two others, New Hampshire and Massachusetts, had abolished slavery. Another two, Pennsylvania and North Carolina, had imposed prohibitive duties on the importation of slaves. Only Georgia continued the slave trade until 1798. South Carolina, which had temporarily ended the slave trade in 1787 because of the impact of its debts on its balance of payments, reopened the slave trade in 1803.[49] North Carolina repealed its prohibitive duty on slave importation in 1790 but in 1794 enacted legislation banning slave importation.

While Congress was prohibited from terminating the slave trade to the United States until 1808, it responded to the petitions of the Quakers to keep Americans out of the foreign slave trade.[50] In 1794 Congress prohibited American citizens and residents from building or equipping ships in the United Statesd or sailing a ship from a U.S. port in order to engage in the slave trade to any foreign country.[51] In 1800 this was supplemented by a statute barring Americans from having any property right in a slave ship or serving on such a vessel in the foreign slave trade.[52]

In 1803, Congress prohibited any person from importing slaves into any state that had laws barring the admission of slaves.[53] This statute was enacted to reinforce the prohibitions on entry of slaves by the state governments, since only the national government had the naval vessels to assist in the enforcement. The penalty for illegal importation was one thousand dollars per slave and forfeiture of the ship. Even though Article I, Section 8, of the Constitution had delegated exclusive power to Congress to regulate foreign commerce, an exception was created by Article I, Section 9. Since the national government could not bar the international slave trade to the United States until 1808, the power to do so was reserved to the states until 1808. The Act of 1803 merely supplemented this narrow state power over the international slave trade.

In March 1807, Congress acted in anticipation of the end of the constitutional limitation in Article I, Section 9. Effective January 1, 1808, Congress prohibited the importation of slaves from abroad into any port or place within the jurisdiction of the United States.[54] The statute also prohibited the building or equipping of ships for the slave trade from abroad to the United States with a penalty of forfeiture of such ships and a fine of $20,000. Persons who purchased or sold slaves that were illegally imported were subject to five to ten years imprisonment and fined from $1,000 to $10,000.

## THE FUGITIVE SLAVE CLAUSE AND EMINENT DOMAIN

The first reason that the slave states accepted a broad power in Congress to regulate domestic commerce in slaves after 1807 was that they felt secure in the laws of property as the legal basis of the institution of slavery. Under the federal system created by the structure of the Constitution, the law of property was reserved to the states. At the time of the Constitutional Convention, slavery was part of the property law of most of the states, North and South.[55] The overwhelming view north of the Carolinas was that the slave trade was barbarous and should be ended, but only a few persons at the convention spoke of eventual abolition of slavery throughout the nation.[56]

The Lockean principle that the primary function of government was to protect property was the foundation for the clauses in the Constitution relating to fugitive slaves and eminent domain.[57] The counting of three-fifths of the slaves for representation in the lower House was not a recognition of the slave owners that slaves were legal persons. It was only a legal fiction that slaves would be represented in Congress by slave owners. From the viewpoint of the Southerners, the partial representation of slaves in the House was solely to protect their property interest in slaves.[58] The Southerners were federalists because they felt that only a strong national government could keep the peace and prevent rebellions, a necessary reinforcement of their property interests in slaves.[59]

The Fugitive Slave Clause of the Constitution was preceded by the one adopted by the Continental Congress in the Northwest Ordinance of 1787.[60] Since all thirteen colonies recognized slavery in 1776, the framers of the Articles of Confederation did not consider the need for a provision relating to fugitive slaves. But then the abolition movement in New England got under way. Steps toward immediate or gradual emancipation of slaves were taken in Vermont, Massachusetts, Connecticut, Rhode Island, and Pennsylvania from 1777 to 1784. For Southerners, this raised the question of what protections those states might offer to fugitive slaves. The Northwest Ordinance was adopted under the unanimous rule of the Articles of Confederation when representatives from eight states were present, half from the South and half from the North. This compromise prohibited slavery in the territory northwest of the Ohio River but did not emancipate slaves already there.[61] It also provided "That any person escaping into the same, from whom labor or service is lawfully claimed in any one of the original States, such fugitive may be lawfully reclaimed, and conveyed to the person claiming his or her labor or service as aforesaid."[62] The language put no affirmative duties on territorial officials in the Northwest, so that procedures for recovery of slaves were left undetermined. Lynd presents substantial evidence that the Northwest Ordinance was adopted by the Continental Congress as an interrelated part of the compromises adopted at the Constitutional Convention at the same time.[63] The

Southerners voted for the Northwest Ordinance because it brought to an end the campaign of some Northern delegates to limit the expansion of slavery throughout the West. The negative implication of the Ordinance was that expansion of slavery south of the Ohio River was approved. The entire Northwest Ordinance was enacted into law by Congress on August 7, 1789.[64]

At the Constitutional Convention, the move for a fugitive slave clause began on August 24, 1787, when Pierce Butler and Charles Pinckney of South Carolina moved "to require fugitive slaves and servants to be delivered up like criminals."[65] James Wilson of Pennsylvania objected, "This would oblige the Executive of the State to do it, at the public expense."[66] Butler withdrew his proposal and on August 29 submitted the following, which was approved without debate: "If any person bound to service or labor in any of the United States shall escape into another State he or she shall not be discharged from such service or labor, in consequence of any regulations subsisting in the State to which they escape, but shall be delivered up to the person justly claiming their services or labor."[67] After rewriting by the Committee on Stile, the final language adopted in Article IV, Section 2, was as follows: "No Person held to Service or Labor in one State, under the Laws thereof, escaping into another, shall, in consequence of any Law or Regulation therein, be discharged from such Service or Labor, but shall be delivered upon Claim of the Party to whom such Service or Labor may be due."[68]

While the language of this clause does not use the word "property," the clause was viewed by the Southerners as a recognition by the nation of their property interests in slaves. While the language of the clause could apply both to slaves and to bond servants, only the latter had contractual relations with their employers. The relation of owner to slave had to be based on the law of property, and the state slave codes confirmed this.

No one at the time seemed to realize that the great abuse of this clause would be against the free Negroes in the North. A falsely sworn statement by any renegade white Southerner could lead to the wrongful enslavement of free Negroes.[69] This illustrates the lower-caste status of all blacks, slave and free, in both the South and the North.

The Fugitive Slave Clause of the Constitution did not receive enforcement until the Act of 1793.[70] The slave owner or his agent was empowered by Congress to seize the slave and take him or her before a federal judge or before any magistrate of a county or city and by oral testimony or written affidavit establish that labor was owed under the laws of the place from which the slave fled. The judge or magistrate was authorized to issue a certificate of ownership. Any person willingly obstructing any seizure by a slave owner or harboring or concealing a fugitive slave was subject to a $500 fine.

Southerners asserted that the Fugitive Slave Clause was a great advance over the prior law. General Pinckney of South Carolina stated, "We have obtained a right to recover our slaves in whatever port of America they may take refuge, which is a right we had not before. In short, considering all circumstances, we have made the best terms for the security of this species of property it was in our power to make."[71] James Madison noted, "This [fugitive slave] clause is a better security than any that now exists. No power is given to the general government to interpose with respect to the property in slaves now held by the states."[72] Madison was emphasizing that in a national government of enumerated powers, property rights in slaves were expressly recognized by the Fugitive Slave Clause so that earlier demands for an express clause prohibiting emancipation of slaves was unnecessary.[73]

The second major protection for property in slaves was the English constitutional principle of eminent domain, that there must be compensation for property taken by the government. While this principle did not become part of our written national Constitution until the ratification of the Fifth Amendment in 1791,[74] it was part of the Rights of Englishmen that the colonists deemed enforceable against any government they created. The privileges and immunities of Englishmen had been preserved in the Charter of Virginia of 1606 and most of the later colonial charters.[75] These constitutional limitations on government had been abridged by the Crown and that had led to the Revolution. No American would suggest that these fundamental rights of citizens against government would not be effective against their new government.

The origins of the right to compensation when property is taken by government can be traced to Chapter 28 of Magna Carta.[76] While this clause was stated in terms of taking of chattels, the later English statutes secured the principle for real property.[77] Justice Story, citing Sir William Blackstone's *Commentaries*, notes the importance of the right to compensation in takings:

> Indeed, in a free government almost all other rights would become utterly worthless if the government possessed an uncontrollable power over the private fortune of every citizen. One of the fundamental objects of every good government must be the administration of justice; and how vain it would be to speak of such an administration, when all property is subject to the will or caprice of the legislature and the rulers.[78]

This statement reflects a basic understanding of the economics of property rights, that rights in property are basic civil rights because property represents someone's savings. If savings, as invested in property, are not protected by law, savings will not exist and the economy will not function. No production for sale or transactions can exist without legal property protections for the means of production and for the output.

Since abolition of slavery was not in issue at the Constitutional Convention, there was no direct debate on compensation. The one incidental mention of compensation was by Gouverneur Morris of Pennsylvania as he objected to slave representation in the House of Representatives. Madison summarized Morris's statement, "He would sooner submit himself to a tax for paying for all the Negroes in the U. States than saddle posterity with such a Constitution."[79]

In the Northern states, where there were small but vocal abolition movements, the argument that confiscation of property rights in slaves required compensation from the state was made in the legislatures.[80] In fact, the proposals for gradual emancipation were based on the concept of compensation. Children of slaves were to be slaves until they reached an age when their completed work compensated the owner for the cost of raising them. The Pennsylvania abolition law of 1780 set the age of emancipation at 28.[81] It thus seems clear that the issue of taking property without compensation was the key barrier to immediate abolition of slavery in the New England states and the Eastern states.

## POLITICAL HORIZONS AND NONAMENDABLE CLAUSES

The political horizons of the delegates to the Constitutional Convention, the period of time over which they could reasonably foresee changes in the structure of national political power, is crucial to understanding the compromise of the Southern delegates. The argument here is that it is very difficult to construct a political horizon of more than ten years and surely not possible to have a political horizon that exceeds twenty years. Power shifts in the House of Representatives were dependent on immigration of Europeans in the various regions and the importation of African slaves in the deep South. The magnitudes of the immigration and importation over the next ten to twenty years was highly uncertain.

The political horizon of 1789 had a geographical limit of expansion to the Mississippi River. The 1803 Louisiana Purchase was not then contemplated and was not the concern of those who favored or those who opposed the expansion of slavery. The Southern states, by claiming lands to the Mississippi, were in a unique position to bargain in their cession of lands to the national government that slavery be protected in those areas. In 1789, North Carolina passed a cession act specifically providing that Congress could make no laws emancipating slaves in the ceded territory.[82] Congress accepted this conditioned grant. In 1789, Virginia consented that the district of Kentucky be established as an independent state.[83] In order to govern the territories pending statehood, Congress in 1790 passed the Southwest Ordinance, applying the ordinance of 1787 to "the territory of the United States south of the river Ohio" but omitting the prohibition on slavery.[84]

The political horizon of the Southerners regarding the slave trade was expanded to twenty years (until 1808) by virtue of the inclusion of Article I, Section 9. Given the opposition to the African slave trade at the Constitutional Convention by all states north of the Carolinas, the slave importers in South Carolina and Georgia should have expected the statute that terminated the African trade to the United States on January 1, 1808. As to the possible congressional regulation of the internal slave trade after 1807, the initiation of bills by Northerners depended on the relative political power of the slave states and the extent to which interested Northerners could build voting blocs to battle the Southerners. At the convention, Charles Pinkney, a leader of members bargaining to protect the slave trade, moved that statutes regulating commerce should be passed only with the assent of two-thirds of the members of each house.[85] The majority of Southerners opposed the motion, noting that the Northern states had compromised on the slave trade and that international trade relations required an ability in Congress to react to policies of other nations.[86] At the Virginia ratifying convention, an amendment was also proposed that regulation of commerce should depend on two-thirds votes of both houses.[87] Madison opposed this, asking if it was reasonable to require the Northern states to "bind themselves to the defence of the Southern States, and still be left at the mercy of the minority for commercial advantages."[88]

The Southerners felt secure in their ability to prevent Congress from enacting onerous regulations of the internal slave trade after 1807. In the short term, their allotment of 44.6 percent of the seats in the House of Representatives was clearly sufficient to protect them.[89] Nevertheless, General Pinkney complained that it was insufficient: "If they [the Southern States] are to form so considerable a minority, and regulation of trade is to be given to the Genl. Government, they will be nothing more than overseers for the Northern States."[90] This was an argument for one more representative for the South, an increment that would not significantly increase the already strong bargaining position of the South.[91]

The political influence of the Southern states in the House of Representatives is illustrated by the defeat of attempts to impose the tax of $10 per head on slaves imported before 1808 as authorized by Article I, Section 9. Bills in the House in 1789, 1804, and 1806 were either withdrawn or dropped in committee so that there was never a vote on the issue.[92]

The one regulation of the interstate slave trade to pass the Congress ended its legislative process by protecting the coastal shipping of slaves between states. The bill that had originated in the Senate and eventually became the law prohibiting the foreign slave trade after January 1, 1808, underwent a number of changes in the House.[93] Just before it was to be voted upon, Peter Early of Georgia realized that part of the language in the bill might apply to coastal shipping of slaves between states. He insisted on addition of a clause protecting the shipment of Negroes not imported into the country contrary to the act. The House accepted this amendment.[94] When the bill was returned to the Senate, they accepted all of it except the last clause. The problem was that Spanish Florida would become the key continental area for import of African slaves, and the issue was how to prohibit these slaves from the coastal trade to the United States. The Senate added a system to regulate the interstate coastal trade to prevent the illegal smuggling of Africans from Florida that became sections 8 and 9 of the Act of March 7, 1807.[95] Slaves were not to be transported on vessels of less than forty tons, and the captains of any ship transporting slaves had to prepare a manifest showing the origin of each slave and showing that he or she had been imported into the United States before January 1, 1808. The manifest had to be delivered to the port official at the place slaves were unloaded.

This application of the Commerce Clause to the regulation of the slave trade "among the several states" was passed in spite of the vigorous opposition of a few

Southern members of the House.[96] This first regulation of the internal slave trade raised the specter in the minds of some outspoken Southerners of further regulation that would reduce the value of slaves. John Randolph of Virginia was reported to have made the following arguments:

> The provision of the bill touched the right of private property. He feared lest, at a future period, it might be made the pretext of universal emancipation. He had rather lose the bill, he had rather lose all the bills of the session, he had rather lose every bill passed since the establishment of the Government, than agree to the provision contained in the slave bill. It went to blow up the Constitution in ruins.[97]

In fact, there was great smuggling of new African slaves from Florida in the coastal trade of the Southern states after enactment of these regulations.[98]

At the Constitutional Convention, the limited political horizon prevented any prediction by the Southern states that their bloc in the House of Representatives would continue to be large and therefore powerful. In 1820, the South's portion of the House was still 42.3 percent.[99] In 1787, the uncertainty of their future power caused the Southerners to bargain for unamendable clauses in the Constitution. On September 10, when the amending power was before the convention, John Rutledge of South Carolina said, "he never could agree to a power by which the articles relating to slaves might be altered by the States not interested in that property and prejudiced against it."[100] The result was an addition to the amending power that in Article V reads: "Provided that no Amendment which may be made prior to the Year One thousand eight hundred and eight shall in any Manner affect the first and fourth Clauses in the Ninth Section of the first Article."[101] Thus the constitutional prohibition on ending the slave trade and barrier to enactment of specific capitation taxes on slaves were removed from possible amendment for twenty years.

The more important limit on amendment required equal representation in the Senate. Though benefiting the slave states as a bloc, this clause arose from the power conflict between large states and small states. The proviso at the end of Article V stated: "that no State, without its Consent, shall be deprived of its equal Suffrage in the Senate."[102] Roger Sherman of Connecticut proposed this clause on behalf of the four small states in the North.[103] The final compromise wording was proposed by a representative of a large state, Gouverneur Morris of Pennsylvania.[104]

The states that demanded prohibition against amendment of the slave-trade clause, South Carolina and Georgia, were not small states in size, but Georgia had a small population. One of the largest states, which opposed the slave trade, was Virginia. But Virginia had more slaves than any other state, and its delegates had a duty to protect the property interests of the slave owners. Equal suffrage in the Senate was long-run protection against political movements of some Northerners for abolition of slavery. While it was not predictable in 1787, the Southern share of the Senate rose significantly from 5 of 13 states in 1789, or 38 percent, to 11 of 22 states in January 1820, or 50 percent.[105]

## CONCLUSION

The African slave trade to the United States was clearly in decline by 1787, as almost all state legislatures prohibited it. Consequently, the proposal at the Constitutional Convention to prohibit the slave trade was not a move for radical change in social policy. This preceded the invention of the cotton gin, and some observers then expected slavery to decline. Of the Southern states, Virginia prohibited the slave trade in 1778; Delaware, in 1776; and Maryland, in 1783.[106] These states had large slave populations relative to their productive land. Given the reproductive rates of their slaves, these states were able to maintain a supply of slaves adequate for the markets.[107] This fact and the view of some leaders that more slave importation would discourage European immigration made for strong economic motivation in these three slave states to join the Northern states in favoring immediate national termination of the African slave trade.

In contrast, South Carolina and Georgia were largely undeveloped areas that could not recruit European immigrants to clear forests and drain swamps. Only slaves could be forced to work at the heavy labor needed to prepare the land for cash crops.[108] With the future economic growth of their states in the balance, the delegates from those two states threatened to remain out of the Union if the African slave trade were immediately prohibited. The result was the compromise of Article I, Section 9.

As to the domestic slave trade, all of the slave states had economic motives to maintain it. Virginia and Maryland, with relatively large slave populations, had relatively low productivity from slave labor. Their land and climate and their main crop, tobacco, could not earn nearly as high a return as the rice, sugar, and indigo grown in South Carolina and Georgia.[109] As a result, there was an economic incentive for Virginians and Marylanders to ship slaves south for sale.

Given the language of Article I, Section 8, there can be no doubt that Southerners at the convention realized that the power vested in Congress to regulate "commerce among the several states" would apply to transactions in slaves. This was the only conclusion consistent with the Southerners' view that slaves were assignable property. Within their political horizon, they may have counted on the size of their strategic bloc of representatives in the House to continue as a bar to burdensome regulation. Greatly expanded European immigration to the North in the future that would dilute their power in the House may not have been within their political horizon. Nevertheless, their ultimate protection against burdensome regulation or even prohibition of interstate commerce in slaves was to be the nonamendable constitutional requirement in Article V of equal suffrage in the Senate. And this clause had been presented to the South by the bargaining of the small states of the North at the Convention.

The future of slavery as an institution was another matter. To those who lived by the language of the Declaration of Independence, slavery as the most severe caste system was an anomaly for the new nation. But to the slave owners in Virginia and other Southern states, their total investment in slaves of approximately

$200 millions was their largest asset.[110] They were determined to secure a constitution that recognized their property interests in slaves, and the Fugitive Slave Clause of Article IV, Section 2, did just that. And though the constitutional limitation of eminent domain was not discussed at the Constitutional Convention, it is clear that this principle was part of the reliances of the slave owners.

## NOTES

1. U.S. Const., Art. I, §§8 and 9. The classic study of the slave trade is W.E.B. Du Bois, *The Suppression of the African Slave-Trade to the United States of America 1638–1870* (New York: Longmans, Green, 1896) (cited hereinafter as Du Bois, *Supression*).
2. U.S. Const., Art. IV, §2. "The role of slavery at the Philadelphia Convention was central, not peripheral. The delegates wrote generous concessions to slavery into the Constitution. These enhanced the political power of the slave states and protected slavery's future." William M. Wiecek, The Witch at the Christening: Slavery and the Constitutional Origins, in *The Framing and Ratification of the Constitution*, 170, Leonard W. Levy and Dennis J. Mahoney, eds. (New York: Macmillan Publishing Co., 1987).
3. U.S. Const., Amend. V.
4. U.S. Const., Art. V.
5. See Donald L. Robinson, *Slavery in the Structure of American Politics 1765–1820*, 168–206 (New York: Harcourt Brace Jovanovich, 1971) (cited hereinafter as Robinson, *Slavery*); Paul Finkelman, Slavery and the Constitutional Convention: Making a Covenant with Death, in R. Beeman, S. Botein, and E.C. Carter, eds., *Beyond Confederation: Origins of the Constitution and American National Identity* 188–225 (Chapel Hill: University of North Carolina Press, 1987).
6. The most comprehensive study is William W. Crosskey, 1 *Politics and the Constitution in the History of the United States* 3–186 (Chicago: University of Chicago Press, 1953) (hereinafter cited as Crosskey, *Politics*).
7. See Robinson, *Slavery, supra,* note 5 at 86–87, 192.
8. *E.E.O.C. v. Wyoming*, 460 U.S. 226, 248–49 (1983).
9. Crosskey, 1 *Politics, supra,* note 6 at 3–186. See Michael Conant, *The Constitution and the Economy: Objective Theory and Critical Commentary* 87–114 (Norman: University of Oklahoma Press, 1991).
10. See George Caines, *An Enquiry into the Law Merchant of the United States; or Lex Mercatoria Americana, on Several Heads of Commercial Importance* (New York: Isaac Collins, 1802); Adam Anderson, *Historical and Chronological Deduction of the Origin of Commerce* (London: J. Walter, 1787). As to transactions in shipping and insurance services and in bills of exchange and promissory notes, see Malachy Postlethwayt, *Universal Dictionary of Trade and Commerce* (London: W. Straham, 1774).
11. Tench Coxe, *A View of the United States of America* 7 (London: J. Johnson, 1794). See Jacob E. Cooke, *Tench Coxe and the Early Republic* 109–31 (Chapel Hill, N.C.: University of North Carolina Press, 1978).
12. 22 U.S. (9 Wheat.) 1, 196 (1824).
13. Hamilton spoke of "treaties among nations" and "hostilities among nations" in the context of nations as governments. A. Hamilton, J. Madison, and J. Jay, *The Federalist*, No. 6 at 35, No. 7 at 42. E. Bourne, ed. (New York: Tudor Publishing, 1947) (hereinafter cited as *Federalist*).

14. The Committee of Style did not alter the language adopted by the Committee of Detail. Max Farrand, 2 *The Records of the Federal Convention of 1787*, 595 (New Haven: Yale University Press, 1913) (hereinafter cited as Farrand, *Records*).

15. Crosskey, *Politics, supra,* note 6 at 50–55.

16. *Gibbons v. Ogden*, 22 U.S. (9 Wheat.) 1, 194 (1824).

17. Madison, in discussing whether the Constitution was adopted as a compact of the states, noted the different uses of the word "states":

It is indeed true that the term "states" is sometimes used in a vague sense, and sometimes applied in different senses, according to the subject to which it is applied. Thus it sometimes means the separate sections of territory occupied by the political societies within each; sometimes the particular governments established by those societies; sometimes those societies as organized into those particular governments; and lastly, it means the people composing those political societies, in their highest sovereign capacity. Although it might be wished that the perfection of language admitted less diversity in the signification of the same words, yet little inconvenience is produced by it, where the true sense can be collected with certainty from the different applications. In the present instance, whatever different construction of the term "states," in the resolution, may have been entertained, all will at least concur in that last mentioned; because in that sense the Constitution was submitted to the "states;" in that sense the "states" ratified it; and in that sense of the term "states," they are consequently parties to the compact from which the powers of the federal government result.

James Madison, *Report on the Virginia Resolutions*, in Jonathan Elliot, ed., 4 *Debates of the Several State Conventions on the Adoption of the Federal Constitution* 547 (Philadelphia: Lippincott, 1836–45) (cited hereinafter as Elliot, *Debates*).

18. See sources cited in Crosskey, *Politics, supra,* note 6 at 55–69 and 1267–74. Crosskey cites a number of dictionaries, including Samuel Johnson, *Dictionary of the English Language* (1756), noting "state" as a group of persons and not citing any use of the term as a territory. It was common parlance of the times to say "I am of Vermont" or "I belong to Vermont." *Id.* at 57–58. See Joseph Story, *Commentaries on the Constitution of the United States* §208 (Boston: Hilliard, Gray, 1833).

19. U.S. Const., Art. I, §3 (emphasis added).

20. See Wilfred J. Ritz, *Rewriting the History of the Judiciary Act of 1789*, 83–86 (Norman: University of Oklahoma Press, 1990).

21. Tench Coxe, *A View of the United States of America, supra,* note 11 at 32–33.

22. *Federalist* No. 42 at 287 (Madison) (emphasis added). At the later conflict over admission of Missouri as a slave state, some Southern spokesmen argued against all federal regulatory power over slaves, urging that commerce "among the several states" in Article I, Section 8, did not include transactions in slaves. In support of this, Madison denied that Article I, Section 9, had applied to interstate importation of slaves. See letter from James Madison to Robert Walsh, November 27, 1819, 3 Farrand, *Records* 436.

23. For an analysis of the politics of the attempt to end the importation of slaves, see Robinson, *Slavery, supra,* note 5 at 295–346.

24. Farrand, 2 *Records, supra,* note 14, at 181.

25. *Id.,* at 183.

26. *Id.*

27. *Id.*, at 220–222.
28. *Id.*
29. *Id.*, at 370
30. *Id.*, at 373.
31. *Id.*, at 374.
32. *Id.*, at 396.
33. *Id.*, at 408–09. The $10 duty on slaves, if imposed, would have been approximately 3 to 5 percent of the average price of a slave and reasonably close to average ad valorem duties on imported goods. *Annals of Congress*, 1st Cong., Sess. 1, 356 (May 14, 1789).
34. See statements of George Nicholas and Edmund Randolph at the Virginia ratifying convention. Elliot, 3 *Debates* 456–57, 464. Chief Justice Marshall, in dictum, later recorded the same view. *Gibbons v. Ogden*, 22 U.S. (9 Wheat.) 1, 216 (1824). See later similar reflections of the co-author of the *Federalist*, former Chief Justice John Jay. Letter of Jay to Elias Boudinot, Nov. 17, 1819, in Henry P. Johnson, ed., 4 *Correspondence and Public Papers of John Jay* 430–431 (New York: Putnam, 1890–93).
35. Berns quotes a minority view among the framers and later congressmen that the scope of the constitutional limitation for slave trade somehow determined the scope of the commerce power in Congress over the slave trade after 1807. He adopts a minority view that "migration" refers to interstate importation of slaves and that this is what empowers Congress to regulate interstate movement of slaves after 1807. Walter Berns, *The Constitution and the Migration of Slaves*, 78 Yale L. J. 198 (1968). The argument that limitations have a "negative pregnant" that creates legislative power violates accepted rules of documentary interpretation. See David B. Davis, *The Problem of Slavery in the Age of Revolution 1770–1823*, 128 n. 33 (Ithaca: Cornell University Press, 1975).
36. The convention members from the Northern states who opposed slavery did not want the word "slave" in the Constitution. See statements of Luther Martin in Farrand, 3 *Records* 310. See William M. Wiecek, *The Sources of Antislavery Constitutionalism in America, 1760–1848*, 76 (Ithaca: Cornell University Press, 1977).
37. See explanation of James Iredell in the North Carolina ratifying convention. Elliott, 4 *Debates,* 102; James Wilson at Pennsylvania Convention, Elliot, 2 *Debates* 452–53; Moncure D. Conway, *Omitted Chapters of History Disclosed in the Life and Papers of Edmund Randolph* 78–79 (New York: Putnams, 1888); Samuel Johnson, 2 *Dictionary of the English Language* (London: J. Knapton et al., 1756), defining "migration" as the act of changing place.
38. The evidence of this usage has been assembled in Crosskey, 1 *Politics, supra,* note 6 at 297–301.
39. *Revised Code of the Laws of Mississippi* 369 (Natchez, 1824), quoted in Du Bois, *Suppression, supra,* note 1 at 254.
40. The history of the "imports and exports" clause of Article 1, Section 10, shows that one of its functions was to prevent duties or other taxes on the interstate movement of goods. See Crosskey, 1 *Politics, supra,* note 6 at 295–323. Compare *Woodruff v. Parham*, 75 U.S. (8 Wall.) 123 (1868).
41. An Act for an amicable settlement of limits with the state of Georgia, and authorizing the establishment of government in the Mississippi territory, 5th Cong., Sess. 2, Ch. 28, §7, 1 Stat. 549 (1798).
42. An Act erecting Louisiana into two territories, and providing for the temporary government thereof, 8th Cong., Sess. 1, Ch. 38, §10, 2 Stat. 283 (1804).

43. See Luther Martin's concern about the size of these states. *General Information*, Farrand, 3 *Records, supra,* note 14, at 224.

44. See Robinson, *Slavery, supra,* note 5 at 54–97.

45. *Id.* at 131–67.

46. On October 18, 1774, the Congress resolved: "We will neither import nor purchase, any slave imported after the first day of December next; after which time, we will wholly discontinue the slave trade, and will neither be concerned in at ourselves, nor will we hire our vessels, nor sell our commodities or manufactures to those who are concerned in it." 1 *Journals of the Continental Congress* 77 (Washington, D.C.: U.S. Government Printing Office, 1904).

    On April 6, 1776, the Congress resolved: "That no slave be imported into any of the thirteen United Colonies." 4 *Journals of the Continental Congress* 258 (1906).

47. See W.E.B. Du Bois, *Suppression, supra,* note 1 at 47–48.

48. See Arthur Zilversmit, *The First Emancipation: The Abolition of Slavery in the North* 106, 108, 152–59 (Chicago: University of Chicago Press, 1967) (hereinafter cited as Zilversmit, *First Emancipation*); Robinson, *Slavery, supra,* note 5 at 299; W.E.B. Du Bois, *Suppression, supra,* note 1, at 51, 72.

49. W.E.B. Du Bois, *Suppression,* at 71, 86–87.

50. The petitions of the Quakers are printed in the *Annals of Congress*, 1st Cong., Sess. 2, 1224 (Feb. 11, 1790); *Id.* at 1239 (Feb. 12, 1790). The second is signed by Benjamin Franklin, President of the Pennsylvania Society for Promoting the Abolition of Slavery.

51. An Act to prohibit carrying on the Slave Trade from the United States to any foreign place or country, 3d Cong. Sess 1., Ch. 11, 1 Stat. 347 (1794).

52. An Act in addition to the act intitled "An Act to prohibit the carrying on of the Slave Trade from the United States to any foreign place or country," 6th Congress, Sess. 1, Ch. 51, 2 Stat. 70 (1800).

53. An Act to prevent the importation of certain persons into certain states, where, by the laws thereof, their admission is prohibited. 7th Cong., Sess. II, Ch. 10, 2 Stat. 205 (1803).

54. An Act to prohibit the importation of Slaves into any port or place within the jurisdiction of the United States, from and after the first day of January, in the year of our Lord one thousand eight hundred and eight. 9th Cong. Sess. 2, Ch. 22, 2 Stat. 426 (1807). The British statute prohibiting the slave trade was enacted at the same time. An Act for the Abolition of the Slave Trade, 47 Geo. 3, c. 36 (1807).

55. See Robinson, *Slavery, supra,* note 5 at 18–21. The state statutes regulating slavery are reported in John C. Hurd, 1 *The Law of Freedom and Bondage in the United States* 228–311, 2 *Id.* 1–218 (Boston: Little, Brown, 1858).

56. Gouverneur Morris was one of the few outspoken foes of the institution of slavery at the Constitutional Convention. Farrand, 2 *Records* 221–23. Many opponents of slavery spoke at the Northern states' ratifying conventions.

57. As to the protection of property rights as a primary function of the Constitution, see Jennifer Nedelsky, *Private Property and the Limits of American Constitutionalism: The Madisonian Framework and Its Legacy* (Chicago: University of Chicago Press, 1990); James W. Ely, Jr., *The Guardian of Every Other Right: A Constitutional History of Property Rights* (New York: Oxford University Press, 1992). As to Locke's part in preparing the charter for South Carolina that provided for a slave owner's absolute power and authority over slaves, see Robinson, *Slavery, supra,* note 5 at 20, 42.

58. Pierce Butler of South Carolina "contended strenuously that property was the only just measure of representation. This was the great object of Governt: the great cause of war, the great means of carrying it on." Farrand, 1 *Records* 542. See Finkelman, *Slavery and the Constitutional Convention, supra,* note 5.

59. Ulrich B. Phillips, *The South Carolina Federalists,* 14 Am. Hist. Rev. 529 (1909).

60. 32 *Journals of the Continental Congress* 334–43 (1936).

61. See Paul Finkelman, Slavery and Bondage in the "Empire of Liberty," in F. D. Williams, ed., *The Northwest Ordinance: Essays on Its Formulation, Provisions and Legacy* 61–95 (East Lansing: Michigan State University Press, 1988).

62. 32 *Journals of the Continental Congress* 343.

63. See Staughton Lynd, *Class Conflict, Slavery, and the United States Constitution* 185–200, 205–213 (Indianapolis: Bobbs-Merrill Co., 1967).

64. An Act to Provide for the Government of the Territory Northwest of the Ohio River, 1st Cong., Sess. 1, ch. 8, 1 Stat. 50, 53 (1789).

65. Farrand, 2 *Records* 443.

66. *Id.*

67. *Id.* at 453–54.

68. U.S. Const. Art. IV, sec. 2.

69. See Robinson, *Slavery, supra,* note 5 at 286–87.

70. An Act respecting fugitives from justice, and persons escaping from the service of their masters, 2d Cong. Sess. 2, ch. 7, 1 Stat. 302 (1793). See *Prigg v. Pennsylvania,* 41 U.S. (16 Peters) 539 (1842). See Robert A. Burt, *Constitution in Conflict* 175–93 (Cambridge: Harvard University Press, 1992); Paul Finkelman, *Prigg v. Pennsylvania* and Northern State Courts: Antislavery Use of a Pro-Slavery Decision, 25 *Civil War History* 5–35 (1979).

71. Farrand, 3 *Records* 254.

72. *Id.,* at 325.

73. See demand of General Pinckney in Farrand, 2 *Records* 95.

74. U.S. Const., Amend V.

75. See Forrest McDonald, *Novus Ordo Seclorum: The Intellectual Origins of the Constitution* 9–55 (Lawrence: University of Kansas Press, 1985).

76. See A. E. Dick Howard, *The Road from Runnymede* 38, 210 (Charlottesville: University of Virginia Press, 1968); J.A.C. Grant, *The Higher Law Background of the Law of Eminent Domain,* 6 Wisconsin Law Review 67 (1931).

77. *Attorney General v. DeKeyser's Royal Hotel* [1920] A.C., 508 H.L.; Philip Nichols, 1 Law of Eminent Domain §1.21 (Albany: Mathew Bender, 3d ed., 1985).

78. Joseph Story, 2 *Commentaries on the Constitution of the United States, §1790* (Boston: Little, Brown, 5th ed., 1891). See James Kent, *2 Commentaries on American Law* 425–35 (Boston: Little, Brown, 10th ed., 1860); Friedrich Hayek, *The Constitution of Liberty* 140–42 (Chicago: University of Chicago Press, 1960).

79. Farrand, 2 *Records* 223.

80. Zilversmit, *First Emancipation, supra,* note 48, at 176–77, 194–97, 203–04.

81. *Id.* at 128.

82. An Act to accept a cession of the claims of the state of North Carolina to a certain district of Western territory, 1st Cong., Sess. 2, Ch. 6, 1 Stat. 106–08 (1790).

83. An Act declaring the consent of Congress, that a new State be formed within the jurisdiction of the Commonwealth of Virginia, and admitted into this Union, by the name of the State of Kentucky, 1st Cong., Sess. 3, Ch. 4, 1 Stat. 189 (1791).

84. An Act for the Government of the Territory of the United States south of the river Ohio, 1st Cong., Sess. 2, Ch. 14, 1 Stat. 123 (1790).

85. Farrand, 2 *Records* 449.

86. *Id.* at 451.

87. Elliot, 3 *Debates* 620.

88. *Id.* at 621.

89. Farrand, 1 *Records* 563.

90. *Id.* at 567.

91. Robinson, *Slavery, supra,* note 5 at 180.

92. See Du Bois, *Suppression, supra,* note 1 at 234, 241, 243.

93. See *Id.* 105–08; Robinson, *Slavery, supra,* note 5 at 333–35.

94. Annals of Congress, 9th Cong. 2d Sess., 484 (Feb. 12, 1807).

95. 2 Stat. 426, 429 (1807), repealed in Appropriations Act, §9, 13 Stat. 353 (1864).

96. See Robinson, *Slavery, supra,* note 5 at 335.

97. Annals, 9th Cong. 2d Sess. 528 (Feb. 18, 1807).

98. See Robinson, *Slavery, supra,* note 5 at 338–46.

99. *Id.*, 180.

100. Farrand, 2 *Records* 559.

101. U.S. Const., Art. V.

102. *Id.*

103. Farrand, 2 *Records* 629–30. See Wiecek, *Sources of Antislavery Constitutionalism, supra,* note 36, at 66–67.

104. Farrand, 2 *Records* 631.

105. Robinson, *Slavery, supra,* note 5 at 180.

106. Du Bois, *Suppression, supra,* note 1 at 224, 226.

107. In the 1790 census, Virginia's population was 40.9 percent African, with 292,000 slaves; Maryland's population was 34.7 percent African, with 103,000 slaves; Delaware's population was 21.6 percent African, with 8,800 slaves. U.S. Department of Commerce, Bureau of the Census, *Negro Population 1790–1915*, at 51, 57 (Washington, D.C.: Government Printing Office, 1918).

108. In the 1790 census, South Carolina's population was 43.7 percent African, with 107,000 slaves; Georgia's population was 35.9 percent African, with 29,000 slaves. *Id.*

109. See Ulrich B. Phillips, *American Negro Slavery* 67–97 (New York: Appleton & Co., 1918).

110. This estimate is derived from reports of slave prices in the period of from $300 to $400. *Id.* at 370–71.

3

# Compromise Opinions on the Equal Protection Clause: Racial Caste System in *Plessy* and *Brown*

In *Brown v. Board of Education of Topeka,*[1] the Supreme Court held state-mandated racial segregation in public schools to violate the Equal Protection Clause of the Fourteenth Amendment. The limited explication in the opinion of Chief Justice Earl Warren for the unanimous Court led to much negative criticism.[2] The failure to overrule expressly the decision in *Plessy v. Ferguson*[3] that had validated a racial caste system in the legal fiction of "separate but equal" was primary. The view of Warren that a unanimous opinion was crucial to general public acceptance of this radical termination of racially segregated public schools meant that he would have to compromise with the justices who refused to overrule *Plessy* expressly. The caste system so roundly condemned by Justice John Harlan in his dissent in *Plessy* continued into the twentieth century with the open denial of equal education, segregation in public places, refusal of employment in most manufacturing and retailing, and even peonage. Sociologists have demonstrated the overwhelming proof that the foremost function of caste systems is to deny equality. Yet this fundamental fact was not a key element in the *Brown* opinion, except in its conclusion that segregated schools generate a sense of inferiority in African-American pupils that creates inherent inequality. A partial explanation is that, in one of the cases in *Brown*, the physical facilities of schools were equal, so that the stigma of inferiority by forced segregation was the issue.

There was overwhelming evidence of the racist ideology of most white Americans after the Civil War, and this racism was expressed as a caste preference against social relations with illiterate former slaves except as servants or sharecroppers.[4] The social background was the institution of slavery and the attempts to perpetuate the caste system after the war with Black Codes. The Civil Rights Act of 1866[5] and the Fourteenth Amendment of 1868[6] were designed to prevent this racism from being extended into law in state regulatory statutes. The standard for application of the Equal Protection Clause was announced by Justice Henry Brown for the majority in *Plessy*. He admitted that "the object of the amendment was undoubtedly to enforce the absolute equality of the two races before the law."[7] Given the social purpose of the Equal Protection Clause in a racist society, the Louisiana segregation statute for trains should have been held unconstitutional. Instead, *Plessy* became the legal foundation for many more racial-segregation laws and perpetuation of a caste system into the next century.[8]

One thesis of this study is that the Equal Protection Clause was designed to mandate total elimination of official race discrimination. All vestiges and badges of the caste system of slavery and Black Codes were to be removed from the law. As Justice John M. Harlan explained in his dissent, state-mandated racial segregation was clearly a state legislative program to enforce a badge of inferiority. In a racist society, this was obvious to all observant persons except a majority of the Supreme Court. The *Plessy* Court erred in asserting that total racial equality and legal segregation of African Americans were consistent policies, and it erred in holding that the Louisiana statute merely concerned the social separation that the majority of white citizens preferred. Social choice is personal, but state law is civil control at its utmost. The *Plessy* opinion was total error.

The series of Supreme Court opinions upholding state segregation laws demonstrated that the Court majority relied on *Plessy* as a precedent. The justices ignored the canon of interpretation that the highest appeals court is not bound by *stare decisis* when making a constitutional interpretation.[9] As Justice Felix Frankfurter proclaimed, "The ultimate touchstone of constitutionality is the Constitution itself and not what we have said about it."[10] Since the whole National Association for the Advancement of Colored People (NAACP) strategy was to challenge every state segregation statute against the Constitution itself, counsel in those cases deserve only small blame for not briefing and arguing the canon of interpretation. It is elementary that the Court must not rely on its own past errors by mistakenly following past constitutional opinions. The hesitancy of the Court to overrule past cases because large sectors of the public have relied on such cases should not apply where the past case has led to inhumane treatment of a minority. The pervasive prevalence of invidious, oppressive state-mandated segregation should have been tested in each case against the meaning of the language in the Equal Protection Clause.

Another thesis of this study is crucial to critical evaluation of the *Brown* opinion. The general language of key constitutional clauses states broad principles of law that, over time, will have many applications to evolving social institutions. The language itself is all that is approved by the ratifying conventions in the states and the language itself is all the judiciary is under oath to interpret. The varying and conflicting statements of the framers in the 39th Congress who drafted the Fourteenth Amendment were not available to most ratifiers in the states and would not have been binding on them even if available. The views of each and every member at all the ratifying conventions on the meaning of "equal protection of the laws" are unavailable because most members who voted approval did not explain their reasons for voting to ratify the amendment. Probably most of the ratifiers did not consider whether the Equal Protection Clause would require desegregated schools either upon ratification or after some period of adjustment. Consequently, a historical search in 1953 for the various views of the ratifiers had to be inconclusive.

The conclusion is that the Supreme Court majority in *Brown* knew that the decision in *Plessy* was wrong when issued and, that Justice John Harlan's views against statutory encoding of racism were clearly correct if equal treatment of African Americans by the states was ever to be realized. The language of the Equal Protection Clause was color-blind. The solution of the Warren Court, if unanimity of the Court was essential to general public acceptance of radical legal change, was to sidestep *Plessy* to obtain the votes of the Court minority. The necessity to end the badge of social inferiority that was symbolized by mandated segregation of African Americans had been ordered by President Harry Truman for the armed forces in 1948. The expanding civil rights movement of the mid-twentieth century dictated that the Supreme Court finally recognize the color-blind Fourteenth Amendment and do the same for public schools.

## EQUAL PROTECTION: ORIGINAL MEANING

The final clause of Section 1 of the Fourteenth Amendment provides "that no state shall deny to any persons within its jurisdiction the equal protection of the laws."[11] Following generally accepted rules of documentary interpretation, the clause must be viewed as a complement to the earlier clauses in Section 1 and also as having a specific function of its own.[12]

The Privileges-or-Immunities Clause was designed to make all national constitutional limitations protecting citizens effective against the states.[13] The Due Process Clause mandated full and fair procedure to any person whose life, liberty, or property was to be taken by a state.[14] The Equal Protection Clause complemented the earlier ones by providing a specific substantive protection for all persons within a state in order to bar oppressive state legislation that would not have contravened the earlier prohibitions. Equal protection does not refer to fundamental civil liberties that are protected by the Privileges-or-Immunities Clause. Rather, it primarily concerns statutes that classify persons in order to regulate human behavior in some substantive way.[15] The most prominent examples of application of the clause have been to the classification of children by race involved in the state regulation of public schools.

Unlike the Privileges-or-Immunities Clause and the Due Process Clause, both of which had hundreds of years of legal-linguistic history, the Equal Protection Clause brought new language to the Constitution.[16] The word "equal" is found in natural-law contexts in the Declaration of Independence and in the "free and equal" clauses of some state constitutions.[17] These clauses were the basis in a few states for the judicial termination of slavery where it was a dying institution opposed by the majority of citizens.[18] The clauses did not function as controlling law on other topics.

The word "protection" is derived from the Latin term meaning "to cover or to save from harm." Equal protection means equal coverage for all persons.[19] The shield of the law is to be the same for any individual or firm found by the courts to come within the definition of "person."[20] The close connection between the idea of equality and its protection by government was stated by Senator Timothy Howe, abolitionist from Wisconsin:

> I have thought that it belonged to republican institutions to carry out, to execute the doctrines of the Declaration of Independence, to make men equal. That they are not equal in social estimation, that they are not equal in mental culture, that they are not equal in physical stature, I know very well; but I have thought the weaker they were the more the government was bound to foster and protect them. If government be designed for the protection or the weak, certainly the weaker men are the more they need its protection.[21]

In this context, the word "laws" must mean both the common law and statutes. The hearings in the 39th Congress demonstrate that one primary purpose of the Equal Protection Clause was to invalidate the Black Codes that had been adopted by many of the southern states.[22] Another primary purpose was to assure equality in the right to contract and to hold property, key elements of the common law.[23] Even the objective of overruling the doctrine of *Scott v. Sandford*[24] vindicated a common-law principle, that persons of African descent could be free and equal citizens of the nation. This was the principle that Lord Mansfield had enunciated in 1772 in *Somerset's Case,*[25] when he held that a slave brought into England could resist return to the colonies and receive a judicial ruling that he was a free person.

The phrase "equal protection of the laws" must mean that persons in like circumstances are to receive the same treatment.[26] There is no issue of inequality if persons are not in like circumstances. Barbers and lawyers do not expect to take the same state licensing examination to enter their professions. Equal protection thus requires classification in order to determine if persons are in like circumstances in relation to a constitutionally valid statutory objective. Legislative classification defines the class to which the law applies. Most statutes are not generally legislation applying to all persons in the state, but rather are special laws regulating a particular group. "Indeed, the greater part of all legislation is special, either in the extent to which it operates, or the objects sought to be attained by it."[27]

The idea of equality before the law in the Anglo-American legal system has its beginnings in chapter 40 of the Magna Carta, which states: "To no one will we sell, to no one will we refuse or delay, right or justice."[28] As one key aspect of the English concept, "Rule of Law" means "equality before the law, or the equal subjection of all classes to the ordinary law of the land administered by the ordinary law courts."[29] The protection was incorporated in the Massachusetts Body of Liberties of 1641 as follows: "Every person within this Jurisdiction, whether Inhabitant or forreiner shall enjoy the same justice and law, that is generall for the plantation, which we constitute and execute one towards another without partialitie or delay."[30] The religion clause of the Massachusetts Constitution of 1780 declared that "every denomination of Christians, demeaning themselves peaceably, and as good subjects of the commonwealth, shall be equally under the protection of the law."[31]

The absence of express Equal Protection Clauses in most state constitutions at that time can probably be attributed to the existence of slavery. After ratification of the Fourteenth Amendment, the dicta on equality became more general. As Chief Justice Morrison Waite observed:

The equality of the rights of citizens is a principle of republicanism. Every republican government is in duty bound to protect all its citizens in the enjoyment of this principle, if within its power. That duty was originally assumed by the States; and it still remains there. The only obligation resting upon the United States is to see that the States do not deny the right. This the Amendment guaranties, but no more. The power of the National Government is limited to the enforcement of this guaranty.[32]

Since the Equal Protection Clause was adopted primarily to protect the legal rights of former slaves, the foremost group of cases under the clause have concerned racial segregation. These cases illustrate the difficult issues of interpretation when a constitutional clause incorporates the ideals of revolutionary change in a society. The language of the clause, drafted by the radical Republicans on the Committee of Fifteen on Reconstruction, was couched in the broadest possible terms in order to express the committee's ideals of a legal system where all persons were absolutely equal.[33] Although the language did not treat social or political equality,[34] its mandate for legal equality was unequivocal.

The inclusive character of the language in the Equal Protection Clause must be emphasized because a few recent scholars have erroneously suggested that the alleged intent of some of the framers controls and narrowly limits its meaning.[35] Their argument is that evidence of the intent of some members of the 39th Congress, though highly controversial and not within the knowledge of the ratifiers, can be used to cut the meaning of the language to a fraction of its facial definition to ordinary readers of those times.[36] By asserting that the comprehensive language of the Fourteenth Amendment was designed solely to constitutionalize the narrower language of the Civil Rights Act of 1866,[37] they conclude that wholly different language is equivalent. This attempt to curtail the meaning of the language of the clause by interpretation violates a basic rule of documentary construction.[38]

Section I of the Civil Rights Act of 1866 provided former slaves with the same right to contract, to sue, and to hold property as whites for "the full and equal benefit of all laws and proceedings for the security of person and property, as is enjoyed by white citizens."[39] This language is narrower in scope than "the equal protection of the laws" in the Fourteenth Amendment. As noted, the latter applies to all laws, both common law and statutes. There is no doubt that one primary function of the Fourteenth Amendment was to supply a constitutional foundation for the Civil Rights Act. Congressman John A. Bingham of Ohio, the radical Republican who was later the primary author of Section 1 of the Fourteenth Amendment, opposed the Civil Rights Act because he thought that Congress was without power to pass such bill.[40] He indicated that a legal foundation for this act and for the original antidiscrimination clause that had been deleted from the final act could be secured only by constitutional amendment. But the equality of civil rights provided in the 1866 act did not include equality under statutes dispersing public benefits. State statutes providing public education only for whites would not violate the 1866 act. The language of the Equal Protection Clause of the Fourteenth Amendment was broader and would apply to all state statutes, including those dispensing state benefits, and to all regulations of the marketplace that might be administered to the detriment of nonwhites.

For efficient judicial review of cases arising under the Equal Protection Clause, the courts should have adopted a two-step process of analysis. The first issue is whether there is a constitutionally valid objective. "The sovereign might not draw distinctions between individuals based solely on differences that are irrelevant to a legitimate governmental objective."[41] This would apply both to trial judges in common-law actions and to legislatures. If a trial judge in common-law litigation should indicate by language or rulings that he or she will grant motions to exclude all members of a certain race, religion, or ethic group from serving on juries, that objective is constitutionally invalid.[42] Similarly, a state statute limiting jury service to whites is also invalid.[43] In these examples, the objective of the judge or the statute is discrimination on the basis of race or some other arbitrary characteristic. The unequal treatment makes the actions unconstitutional, whether or not prohibited by federal statute.[44] The Supreme Court has consistently held that the judiciary has the power to enforce the Fourteenth Amendment whether or not Congress has passed an enforcement statute pursuant to Section 5.[45]

The second step to test conformity to the Equal Protection Clause is necessary only if there has been a finding of a constitutionally valid objective of the common-law rulings or statute in question. If such finding has been made, the second test is whether the classification that has been adopted assigns all persons who are in like circumstances or "similarly situated" to the same class.

In applying this two-step analysis to the case of school segregation by race, for example, the first finding should be whether the objective of the statutes was arbitrary separation on the basis of race. If so, an immediate conclusion of unconstitutionality should follow. But if the court should find that the statutory objective was to subsidize elementary and secondary education and regulate quality in the operation of schools, then the second test would have to be applied: the determination if all persons similarly situated were treated equally. The persons similarly situated for purpose of education are all children. Separating any one or group of them on the basis of noneducational criteria would be arbitrary and therefore unequal. Legislative segregation on the basis of race, religion, height, weight, country of ancestor's origin, or any other noneducational criterion is a badge of differentiation that indicates inequality.

## EQUALITY OF PERSONS: RACIAL SEGREGATION

The economic theory of racial discrimination postulates that there exists a dominating ethnic group in a society and that many of the members of that group have a taste not to associate with members of the other ethnic groups.[46] To the extent that members of the dominant group refuse to engage in value-increasing exchanges with other groups, incomes of both groups are reduced. Before World War I in the United States, African Americans were largely barred from skilled trades and factory work and were relegated by a caste system to the lowest income levels.[47] In a caste society, transactions between dominant and dominated members are not discouraged so long as minority members remain in the areas and tasks assigned by the system of their group. Contractual relations between whites and African Americans after the Civil War were necessary for the functioning of the economy in the south. Whites entered sharecropping agreements with African Americans in rural areas and hired them as unskilled labor in urban areas.[48] Large numbers of African-American women worked as domestic laborers in white homes.

A key factor maintaining the lower caste status of African Americans after the Civil War was separate and unequal education.[49] Before passage of the Fourteenth Amendment, there were few public schools in the South, and most states provided public schools only for whites. Other states required African Americans to pay separate taxes for their own schools. The percentage of African-American children in school rose from 1.9 in 1860 to 9.9 in 1870 and to 33.8 in 1880, but it dropped to 31.1 in 1900.[50] Even though some courts held that dual systems of taxes violated equal protection,[51] county administrators allocated general tax funds on an unequal per capita basis, largely in favor of white schools.[52] Thus, the assumption in the South that African Americans were being educated at the expense of whites was false.

Racial segregation and economic deprivation were interrelated phenomena. In those Southern states with large African-American populations, the underinvestment in public education left the economy with a large segment of semiliterate persons, ill prepared to hold jobs in an industrializing economy.[53] Part of the lag in economic development in the South must be attributed to this limited invest-ment in African-American public education.

If the courts had followed the original meaning of the Equal Protection Clause, statutes requiring racial separation would have been invalidated upon the enact-ment of the Fourteenth Amendment. Such laws are today immediately suspect because their objective is discriminatory—treating some persons as second-class citizens.[54] But the invidious character of statutory racial classification had been recognized by the Court as early as the *Strauder* case of 1870, where Justice William Strong observed:

> The words of the Amendment, it is true, are prohibitory, but they contain a neces-sary implication of a positive immunity, or right, most valuable to the colored race—the right to exemption from unfriendly legislation against them distinctively as col-ored,—exemption from legal discriminations which are steps toward reducing them to the condition of a subject race.[55]

A few racial segregation laws have an antebellum origin.[56] Although the rural South had the ultimate caste system in slavery, a few major cities had large num-bers of free African Americans. Segregation laws and ordinances were enacted in these cities to define and defend the caste system for free African Americans. The Civil War brought an end to the slavery and an end to statutory racial segregation in public places for a long period of time. It was more than ten years after the federal troops left the South in 1877 that the first state segregation statute for public places was passed.[57] The capitulation to racism allowed extremist views to take control of social relations through legislation. The essence of white supremacy was to relegate and maintain African Americans in a lower caste, which was the function of segregation laws.[58]

The background to the state-mandated racial segregation in *Plessy* is a set of inconsistent Supreme Court opinions that demonstrate the interactions between the Commerce Clause and the Equal Protection Clause of the Fourteenth Amend-ment. The national case law began during reconstruction in Louisiana in *Hall v. De Cuir*.[59] The constitution of Louisiana provided that "All persons shall enjoy equal rights and privileges upon any conveyance of a public character."[60] The statute of 1869 concerning exclusion of passengers who refused to pay or who misbe-haved had a proviso: "Said rules make no discrimination on account of race or color."[61] Mrs. De Cuir, "a person of color," was an intrastate passenger on de-fendant's interstate steamboat on the Mississippi River. She was denied a cabin on the upper deck, which was reserved for white persons. She sued for damages under the statute and prevailed in the state courts. The Louisiana Supreme Court held that the state constitutional clause and statute did not regulate commerce but merely reinforced a standing duty under common and civil law that common carriers treat all passengers alike.[62]

On writ of error, the U.S. Supreme Court reversed the Louisiana ruling, hold-ing the state law to violate the Commerce Clause of Article I, Section 8. Since different states along the route could have different rules on racial mixing, the state law was held an unconstitutional burden on commerce. "If the public good requires such legislation, it must come from Congress and not from the States."[63] The vessel was duly enrolled and licensed under federal law to engage in the coasting trade. As Chief Justice John Marshall had explained in *Gibbons v. Ogden*,[64] the integration of interstate and intrastate commerce on public carriers barred state regulation.

The key problem with this case is that Congress had acted, but too late for this legal action. The Civil Rights Act of March 1, 1875, provided:

> That all persons within the jurisdiction of the United States shall be entitled to the full and equal enjoyment of the accommodations, advantages, facilities, and privileges of inns, public conveyances on land or water, theatres, and other places of public amusement; subject only to the conditions and limitations established by law, and applicable alike to citizens of every race and color, regardless of any previous condition of servitude.[65]

While this statute was passed after the trial in *De Cuir* and two months after the Louisiana Supreme Court opinion, its existence apparently was not pleaded on appeal by counsel for De Cuir as a national policy deserving equitable consideration. Since the federal statute was remedial, providing for $500 damages, the Supreme Court could have taken notice of it as a national antidiscrimination policy and then given recognition to operation of the state statute with the same policy for intrastate trips prior to March 1, 1875. This would have recognized concurrent state and federal jurisdiction over local commerce until Congress exercised its plenary power over commerce to preempt local regulation.[66]

An alternative approach by the Supreme Court would have been a structural analysis holding that constitutional limitations such as the Fourteenth Amendment take a higher status in law than delegated powers such as the commerce power. The state law against discrimination on public conveyances had the same objective as the more general Equal Protection Clause of the Fourteenth Amendment for all state laws. The court at that time only hypothesized segregation statutes in adjacent states. It is those hypothetical segregation statutes that would have violated equal protection and burdened commerce among the several states, not the Louisiana statute enforcing equal protection in public conveyances.

In the *Civil Rights Cases*[67] of 1883 the Supreme Court invalidated the Civil Rights Act of 1875 without consideration of the Commerce Clause.[68] As quoted earlier, the act provided for full and equal accommodations in common carriers, inns, theaters, and places of amusement. Only one of the five cases concerned carriers, that is, *Robinson v. Memphis & Charleston R. Co.* The railroad's main line ran from Memphis to Chattanooga in Tennessee, but it was connected to three successive lines that extended to Lynchburg, Virginia, so that the four lines together operated as a major east-west route in interstate commerce.[69] Robinson sued for statutory damages of $500 because the railroad conductor refused to allow

Robinson's wife to ride in the ladies' car as she appeared to be a person of African descent.[70]

Since the Civil Rights Act was adopted pursuant to Section 5 of the Fourteenth Amendment, the briefs of counsel and the opinions centered on equal protection and did not treat the Commerce Clause. Justice Joseph Bradley, for the majority, held sections 1 and 2 of the Civil Rights Act unconstitutional because the Fourteenth Amendment applied to state action and not usually to the behavior of private firms.[71] "It does not authorize Congress to create a code of municipal law for the regulation of private rights; but to provide modes of redress against operation of state laws, and action of state officers, executive or judicial, when these are subversive to fundamental rights specified in the amendment."[72] The inference is that if a federal court found a state statute mandating racial discrimination to violate the Fourteenth Amendment, then the Civil Rights Act could be a valid remedy against persons or firms. Or if a state constitution or statute provided for nondiscrimination on the basis of race and state officers failed to enforce it, the Civil Rights Act would be a valid remedy against persons or firms. This same analysis was utilized later in the opinion when Justice Bradley held the Thirteenth Amendment could not be a basis for the Civil Rights Act.[73] The mere refusal of firms to sell services to individuals, even in regulated industries such as common carriers, was held not to be a badge of slavery or servitude. The scope of common-law remedies for refusal of service was a matter of state law.

Since the Court held that the Equal Protection Clause applied only to discriminatory state statutes, it ruled that it was not necessary to examine arguments based on the legal theory of Senator Charles Sumner and his associates in proposing the civil rights bill that carriers and inns were regulated by common-law duties to serve all paying travelers decent in appearance and conduct.[74] Under Sumner's view, the Civil Rights Act was merely a supplemental national control for regulated industries to effect directly the ban on racial discrimination mandated by the Equal Protection Clause.[75] Sumner had argued that "The pending bill simply reinforces this rule, which without Congress ought to be sufficient. But since it is set at naught by an odious discrimination, Congress must interfere."[76]

The relation of the common-law duties of carriers to the Civil Rights Act had special meaning in the *Robinson* case. Tennessee had enacted a statute in 1875 abrogating the common-law duty of common carriers, innkeepers, and proprietors of public amusements to serve all persons, removing the duty to serve all potential patrons.[77] This enactment demonstrated that the Tennessee legislature understood that the constitutional basis for the common carrier provisions of the Civil Rights Act was to reinforce common-law duties by preventing racial discrimination. Hence, the elimination of common-law duties was enacted to facilitate racial discrimination. Consequently, in 1880 a federal circuit court held the state statute unconstitutional as applied to interstate travel.[78] In fact, only a few African-American plaintiffs obtained legal redress for exclusion from segregated facilities.[79]

The lone dissent of Justice Harlan in the *Civil Rights Cases*, covering thirty-seven pages in the official reports, rejects the stilted formalism of the majority and emphasizes constitutional and statutory purposes.[80] Harlan reviewed the antislavery origins of the Thirteenth and Fourteenth Amendments to show the breadth of their purposes. The express power in Section 2 of the Thirteenth Amendment for congressional enforcement was for eradication of slavery and all burdens and disabilities that constituted badges of slavery and servitude.[81] The Civil Rights Act of 1866 was the first legislative act to protect fundamental rights that were the essence of civil freedom.[82] Harlan concluded that freedom for former slaves "necessarily involved immunity from, and protection against, all discriminations against them, because of their race, in respect of such civil rights as belong to freemen of other races."[83] Harlan reviewed the precedents describing the common-law obligations of operators of common carriers, inns, and places of public amusement. He concluded that racial discrimination in these regulated industries was a badge of servitude and that the Thirteenth Amendment by itself was a constitutional foundation for the Civil Rights Act of 1875.

Harlan then reviewed the purposes of the Fourteenth Amendment. He centered his analysis on privileges or immunities of citizens of the United States and suggested analogies from the interstate Privileges-and-Immunities Clause of Article IV, Section 2. He asserted that "citizenship in the country necessarily imports equality of civil rights among citizens of every race in the same state."[84] He thus considered the interstate Privileges-and-Immunities Clause to be a type of Equal Protection Clause, an idea found in abolitionist constitutional theory. He then cited key Supreme Court opinions that assert that equality requires that there be no discrimination on the basis of race.[85] Unfortunately, Harlan failed to make an analysis based on the meaning of the language in the Equal Protection Clause.

Harlan reviewed the standing rules of documentary construction. "This court has always given a broad and liberal construction to the constitution, so as to enable congress, by legislation, to enforce rights secured by that instrument."[86] The view of the majority opinion that congress may act to correct invidious racial discrimination in regulated industries only after a state statute has been enacted to force such discrimination presumes

> that the general government has abdicated its authority, by national legislation, direct and primary in its character, to guard and protect privileges and immunities secured by that instrument. . . . Such an interpretation of the amendment is plainly repugnant to its fifth section, conferring upon congress power, by appropriate legislation, to enforce, not merely the provisions containing prohibitions on the states, but all provisions of the amendment, including provisions, express and implied, of the grant of citizenship in the first clause of the first section of the article.[87]

The judiciary could annul state legislation mandating racial discrimination. The power in Congress in the fifth section was to do something in addition, a power to stop hostile racial discrimination by corporations and individuals. The rights secured by the Civil Rights Act of 1875 belonged to all citizens in common and equally with all other citizens in each of the states.

The failure of counsel to plead the Commerce Clause as an additional constitutional basis of the Civil Rights Act of 1875 and the failure of Justice Harlan to argue the Commerce Clause missed what could have been the strongest argument. Transactions of common carriers are in commerce among the several states, and this was later illustrated by the broad construction of the commerce power that the Supreme Court applied to railroads after passage of the Interstate Commerce Act of 1887.[88] The *Shreveport Cases*[89] and others embodied the principle that commerce among the several states extended to local activities that affected rail movements between states. This was in effect the application of the broad principles enunciated by Chief Justice John Marshall in *Gibbons v. Ogden*.[90] Ninety years after passage of the Civil Rights Act of 1875, Congress exercised its restored plenary power over commerce and enacted legislation similar to the 1875 Act, barring racial discrimination in places of public accommodation. This part of the Civil Rights Act of 1964[91] was held constitutional.[92]

The next major interstate carrier opinion was inconsistent with the commerce rule of *Hall v. De Cuir*[93] and hence inconsistent with the original constitutional policy explicated in *Gibbons*. In *Louisville, New Orleans, and Texas Ry. Co. v. Mississippi*,[94] the Court upheld a Mississippi statute of 1888 requiring railroads to provide separate accommodations for the "white and colored races." The statute applied only to intrastate commerce, and the litigation tested only the carrier's duty to provide facilities, not the segregation of passengers. The carrier demonstrated that adding coaches at the state line would increase operating expenses and claimed that this would burden interstate commerce. Justice David Brewer, for the Court, accepted as authoritative the Mississippi court's construction of the statute that discounted the effect of the added expenses. Justice Harlan, joined by Justice Bradley, dissented,[95] arguing correctly that the facts were within the rule of *Hall v. De Cuir*. The defendant was an interstate carrier, and the clear objective of the statute was to segregate all passengers, including interstate travelers.

While the racist ideology permeating white society may have affected the majority justices, another possible explanation of these discrepant cases is that between the two trials the Supreme Court had begun its assumption of power to cut the scope of the Commerce Clause to a fraction of its original meaning.[96] After 1870, the Court issued opinions that excluded most local commerce from national regulation. An exception after 1890 was the national control of intrastate freight rates under the Interstate Commerce Act. State statutes in the South requiring racial segregation on all passenger trains were enforced as regulations of local commerce. Beginning in 1937, the Court restored the Commerce Clause to its broad original meaning, applying to all local commerce that affected other states, and in 1946 state segregation statutes for transport of persons were invalidated. In *Morgan v. Virginia*,[97] a state segregation statute applying both to intrastate and interstate buses was held to burden commerce among the several states. "It seems clear to us that seating arrangements for the different races in interstate motor travel require a single, uniform rule to promote and protect national travel."[98]

## *PLESSY* WAS ERROR

The Louisiana legislature passed the rail segregation statute in 1890, requiring carriers to provide "equal but separate accommodations for the white, and colored races, by providing two or more coaches for each passenger train, or by dividing the passenger coaches by a partition."[99] An exception, demonstrating that some close racial mixing, conforming to the caste system, was approved, provided that the act would not apply "to nurses attending children of the other race." The railroads had opposed the statute because of the increased costs of providing separate cars. An African-American Citizens Committee was organized to raise funds in order to challenge the constitutionality of the statute.[100]

In June, 1892, Homer A. Plessy purchased a first-class ticket for the East Louisiana Railway, an intrastate carrier, for a trip from New Orleans to Covington, Louisiana. When he insisted on boarding the first-class coach, which was reserved for whites, Plessy was arrested for violating the segregation statute. The prosecution filed an information, and Plessy was arraigned in October. Counsel for Plessy promptly filed a motion to dismiss the action, a fourteen-point plea to the jurisdiction of the criminal court. The state's demurrer to the plea was allowed, but the case was not set for trial. Since the state law would not have allowed any appeal from a criminal conviction, counsel for Plessy immediately petitioned the Supreme Court of Louisiana for a writ of certiorari and prohibition against trial judge Ferguson to review the denial of the motion to dismiss the information.

The Supreme Court of Louisiana granted certiorari and, after hearing the appeal, decided against Plessy in his plea for a writ of prohibition against Judge Ferguson.[101] Two important facts were not put in issue in the district court and were thus not heard on appeal. Neither the information nor the defendant's plea to the jurisdiction noted Plessy's race, that he was seven-eighths white, so that the definition of "white" was not put in contest. Plessy's skin pigmentation illustrated the arbitrary nature of legislation that sought to classify people according to race.[102] The fact the train had no first-class carriage for African Americans and that the second-class carriage available to them was greatly inferior was not noted in the pleadings, so that violation of the statutory requirement for equal physical facilities was not put in contest. The very essence of the legal fiction that African Americans would ever be treated equally was not demonstrable to a court. The case would be a contest of the statutory mandate for racial segretation

As to Plessy's claim under the Thirteenth Amendment that enforced racial segregation imposed a badge of servitude, perpetuating a caste system on the races, the court held that the amendment related only to slavery and involuntary servitude, citing the *Civil Rights Cases*.[103] As to the Fourteenth Amendment, the court held that the issue was whether a statute requiring railroads to furnish equal accommodations for the two races also required identity or community of accommodations. The court ruled that so long as separate facilities and accommodations were substantially equal, they did not abridge any privilege or immunity of citizens or otherwise contravene the Fourteenth Amendment.[104] The court cited numerous state court opinions to this outcome. The two state cases quoted extensively had occurred before the adoption of the Fourteenth Amendment and hence missed the key issue of defining and interpreting the language of the Equal Protection Clause.[105]

A writ of error was filed in the Supreme Court of the United States in 1893, but Plessy's counsel encouraged delay because he thought the current majority of the Court had views favoring segregation. The delay was not helpful. The opinion of Justice Brown in 1896 affirmed the Louisiana decision, with only Justice Harlan dissenting.[106] As to the Thirteenth Amendment, the Court followed the Louisiana opinion in holding it was limited to slavery and involuntary servitude. Segregation laws were held not to be of that class.[107] Like the Louisiana Court, the Court cited *obiter dicta* from the *Civil Rights Cases* as authority.[108]

As to the Fourteenth Amendment, Justice Brown's opinion contained major errors about the social context of the racism that led to Jim Crow laws. He ignored the argument in the brief for Plessy by Albion W. Tourgee that emphasized that the social purpose of racial segregation statutes for enterprises enjoying a public franchise was the legalization of a caste system. Tourgee pointed out that before the postwar amendments, slaves had no legal rights and that "free persons of color" had only such rights as the white community where they resided saw fit to confer on them.[109] Under the law of the *Dred Scott* case,[110] neither could become a citizen of the United States and, in the South, neither could become a citizen of any state. Tourgee concluded:

> The effect of the words of the XIVth Amendment was to put *all* these classes on *the same level of right*, as *citizens*; and to make this Court the final arbiter and custodian of the rights. The effect of a law distinguishing between citizens as to race, in the enjoyment of a public franchise, is to legalize caste and restore, in part at least, the inequality of right which was an essential incident of slavery.[111]

Justice Brown's first major error concerned the social psychology of caste systems. The statute specified "separate but equal" and this case did not put in issue provable facts that the rail cars for the lower-caste African Americans were greatly inferior. This lawsuit and similar legal actions demonstrated that segregation itself was highly resented. Justice Brown, for the majority, thus made an assumption of fact that was clearly against the manifest weight of the available evidence. Justice Brown first admitted that "the object of the amendment was undoubtedly to enforce the absolute equality of the two races before the law."[112] But he erroneously concluded: "We consider the underlying fallacy of the plaintiff's argument to consist in the assumption that the enforced separation of the two races stamps the colored with a badge of inferiority. If this be so, it is not by reason of anything found in the act, but solely because the colored race chooses to put that construction upon it."[113] But from time immemorial, the primary function of caste systems has been to impose and perpetuate inequality.

Justice Brown's erroneous assumption that enforced segregation was not racial discrimination had been repudiated by a unanimous Court twenty-three years before *Plessy*. In *Railroad Co. v. Brown*,[114] the Court had recognized the congressional declaration that segregation in transportation was negative discrimination, not equality. The charter to the railroad included a clause that "no person shall be excluded from any car on account of color."[115] The carrier provided separate-but-equal cars for white and colored. Mrs. Brown, a "colored" woman, attempted to sit in the "white" car and was ejected. A judgment for Mrs. Brown against the railroad was affirmed by a unanimous Supreme Court. The inequality was explained: "Congress, in the belief that this discrimination was unjust, acted. It told this company, in substance, that it could extend its road in the District as desired, but that this discrimination must cease, and the colored and white race, in the use of the cars, be placed on an equality."[116]

Justice Brown's second major error was to assert that a state statute mandating racial segregation on common carriers merely denied "social equality," as distinguished from "political equality" that would raise constitutional civil rights under the Fourteenth Amendment.[117] He asserted that segregated schools in the South and North were examples of social separation.[118] He concluded that the issue was whether the statute of Louisiana was a reasonable regulation in good faith for the public good and that there must necessarily be a large discretion in the legislature when determining reasonableness.[119] Tourgee's brief had argued that the state that has a right to distinguish citizens on the basis of race might instead segregate red-headed people or other arbitrary policies such as forcing "colored people" to walk on one side of the street or paint their houses black.[120] Justice Brown's reply was "that every exercise of the police power must be reasonable and extend only to such laws as are enacted in good faith for promotion of the public good, and not for the annoyance or oppression of a particular class."[121] He cited *Yick Wo v. Hopkins*,[122] where a San Francisco ordinance regulating public laundries was held to make an arbitrary and unjust discrimination against the Chinese race. He then reasserted the fallacy that racial segregation of African Americans was reasonable because it was not a badge of inferiority.

Justice Harlan was the lone dissenter. His opinion centered on the Thirteenth and Fourteenth Amendments as a combined protection of individual liberty, which meant he failed to analyze the meaning of the language in the crucial Equal Protection Clause that applied to wrongful discrimination. He first noted the statutory exemption for "nurses attending children of the other race," an example of approving interracial contact so long as caste relationships prevailed.[123] He then cited the authorities that common carriers were public highways delegated the right to eminent domain. He concluded that the civil rights of citizens do not permit such a public authority to know the race of those entitled to patronize them.[124] Racial distinctions are inconsistent with equality of civil rights of citizens and with personal liberty. The purpose of the amendments was to secure to former slaves and their descendents the civil rights that the white race enjoyed.[125] Everyone knew that the purpose of the racial segregation statute was to interfere with personal liberty so that whites and blacks could not choose to occupy the same public conveyance on a public highway.[126]

Justice Harlan concluded that racial segregation of former slaves was a badge of second-class citizenship and therefore a denial of equal protection. "There is no caste here. Our constitution is color-blind, and neither knows nor tolerates classes among citizens. In respect of civil rights, all citizens are equal before the law."[127] He concluded: "In my opinion, the judgment this day rendered will, in time, prove to be quite as pernicious as the decision made by this tribunal in the *Dred Scott* case."[128] As many commentators predicted, Justice Harlan has been vindicated on the meaning of equal protection.[129] The modern Court has unqualifiedly asserted that: "The Equal Protection Clause was intended to work nothing less than the abolition of all caste-based and invidious class-based legislation."[130]

If the *Plessy* Court had adopted Justice Harlan's opinion as that of the Court, it would have been an elementary application of social jurisprudence. The Equal Protection Clause as a constitutional response to the perpetuation of a caste system was designed to prevent social racism from being enforced by legislatures or courts. The opinion in Plessy was clearly fallacious and should not have been considered settled law by any court.[131] Yet the Supreme Court not only chose to follow *Plessy* as to intrastate trips but also later construed the Commerce Clause so that interstate African-American patrons could be racially segregated.[132]

The *Plessy* decision fostered the ideology of racial separation and statutes enforcing racial segregation for almost sixty years. The decision was more than just a travesty of justice. It was part of the common understanding of Americans in 1890 that racial segregation was a badge of inferior status. This truth is confirmed by historians and sociologists who in this century have made scientific studies of the origins of "jim crow."[133] Charles Black has characterized the acceptance of the separate-but-equal doctrine as the point where "the curves of callousness and stupidity intersect at their respective maxima."[134] Robert Harris has labeled *Plessy* "a compound of bad logic, bad history, bad sociology, and bad constitutional law."[135]

## SEGREGATION IN PUBLIC EDUCATION

The doctrine of *Plessy* confirmed the constitutionality of a caste society. Applied to education, it validated existing segregation of public schools[136] and discouraged legal attacks on segregation because all trial courts would be bound to follow the precedent of *Plessy*. An African-American community, one generation out of slavery and largely illiterate, was at the mercy of the white supremacists who had instigated the passage of segregation statutes. The result was not a society that was separate and equal. Like other caste systems, it was a society that was separate and unequal.[137] The most pronounced aspect was highly inferior schools for African Americans and in many areas the absence of public high schools for them.[138]

The school segregation cases began in 1850, long before the Fourteenth Amendment, with a key Massachusetts decision that was overruled by legislative action. *Roberts v. City of Boston*[139] challenged regulations of the Boston School Committee assigning "colored" children to two of the 161 primary schools in Boston. The plaintiff, a five-year-old "colored" girl, attempted to enter the school nearest her home, a distance of 900 feet, and was denied admission.[140] The segregated school was 2,100 feet from her home. The qualification of instructors in white and "colored" schools was equal, and the physical deficiencies of the "colored" school appear not to have been put in issue. Chief Justice Lemuel Shaw, for the Supreme Judicial Court, upheld the Boston School Committee. The clause of the Massachusetts Declaration of Rights, "All men are born free and equal,"[141] was a natural-law proclamation, not operative law. "The province of a declaration of rights and constitution of government, after directing its form, is to declare great principles and fundamental truths, to influence and direct the judgment and conscience of legislators in making laws, rather than to limit and control them, by directing what precise laws they shall make."[142] Charles Sumner, for the plaintiff, had argued that discrimination on the basis of race was a perpetuation of caste and necessarily a violation of equality.[143] The court upheld the discretion of the School Committee and held that separate schools did not violate any constitutional rights. But the *Roberts* decision was law for only five years. Citizens organized and convinced the legislature that separate schools were in their nature unequal. In 1855 the Massachusetts legislature enacted a statute prohibiting the separation of children in schools on the basis of race, color, or religious opinion.[144] Given the factual basis of the legislative rejection of the *Roberts* decision, the opinion should never have stood as a precedent for separate-but-equal schools.

After the Civil War, radical Republicans began what was to be an unsuccessful campaign to end racial segregation in the public schools. The new constitutions of 1868, drafted by the conventions controlled by the radicals in Louisiana and South Carolina, expressly prohibited racial segregation in public schools.[145] In 1870, the radicals in Congress were successful in incorporating bars against racial segregation in state schools as a condition subsequent in the acts to readmit Mississippi, Texas, and Virginia to the Union.[146] These conditions were subsequently evaded.

The controversies over school segregation in Congress demonstrate that most members recognized that the power to order racially mixed schools was within the power of Congress under Section 5 of the Fourteenth Amendment.[147] Under the leadership of Senator Sumner, the proposal for what would become the Civil Rights Act of 1875 contained a clause for equal rights in common schools and institutions of learning authorized by law, but this was deleted from the final bill.[148]

Even some Southern Republicans opposed such bills. Thus, though there was recognition that the Fourteenth Amendment could apply to schools, it was politically impossible to pass national statutes mandating mixed schools. This left open the issue of whether the courts could hold segregated schools in any state or district to violate the Equal Protection Clause in the absence of congressional legislation. In fact, the grant to Congress could not be exclusive if the Equal Protection Clause were to be meaningful. If Congress was divided in blocs and there was an impasse on antisegregation legislation, only the judiciary could block flagrant violation of equality of the races.

For fifty years after *Plessy*, the African-American community, with few lawyers and few friends among skilled white lawyers who would donate time to an impoverished group, did not begin a direct attack on school segregation. Instead, most actions centered on showing the inequality of schools for African Americans. In *Cumming v. County Board of Education*,[149] a Georgia high school for 60 African Americans was closed in order to convert the building to a primary school for about 300 African Americans. The Constitution of Georgia mandated primary schools for all children, supported by taxation. "The schools shall be free to all children of the state, but separate schools shall be provided for the white and colored races."[150] In violation of this clause, 400 or more "colored" children had been turned away from primary education for lack of buildings and teachers.[151] Closure of the African-American high school was adopted as the only financially feasible remedy for this denial. The county provided a high school for white girls and assisted a county denominational high school for white boys.[152] The African-American plaintiffs, alleging violation of the Fourteenth Amendment to the Constitution but failing to center on the Equal Protection Clause, sued to enjoin the collection of taxes to support white high schools until a public high school was also provided for African Americans. The school board denied that African Americans were barred from high school since, for the same small tuition of the public high school for white girls, nonwhites could attend any one of three "colored" denominational high schools in Augusta.[153]

The Supreme Court affirmed a decision for defendants. Plaintiffs had made no objection to the segregated school system. The entire case turned on plaintiff's prayer for a remedy detrimental to education. Justice Harlan, for the Court, stated that if plaintiffs had drafted a prayer that the school board, out of funds under its control, be ordered to establish and maintain a high school for "colored" children and if the board refused because of their race, "different questions might have arisen in the state court."[154] This case is surely not a retreat from Justice Harlan's powerful dissent in *Plessy*. It is clear that this ruling created a very narrow precedent for lower courts.

In *Berea College v. Kentucky*,[155] the state mandate of racial segregation was extended to private colleges. The state statute made it a crime "for any person, corporation, or association of persons to maintain or operate any college, school or institution, where persons of the white and negro races are both received as pupils for instruction."[156] Berea was a private sectarian college dedicated to Christian equality that admitted African Americans equally with whites and had thereby violated the statute. The college was fined $1,000 for teaching whites and nonwhites in the same place at the same time. The Supreme Court sustained the conviction by a vote of 7 to 2 on the ground that the college had failed to change its charter to exclude African Americans. Justice Brewer, for the Court, upheld the state statute on the theory that it had been applied only to the corporate entity, the college.[157] Artificial entities created by the state were without claims against the state, their creator. "Such a statute may conflict with the Federal Constitution in denying to individuals power which they might rightfully exercise, and yet, at the same time, be valid as to a corporation created by the State."[158]

Justices Harlan and William Day dissented, with only Harlan writing an opinion. Harlan disagreed with Brewer's view that the statute was severable and could be applied only to the college. He viewed the statute as a unified whole and insisted it was time to judge its constitutionality as applied to individuals. The statute invaded the liberty of individuals to teach and to learn. "I am of the opinion that in its essential parts the statute is an arbitrary invasion of the rights of liberty and property guaranteed by the Fourteenth Amendment against hostile state action and is, therefore, void."[159] This was an application of substantive due process, as distinguished from the equal protection emphasis in *Plessy* that had centered on perpetuation of the caste system.

The *Berea College* opinion was a significant expansion of the doctrine of *Plessy* to nonregulated industries. As a result, laws were passed throughout the South requiring racial segregation in public places, including privately operated facilities such as restaurants, theaters, and pool halls.[160]

The validity of state racial segregation was assumed in *Gong Lum v. Rice*.[161] The Court affirmed the denial of admission of a Chinese-American girl age nine to a white consolidated high school in Mississippi that apparently included the primary grades. Plaintiffs did not challenge the state segregation statute but only the refusal to admit Martha Lum to the white school. Plaintiffs failed to plead that there was no "colored" school in the county near the white school. Consequently, Chief Justice Taft, for the Court, accepted the assumption of the state supreme court that such a school existed.[162] The Court held that denial of admission of a Chinese citizen of the United States to the white school was not a denial of equal protection of the law, citing *Plessy v. Ferguson*.[163]

## *BROWN V. BOARD OF EDUCATION*

The background to *Brown v. Board of Education of Topeka* was a set of Supreme Court opinions from 1938 to 1950, all of which concerned admission to law schools or graduate schools. These cases centered on unequal treatment of African Americans, and plaintiffs did not directly challenge the *Plessy* ruling on separate but equal. In 1938, the Court, by a vote of 6 to 2, ordered the segregated University of Missouri Law School to admit African-American Lloyd Gaines, holding that the state's offer to subsidize Gaines's tuition to an out-of-state law school was not equal treatment.[164] In 1948, the Court ordered the Oklahoma Board of Regents to provide Ada Sipuel with a legal education in conformity with the Equal Protection Clause.[165] Rather than admit her to the University of Oklahoma Law School, the Board set aside a small section of the state capitol and assigned three law teachers to teach nonwhite students. Upon challenge to this sham of a law school, the Court held that the issue of a separate law school had not been raised on appeal in the action and denied mandamus to compel compliance with its earlier opinion.[166] After one year, the Oklahoma officials stopped financing the one-student law school and Ada Sipuel was admitted to the University of Oklahoma Law School. She was graduated in 1951.

In 1950, two opinions were issued on the same day concerning unequal graduate education. In *Sweatt v. Painter*,[167] Chief Justice Fred Vinson, for a unanimous court ordered plaintiff's admission to the University of Texas Law School. He held that the small separate law school that the state had created for African Americans was unequal to that at the University of Texas, citing size of faculty and student body, law review, moot court, scholarship funds, national honors, and relations of students to leading alumni. He also refused "petitioner's contention that Plessy *v.* Ferguson should be reexamined in the light of contemporary knowledge respecting the purposes of the Fourteenth Amendment and the effects of racial segregation."[168] In *McLaurin v. Oklahoma S. Regents*,[169] the unanimous Court ordered the University of Oklahoma to cease the internal segregation of a doctoral student in education pursuant to a state statute. He had been ordered to sit apart in an anteroom next to the classroom and at specified separate tables in the library and cafeteria. McLaurin was handicapped in his pursuit of education by the prohibition of intellectual commingling with other students. Like Sweatt, McLaurin had been denied a personal and present right of equal protection.[170]

In *Henderson v. United States*,[171] racial segregation in the dining cars of Southern Railway was tested against section 3(1) of the Interstate Commerce Act. The statute made it unlawful for a railroad in interstate commerce "to subject any particular person . . . to any undue or unreasonable prejudice or disadvantage in any respect whatsoever."[172] In this case, an African American was denied dining-car service because the one table in the car that was conditionally reserved for "Negroes" held some white passengers and plaintiff was not allowed to occupy the one empty seat. This clearly violated the statutory standard, and the district court's dismissal of plaintiff's action was reversed. The unusual procedure of this case was the intervention of the Justice Department on behalf of Henderson and in opposition to the Interstate Commerce Commission.

From a historical viewpoint, there was great significance to the intervention of the Justice Department in the last three cases. In the *Sweatt* and *McLaurin* cases, the Solicitor General filed a single combined brief in which counsel analyzed the original meaning of the Equal Protection Clause of the Fourteenth Amendment.[173] The brief then reviewed *Strauder v. West Virginia*[174] and other cases that noted the requirement for broad construction of the Fourteenth Amendment. The conclusion here and in the *Henderson* brief filed shortly before was that the "separate but equal" doctrine of *Plessy v. Ferguson* was wrong as a matter of law, history, and policy. For the first time, U.S. attorneys urged the Court to repudiate the doctrine and overrule *Plessy*.[175] While the Court sidestepped the fundamental issue of "separate but equal," these briefs document the views of the Justice Department in 1950.

After World War II, the National Association for the Advancement of Colored

People (NAACP) stepped up legal attacks on unequal education for African Americans in segregated public schools. But in some cases, radically inadequate physical facilities for African Americans were found by federal judges to be substantially equal to the greatly superior ones for whites.[176] In other cases, where courses or facilities in the white high school were not available in the segregated African-American school, the Court of Appeals reversed judgments for defendant, but admission to the white high school was not ordered as a remedy.[177]

Finally, four cases in which the prayer for remedy was immediate admission of African Americans to white schools in segregated states were heard on appeal in *Brown v. Board of Education*.[178] The facts of the cases differed greatly. In *Brown v. Board of Education of Topeka*,[179] physical facilities, curricula, and qualification of teachers were found equal in African-American and white schools, and African Americans who had to travel much greater distances were provided free transport. The trial court dismissed the action by African-American parents, relying on *Plessy* in spite of its finding of fact from expert testimony on the demeaning character of enforced segregation of minority students.[180]

In *Briggs v. Elliot*,[181] the South Carolina case, the defendants admitted what historians and sociologists knew had existed for eighty years, that "the educational facilities, equipment, curricula and opportunities" afforded African-American pupils in the public schools of the district were "not substantially equal" to those afforded white pupils.[182] The defendants contended white students in the rural parts of the district suffered the same inequalities, implying that two wrongs made a right. In face of the threat of this and similar litigation, Governor James Byrnes, a former justice, and the state legislature made provision for a $75 million bond issue in order finally to equalize educational facilities and opportunities throughout the state. The district court, by a vote of 2 to 1, relied on *Plessy* and denied the plea to end racial segregation and issued an injunction ordering equalization of facilities of the races. Judge Julius W. Waring dissented, arguing that racial segregation is per se inequality in violation of the Fourteenth Amendment.[183] Upon an earlier appeal, the Supreme Court remanded the case to the district court so that it could take action on the basis of reports of the school board on the progress of equalization of schools.[184] The district court found that the educational facilities of the races would be equalized by the beginning of the next school year. That court again denied an injunction abolishing segregation.[185]

In *Davis v. County School Board*,[186] the Virginia case, it was also demonstrated that there were inequalities between the races in facilities, curricula, and transportation of pupils. Like *Briggs*, the Court denied the plea for an injunction against racial segregation, citing *Plessy*, *Gong Lum*, and *Cumming*. Instead, the Court issued an immediate injunction against differences in curricula and transportation between the races and ordered the school board to complete with diligence and dispatch the new high school for African Americans.[187]

In *Belton v. Gebhart*,[188] the Delaware case, in the trial court Chancellor Collins J. Seitz had found that racial segregation itself resulted in inferior education of

African Americans, but because of the rule of *Plessy*, he could not rest his decision on that finding. The Chancellor had found the teacher training, pupil teacher ratio, extracurricular activities, physical plants, and aesthetic considerations at the African-American school to be inferior. He also had found the travel times imposed on African-American students to be an unequal burden. Consequently, he had ordered immediate admission of the African Americans to the white school, and his order was affirmed by the state supreme court.[189]

In the Supreme Court, the oral argument in *Brown v. Board of Education*[190] was heard on December 9, 1952, and the justices met in conference four days later. The notes of the justices, later revealed, showed a sharp division between the justices; following the suggestion of Justice Robert Jackson, no vote was taken at that time.[191] The issues of law, especially the disposition of the *Plessy* doctrine, were confounded with possible remedies and the possible social reactions in the South to desegregation. Chief Justice Fred Vinson was against overruling *Plessy* and seemed to favor segregation to the possible social conflict resulting from desegregation.[192] At that time, Justices Tom Clark and Stanley Reed indicated agreement with Vinson. Justice Jackson felt all possible remedies should be left to Congress. At that time, Hugo Black, William Douglas, Harold Burton, Sherman Minton, and Felix Frankfurter clearly favored either overruling *Plessy* or avoiding it and ordering desegregation. But the issue of remedies was more difficult. Only Black and Douglas supported express overruling of *Plessy*, in effect a declaration of personal and present rights of African-American pupils to enter white schools.

Justice Frankfurter, along with Justice Jackson, while in favor of a desegregation ruling, felt that it was of prime importance to work for total judicial consensus.[193] A unanimous opinion was needed so that the Court, as an institution, could withstand the attacks from southern politicians that might even lead to social disruption. So Frankfurter and Jackson wanted to postpone a final decision for as long as it took to achieve total unity. If only Congress had shown response to the civil rights movement and had passed a statute to end federally enforced public school segregation in the District of Columbia, the task of the Court in *Brown* would have been much easier. But the political power of long-term Southern senators and threat of filibusters to block such legislation made congressional leadership impossible.

In May 1953, the divided Court could only agree to set the school segregation cases for reargument in the fall term. Justice Frankfurter had prepared and submitted to the justices a first draft of a set of five questions to be distributed to the parties as issues for reargument.[194] On June 8, the Court unanimously restored the segregation cases to the docket for reargument on October 12. The revised five questions they were asked to treat can be summarized: (1) had the 39th Congress or the state legislatures that ratified the Fourteenth Amendment contemplated that it would abolish public school segregation? (2) If not, was Congress delegated the power under Section 5 of the amendment to abolish school segregation? (3) Was it within the judicial power, in construing the amendment, to abolish school segregation? (4) Presuming segregation unconstitutional, would a decree requiring Negro children immediate admission to schools within normal geographic districts necessarily follow, or could the Court exercise its equity powers to permit gradual adjustment? (5) Should the Court formulate detailed decrees, or should it appoint a special master to hear evidence toward recommending such decree?

The NAACP assembled a group of leading lawyers to respond to the Court's questions. The result was a 235-page brief that first argued that the purpose of the Equal Protection Clause was to prohibit state laws imposing racial discrimination.[195] Second, *Plessy* was the judicial approval of a fallacy that became a key symbol of white superiority, and the result was a continued caste system, the opposite of equal protection. The compromise of 1877 put the white supremacists in control of the South and brought disenfranchisement, segregation, and even terror to the African-American masses. The Supreme Court opinions recorded the oppressive peonage in the rural South all the way up to World War II.[196] Thus, the argument that "separate but equal" was a legal fiction that hid the oppression of a caste system for African Americans was clearly and completely before the Court in *Brown*.

An event of momentous consequence occurred one month before the Court reconvened for the fall term. On September 8, 1953, Chief Justice Vinson died of a heart attack, and the largest obstacle in the judicial impasse to terminating segregation was gone. Justice Frankfurter is reported to have remarked to a former law clerk, "This is the first indication I have ever had that there is a God."[197] When Chief Justice Warren was appointed, he needed time to read the record and briefs in the *Brown* cases, and the oral reargument was postponed until December 7, 1953. After the oral arguments, the Court met in conference on December 12, 1953, and Chief Justice Warren urged that no vote be taken at that time. Warren indicated his views that state racial segregation laws were unconstitutional.[198] Black, who was away, left word that his view was the same. Douglas, Burton, Minton, and Frankfurter also expressed that view. Clark shifted his position from 1952 and indicated he would join the consensus so long as the terms of relief were flexible. Jackson indicated he would agree as long as the Court openly declared it was making new law for a new day.[199] This left only Justice Reed, who stated that his views were unchanged and that racially segregated schools were constitutional.

In the December 12 conference the issue of the legislative history of the Fourteenth Amendment, which had received much discussion in 1952, was mostly ignored. This was because, during the 1952 term, Justice Frankfurter had delegated to his clerk, Alexander Bickel, the task of analyzing all of the legislative history of the amendment and writing a memorandum on his research.[200] On December 3, Frankfurter circulated the sixty-three-page printed memo to the Court. The report stated that, since there had been almost no congressional discussion of schools, the views of the 39th Congress as a body on school segregation were inconclusive.

Chief Justice Warren, like Frankfurter before him, was determined to have a unanimous opinion. His task was how to persuade the hold-out, Justice Reed. Meanwhile, from December 1953 to February 1954, Reed assigned his two clerks the task of researching for his expected dissent.[201] It may have been the interaction with his clerks and many meetings with the Chief Justice that caused Reed finally to see the light. A dissent would add nothing to future law because the civil rights movement was toward equality for African Americans. A desire for the peaceful acceptance of an end to school segregation and the force of the majority opinion on the position of the United States in the community of nations were factors that presumably caused Reed to join the Chief Justice in his compromise opinion.[202]

## COMPROMISE OPINION

The compromise opinion of Chief Justice Warren is negatively criticized for not announcing a general principle that would apply to a class of similar cases.[203] We do not know whether Warren proposed such a principle in conference and, if so, how many other justices opposed this language and threatened to write concurring opinions or even a dissent. It is clear that the neutral principles that would apply to all classes of state racial discrimination are those explaining the broad construction of the Equal Protection Clause of the Fourteenth Amendment, as noted herein.[204] As has been noted, Justice Brown in *Plessy* stated the first such principle before he proceeded to misapply it. He admitted that "the object of the amendment was undoubtedly to enforce the absolute equality of the two races before the law."[205]

The problem that Chief Justice Warren had to face if he attempted a full explanation of meaning of "equal protection of the laws" was that a broad construction of the language would lead directly to the conclusion that the decision in *Plessy* was error and had to be overruled. But expressly overruling *Plessy* would mean that the Court would have to conclude that all the progeny cases following *Plessy* were error. Consequently, plaintiffs in *Brown* would have a personal and present right to enter schools without reference to their pigmentation. Since some justices opposed an express overruling of *Plessy* and agreed to a unanimous opinion only on the condition that the equitable powers of the court be exercised to give the states time to adjust to radical change in school law, Warren had to sidestep *Plessy*. "In approaching this problem, we cannot turn the clock back to 1868 when the amendment was adopted, or even to 1896 when Plessy v. Ferguson was written. We must consider public education in the light of its full development and its present place in American life throughout the nation."[206]

Warren pointed out that reargument had been largely devoted to circumstance surrounding adoption of the Fourteenth Amendment in 1868.[207] He noted that, in the Congress, proponents who drafted the amendment were determined to remove all racial distinctions between citizens. Opponents wished the amendment to have the most limited effect. The views of the state legislators who turned the proposed amendment into law could not be determined. At best, the expected effects of the amendment on schools was probably not considered by most ratifiers. The evidence was inconclusive.

Bickel has demonstrated that history cannot answer the question of whether a particular set of acts occurring today do or do not violate broad general constitutional principles such as the Equal Protection Clause of the Fourteenth Amendment: "It is thus quite apparent that to seek in historical materials relevant to the framing of the Constitution, or in the language of the Constitution itself, specific answers to specific present problems is to ask the wrong questions. With adequate scholarship, the answer that must emerge in the vast majority of cases is no answer."[208] Even if the majority of ratifiers of the Equal Protection Clause had been surveyed and had replied that the immediate schooling for ex-slaves and their children had to be separate in order to bring them into literate society, this would not determine the long-run meaning of the language of the clause. Warren correctly applied the principled language of the Equal Protection Clause to the behavior of school boards in the 1950s.

Likewise, the antebellum status of schooling could not determine the meaning of equal protection of the laws. In the South, the movement toward free common schools supported by taxation had not taken hold,[209] and slaves were denied education. Racially segregated public schools in the North were not the model for the absolute equality mandated by the new amendment. Constitutional amendments are designed to change human behavior.

In the four trial courts in the *Brown* cases, attorneys for the plaintiffs seeking admission to white schools presented testimony of many expert social scientists on the demeaning character of enforced segregation of minority students.[210] The stigma of being a member of a lower caste was thoroughly demonstrated,[211] so that Chief Justice Warren's conclusion was clearly supported by the records of the four cases. "To separate them from others of similar age and qualifications solely because of their race generates a feeling of inferiority as to their status in the community that may affect their hearts and minds in a way unlikely ever to undone."[212] Warren quoted the findings of fact to this effect by two of the trial courts.[213] In addition, the resounding dissent of Judge Waring in the South Carolina case explained the per se inequality of racial segregation.[214]

"We conclude that in the field of public education the doctrine of 'separate but equal' has no place. Separate education facilities are inherently unequal."[215] Critics of Warren who label this conclusion as unprincipled have failed to reflect on the fatal errors of reasoning by Justice Brown in *Plessy*. Warren's opinion is based on the rejection of a caste system articulated by Justice Harlan in dissent in *Plessy*. Equal protection of the laws required a color-blind Constitution. Judicial compromises made it impossible for Warren to be as articulate as Harlan had been in dissent and write a full explanation of equal protection.

Many critics of Chief Justice Warren fail to note that the Court followed *Brown* with a per curiam overruling of *Plessy*. But it is an elementary application of epistemic principle that inconsistent applications of a given constitutional clause cannot both be correct law. State laws requiring racial segregation in intrastate public transportation cannot be both constitutional and also unconstitutional. In 1956, when *Plessy* was finally overruled in the intrastate bus case, *Gayle v. Browder*,[216] *Plessy* was demonstrated to have been erroneous law. The error took place in 1896, not in 1954, when Warren refused to follow it. Consequently, all lower-court decisions that had relied on the generalizations of *Plessy* to uphold state segregation laws in many areas of state activity were also erroneous.[217] It is truly unfortunate that the Court in *Browder* did not write an opinion explaining its overruling, but this also may have been a compromise decision.

In *Bolling v. Sharpe*,[218] the companion case to *Brown,* the Court held that the segregation of public schools in the District of Columbia violated the Due Process Clause of the Fifth Amendment. Since "due process" means "required procedure" and there is no Equal Protection Clause in the Fifth Amendment, the reasoning of *Bolling* is much more difficult than *Brown*.[219] The Court resorted to substantive due process: "Classifications based solely upon race must be scrutinized with particular care, since they are contrary to our traditions and hence constitutionally suspect."[220] Chief Justice Warren concluded: "Segregation in public education is not reasonably related to any proper governmental objective, and thus it imposes on Negro children of the District of Columbia a burden that constitutes an arbitrary deprivation of their liberty in violation of the Due Process Clause."[221] A more direct approach would have established a national civil right to equal protection from the English right to equal justice as founded in chapter 40 of the Magna Charta and preserved by the Ninth Amendment.[222] It is argued that in a true democracy, equal protection of the laws is a self-evident truth.[223] In this framework, the proclamation of equality in the Declaration of Independence can be viewed as a statement both of natural law and of positive law.

## NOTES

1. 347 U.S. 483 (1954).
2. Learned Hand, *The Bill of Rights: The Oliver Wendell Holmes Lectures 1958*, 54 (1958); Herbert Wechsler, *Toward Neutral Principles of Constitutional Law*, 73 Harv. L. Rev. 1, 31–34 (1959).
3. 163 U.S. 537 (1896).
4. See Leon F. Litwack, *Been in the Storm So Long: The Aftermath of Slavery* (New York: Vintage Books, 1979); C. Vann Woodward, *Reunion and Reaction: The Compromise of 1877 and the End of Reconstruction* (New York: Oxford University Press, 1966); David A. J. Richards, *Conscience and the Constitution: History, Theory, and Law of the Reconstruction Amendments* 150–56 (Princeton: Princeton University Press, 1993).
5. Civil Rights Act of 1866, ch. 31, §1, 14 Stat. 27 (1866).
6. U.S. Const., Amend. 14.
7. *Plessy v. Ferguson*, 163 U.S. at 544.
8. Kenneth L. Karst, *Belonging to America: Equal Citizenship and the Constitution* 21–27, 64–69 (New Haven: Yale University Press, 1989). "The fact is that *Plessy* may have been stillborn, for it never developed beyond a fictional excuse for discrimination. The states adhered to the 'separate' part of the doctrine but never took notice of

the 'equal' proposition." Philip B. Kurland, *Politics, the Constitution and the Warren Court* 89 (Chicago: University of Chicago Press, 1970).

9.  See Edward H. Levi, *An Introduction to Legal Reasoning* 57–61 (Chicago: University of Chicago Press, 1961); Albert R. Blaustein and Andrew H. Field, *"Overruling" Opinions in the Supreme Court*, 57 Mich. L. R. 151 (1958).

10. *Graves v. New York*, 306 U.S. 466, 491–92 (1939).

11. U.S. Const., Amend. 14, §1. See William E. Nelson, *The Fourteenth Amendment: From Political Principle to Judicial Doctrine* (Cambridge: Harvard University Press, 1988).

12. Chief Justice Marshall noted the rule of construction: "It cannot be presumed that any clause in the Constitution is intended to be without effect; and, therefore, such a construction is inadmissible, unless the words require it," *Marbury v. Madison*, 5 U.S. (1 Cranch) 137, 174 (1803).

13. Congressman John A. Bingham, who drafted section 1 of the Fourteenth Amendment, asserted that the prime purpose of the Privileges-or-Immunities Clause was to overrule the Supreme Court's opinion in *Barron v. Baltimore*, 32 U.S. (7 Pet.) 243 (1833) and make the immunities that are enumerated in the Bill of Rights effective against the state governments. Cong. Globe, 39th Cong., 1st Sess., 1089–90 (Feb. 28, 1866); *Id.* 1292 (Mar. 8, 1866). The senate leader on the Fourteenth Amendment, Jacob M. Howard, asserted the same point and added that enforcement of the Bill of Rights against the states together with the Equal Protection Clause were necessary to protect the black man in his fundamental rights as a citizen and wipe out the caste system. Cong. Globe, 39th Cong., 1st Sess., 2765–66 (May 23, 1866). See Akhil Reed Amar, *The Bill of Rights: Creation and Reconstruction* 163–87 (New Haven: Yale University Press, 1998); Michael Kent Curtis, *No State Shall Abridge: The Fourteenth Amendment and the Bill of Rights* 57–91 (Durham: Duke University Press, 1986); Richard L. Aynes, *On Misreading John Bingham and the Fourteenth Amendment*, 103 Yale L. J. 57 (1993); Michael Conant, *Antimonopoly Tradition Under the Ninth and Fourteenth Amendments: Slaughter-House Cases Re-examined*, 31 Emory L.J. 785 (1982).

14. See authorities cited in William W. Crosskey, 2 *Politics and the Constitution in the History of the United States* 1103–16, 1377–78 (Chicago: University of Chicago Press, 1953).

15. It also bars unequal application of common-law rules. *Jersey Shores, etc. v. Estate of Baum*, 84 N.J. 137, 417 A.2d 1003, 1007 (1980).

16. On the early meanings of political equality as a self-evident truth, see Jack R. Pole, *The Pursuit of Equality in American History*, ch. 2 (Berkeley: University of California Press, 1978).

17. Francis Thorpe, ed., *The Federal and State Constitutions, Colonial Charters and Other Organic Laws*, vol. 7 at 3812–13 (1909) (Virginia); id., vol. 5 at 3081–82 (Pennsylvania); id., vol.6 at 3739 (Vermont); *id.*, vol. 4 at 2453 (New Hampshire); *id.*, vol. 3 at 1888–1889 (Massachusetts); *id.*, vol. 1 at 536–37 (Connecticut), *id.*, vol. 5 at 2599 (New Jersey).

18. Robert M. Cover, *Justice Accused: Antislavery and the Judicial Process*, ch. 3 (New Haven: Yale University Press, 1975).

19. See Jacobus tenBroek, *The Antislavery Origins of the Fourteenth Amendment* 175–79 (Berkeley: University of California Press, 1951).

20. See Alfred Avins, *The Equal "Protection" of the Laws*, 12 N.Y.L. Forum 385 (1966).

21. Cong. Globe, 39th Cong., 1st Sess., 438 (Jan. 26, 1866).

22. See tenBroek, *supra,* note 19, at 163–64.

23. Cong. Globe, 39th Cong., 1st sess., 2764–65 (May 23, 1866).

24. 60 U.S. (19 How.) 393 (1857).

25. 1 Lofft's Rep. 1, 20 Howell's State Trials 1, 98 Eng. Rep. 499 (1772). See William M. Wiecek, *Somerset: Lord Mansfield and the Legitimacy of Slavery in the Anglo-American World,* 42 U. Chi. L. Rev. 86 (1974).

26. *Plyler v. Doe,* 457 U.S. 202, 216 (1982); *Royster Guano Co. v. Virginia,* 253 U.S. 412, 415 (1920). See Joseph Tussman and Jacobus tenBroek, *The Equal Protection of the Laws,* 37Calif.LRev. 341, 345 (1949). As to the questionable utility of a rational basis test in modern equal protection opinions of the Supreme Court, see Robert F. Nagel, *Constitutional Cultures: The Mentality and Consequences of Judicial Review* 84–105 (Berkeley: University of California Press, 1989).

27. *Home Insurance Co. v. New York,* 134 U.S. 594, 606 (1890).

28. William McKechnie, *Magna Carta* 395 ( Glasgow: J. Maclehose, 2d ed. 1914). Note the judicial citation of Magna Carta for equal protection in *Malinski v. New York,* 324 U.S. 401, 413–14 (1945) (Frankfurter, J.); *Griffin v. Illinois,* 351 U.S. 12, 16–17 (1956) (Black, J.). See A. E. Dick Howard, *The Road from Runnymede* 311–15 (Charlottesville: University Press of Virginia, 1968).

29. A. Dicey, *Introduction to the Study of the Law of the Constitution* 202 (London: Macmillan, 10th ed. 1962). As to colonial Americans' claims to equality of rights with citizens in England, see John A. Reid, *Constitutional History of the American Revolution* 60–64, 82–86 (Madison: University of Wisconsin Press, 1986).

30. Richard L. Perry and John C. Cooper, *Sources of Our Liberties* 148 (Chicago: American Bar Foundation, 1959).

31. *Id.* at 375.

32. *United States v. Cruikshank,* 92 U.S. 542, 555 (1876).

33. John P. Frank and Robert Munro, *The Original Understanding of "Equal Protection of the Laws,"* 1972 Wash. U.L.Q. 421, 432.Compare, Bickel, *The Original Understanding of the Segregation Decision,* 69 Harv. L. Rev. 1 (1955)

34. Political rights of former slaves were protected in U.S. Const., amend. XIV, §2, and in amend. XV.

35. Paul Dimond, *Strict Construction and Judicial Review of Racial Discrimination under the Equal Protection Clause,* 80 Mich. L. Rev. 462, 494–502 (1982).

36. See, e.g., Raoul Berger, *Government by Judiciary,* ch. 10 (Cambridge: Harvard University Press, 1977); Charles Fairman, *Does the Fourteenth Amendment Incorporate the Bill of Rights?* 2 Stan. L. Rev. 5, 44 (1949).

37. Act of April 9, 1866, c. 31, 14 Stat. 27.

38. *United States v. Wong Kim Ark,* 169 U.S. 649, 699 (1898).

39. See *supra,* note 37.

40. Cong. Globe, 39th Cong, 1st sess., 1290–92 (Mar. 9, 1866). See Horace E. Flack, *The Adoption of the Fourteenth Amendment* 30–31 (Baltimore: Johns Hopkins Press, 1908).

41. *Reed v. Reed,* 404 U.S. 71, 76 (1971); *Lehr v. Robertson,* 463 U.S. 248, 265 (1983).

42. *Ex parte Virginia,* 100 U.S. 339 (1879).

43. *Strauder v. West Virginia,* 100 U.S. 303 (1880).

44. *Ex parte Virginia,* 100 U.S. 339 (1879)

45. See *Oregon v. Mitchell,* 400 U.S. 112, 264n (1970) (Brennan, J.).

46. See Gary Becker, *The Economics of Discrimination* (Chicago: University of Chicago

Press, 2d ed. 1971); Richard Posner, *The Economics of Justice* 351–63 (Cambridge: Harvard University Press, 1983).

47.  Richard Kluger, *Simple Justice* 52–53 (New York: Alfred A. Knopf, 1975); Gunnar Myrdal, 1 *An American Dilemma*, ch. 13 (New York: Harper & Bros., 1944), Charles Johnson, *Patterns of Negro Segregation*, ch. 4 ( New York, Harper & Bros., 1943).

48.  C. Vann Woodward, *Origins of the New South* (Baton Rouge: Louisiana State University Press, 1951); Eli Ginzberg and Alfred S. Eichner, *The Troublesome Presence*: *American Democracy and the Negro*, ch. 8 (New York: Free Press, 1964).

49.  Meyer Weinberg, *A Chance to Learn: The History of Race and Education in the United States*, ch. 2 (New York: Cambridge University Press, 1977).

50.  *Id.* at 44. The percentage of Negro children enrolled in school rose to 44.8 in 1910; 53.5 in 1920; 60.3 in 1930; and 68.4 in 1940. *Id.*

51.  *Claybrook v. Owensboro*, 16 F. 297, 302 (D.C.Ky. 1883); *Puitt v. Commissioners*, 94 N.C. 514, 519 (1886) (ruling under Art. 9, §2 of N.C. Constitution).

52.  Weinberg, *A Chance to Learn, supra,* note 49, at 48. In 1920–1921, in the nineteen Black counties of Mississippi where 78. 1 per cent of the population was Negro, per capita public school expenditure on white children was $30.22, while the per capita expenditure on Negro children was $3.59. The latter was 11.9 per cent of the former. *Id.* at 60

53.  On the optimum social investment in education, see Gary Becker, *Human Capital* (New York: National Bureau of Economic Research, 2d ed., 1975).

54.  Suspect classification has been explained by the Court:

Some classifications are more likely than others to reflect deep-seated prejudice rather than legislative rationality in pursuit of some legislative objective. Legislation predicated on such prejudice is easily recognized as incompatible with the constitutional understanding that each person is to be judged individually and is entitled to equal justice under the law. Classifications treated as suspect tend to be irrelevant to any proper legislative goal. . . . Legislation imposing special disabilities upon groups disfavored by virtue of circumstances beyond their control suggests the kind of "class or caste" treatment that the Fourteenth Amendment was designed to abolish.

*Plyler v. Doe*, 457 U.S. 202, 216 n. 14 (1982). See Judith Baer, *Equality Under the Constitution*, ch. 5 (Ithaca, N.Y.: Cornell University Press, 1983); Hans Linde, *Due Process of Lawmaking*, 55 Neb. L. Rev. 197, 201–2 (1976).

55.  *Strauder v. West Virginia*, 100 U.S. 303, 307–8 (1880).

56.  See Roger A. Fischer, *The Segregation Struggle in Louisiana*, ch. 1 (Urbana: University of Illinois Press, 1974).

57.  C. Vann Woodward, *The Strange Career of Jim Crow* 16 (New York: Oxford University Press, rev. ed., 1957); Howard N. Rabinowitz, *Race Relations in the Urban South*, ch. 8 (New York: Oxford University Press, 1978).

58.  Gion Johnson, The Ideology of White Supremacy, 1876–1910, in James Sprunt, *Studies in History and Political Science*, 31, *Essays in Southern History*, 124, 136–140 (F. M. Green, ed., 1949).

59.  95 U.S. 485 (1878).

60.  *Id.*

61.  *Id.* at 486.

62. *De Cuir v. Benson*, 27 La. Ann. 1, 5 (1875).

63. 95 U.S. at 490.

64. 22 U.S. (9 Wheat.) 1 (1824).

65. Civil Rights Act of 1875, ch. 14, 18 Stat. 335 (1875).

66. See *Wilson v. Black Bird Creek Marsh Company*, 27 U.S. (2 Pet.) 245, 252 (1829), where Chief Justice Marshall upheld Delaware control of a small, navigable creek but noted that Congress could exercise its plenary power over commerce in such cases and the national law would preempt that of a state.

67. 109 U.S. 3 (1883).

68. See Michael W. McConnell, *Originalism and the Desegregation Decisions*, 81 Virginia L.Rev. 949, 984–1086 (1995), for a complete history of the enactment of the Civil Rights Act.

69. John F. Stover, *American Railroads* 42–3 (Chicago: University of Chicago Press, 2d ed., 1997).

70. *Civil Rights Cases*, 109 U.S. at 5.

71. *Id.* at 11 to 15.

72. *Id.* at 11.

73. *Id.* at 20–25.

74. *Id.* at 19.

75. Cong. Globe, 42d Cong., 2d Sess. 383 (Jan. 15, 1872).

76. *Id.* Sumner had quoted as authority on common carrier duties Justice Story's *Commentaries on the Law of Bailments* and Parson's *Contracts. Id.*

77. Act of Mar. 24, 1875, ch. 130, §1, 1875 Tenn. Acts 216.

78. *Brown v. Memphis & C. Ry. Co.*, 5 F. 499, 501 (C.C.W.D. Tenn. 1880).

79. See *Gray v. Cincinnati S. Ry. Co.*, 11 F. 683, 686 (C.C.S.D. Ohio 1882) (charging jury that defendant railroad company was liable under the Civil Rights Act if it denied plaintiff seating in the ladies' car because of her race); see also John Hope Franklin, *The Enforcement of the Civil Rights Act of 1875*, 6 Prologue 225, 229–34 (1974).

80. *Civil Rights Cases*, 109 U.S. at 26.

81. *Id.* at 35.

82. Civil Rights Act of 1866, ch. 31, §1, 14 Stat. 27 (1866).

83. *Civil Rights Cases*, 109 U.S. at 36. This view of Justice Harlan was finally vindicated in *Jones v. Alfred H. Mayer Co.*, 392 U.S. 409 (1968) (Civil Rights Act of 1866 was a valid enforcement pursuant to Section 2 of the Thirteenth Amendment and forbids private racial discrimination in real estate transactions).

84. 109 U.S. at 48.

85. *United States v. Cruikshank*, 92 U.S. 542, 555 (1876); *Ex Parte Virginia*, 100 U.S. 339, 344 (1879); *Strauder v. West Virginia*, 100 U.S. 303, 306 (1880); *Neal v. Delaware*, 103 U.S. 370, 386 (1880).

86. *Civil Rights Cases*, 109 U.S. at 50–51, citing Chief Justice Marshall in *McCulloch v. Maryland*, 17 U.S. (4 Wheat.) 316, 423 (1819).

87. 109 U.S. at 53–54.

88. 24 Stat. 379 (1887).

89. *Houston, E. & W. Texas Ry. v. United States*, 234 U.S. 342 (1914).

90. 22 U.S. (9 Wheat.) 1 (1824).

91. 78 Stat. 214 (1964), 42 U.S.C.A. 2000a-2000a-6 (1994).

92. *Heart of Atlanta Motel v. United States*, 379 U.S. 241 (1964); *Katzenbach v. McClung*, 379 U.S. 294 (1964).

93. 95 U.S. 485 (1878) See *supra*, notes 59 to 63 and accompanying text.

94. 133 U.S. 587 (1890).

95. *Id.* at 593–95.

96. See Michael Conant, *The Constitution and the Economy: Objective Theory and Critical Commentary* 100–105 (Norman: University of Oklahoma Press, 1991).

97. 328 U.S. 373 (1946).

98. *Id.* at 386.

99. Louisiana Acts, 1890, no. 111.

100. See Otto H. Olsen, *Carpetbagger's Crusade: The Life of Albion Winegar Tourgee* 312–31 (Baltimore: Johns Hopkins University Press, 1965).

101. Ex parte Plessy, 45 La. Ann. 80, 11 So. 948 (1892). See Charles A. Lofgren, *The Plessy Case: A Legal-Historical Interpretation*, ch. 3 (New York: Oxford University Press, 1987).

102. See Barbara J. Fields, *Ideology and Race in American History*, in J. Morgan Kousser, *Religion, Race and Reconstruction: Essays in Honor of C. Vann Woodward* 143, 144 (New York: Oxford University Press, 1982); Ashley Montagu, *Man's Most Dangerous Myth: The Fallacy of Race*, (New York: Oxford University Press, 5th ed., 1974); Ashley Montagu, *The Myth of Blood*, 6 Psychiatry 15–19 (1943).

103. 109 U.S. 3 (1883).

104. *Plessy*, 11 So. at 950.

105. *Roberts v. City of Boston*, 5 Cush. 198 (Mass., 1849); *Railroad Co. v. Miles*, 55 Pa. St. 209 (1867).

106. *Plessy v. Ferguson* 163 U.S. 537 (1896). See Lofgren, *Plessy Case, supra*, note 101 at 148–95; Benno C. Schmidt, Jr., *Principle and Prejudice: The Supreme Court and Race in the Progressive Era. Part 1: The Heyday of Jim Crow*, 82 Colum L. Rev. 463, 465–70 (1982).

107. *Plessy*, 163 U.S. at 642.

108. On the precedential value of the *Civil Rights Cases*, see Owen M. Fiss, *Troubled Beginnings of the Modern State, 1888–1910*, vol. 8 of the *History of the Supreme Court of the United States* 362 (New York: Macmillan Publishing Co., 1993).

109. *Plessy v. Ferguson*, Brief for the Plaintiff in Error 14.

110. *Scott v. Sandford*, 60 U.S. (19 How.) 393 (1857).

111. *Plessy*, Brief for Plaintiff in Error 14.

112. *Plessy*, 163 U.S. at 544.

113. *Id.* at 551.

114. 84 U.S. (17 Wall.) 445 (1873).

115. *Id.* at 452.

116. *Id.* at 452–53.

117. *Plessy*, 163 U.S. at 544, 551.

118. *Id.* at 544. Upon adoption of the Fourteenth Amendment, twenty-four of the thirty-seven states then in the union either required or permitted racially segregated schools. Michael Klarman, *An Interpretive History of Modern Equal Protection*, 90 Mich. L. Rev. 213, 252 (1991).

119. *Plessy*, 163 U.S. at 550.

120. *Plessy*, Brief for Plaintiff in Error 29.

121. *Plessy*, 163 U.S. at 550.

122. 118 U.S. 356 (1886).

123. 163 U.S. at 553.

124. *Id.* at 554.

125. *Id.* at 556.

126. *Id.* at 557.

127. *Id.* at 559.

128. *Id.*

129. Richard Watt and Richard Orlikoff, *The Coming Vindication of Mr. Justice Harlan,* 44 Ill. L. Rev. 13 (1949); Alan F. Westin, *John Marshall Harlan and the Constitutional Rights of Negroes: The Transformation of a Southerner,* 66 Yale L.J. 637 (1957).

130. *Plyler v. Doe,* 457 U.S. 202, 213 (1982). See Paul R. Dimond, *The Anti-Caste Principle—Toward a Constitutional Standard for Review of Race Cases,* 30 Wayne L. Rev. 1 (1983).

131. See Earl M. Maltz, *"Separate But Equal" and the Law of Common Carriers in the Era of the Fourteenth Amendment,* 17 Rutgers L.J. 553 (1986).

132. *Chesapeake & Ohio Ry. Co. v. Kentucky,* 179 U.S. 388 (1900); *Chiles v. Chesapeake & Ohio Ry. Co.,* 218 U.S. 71 (1910); *McCabe v. Atchison T. & S.F. Ry. Co.,* 235 U.S. 151 (1914). It is ironic that even the Louisiana Supreme Court in the Plessy era had held application of the state rail segregation statute, when applied to interstate passengers, was unconstitutional. *State ex rel. Abbott v. Hicks,* 44 La. Ann. 770 778, 11 So. 74, 76 (1892).

133. Eric Foner, *Reconstruction: America's Unfinished Business, 1863–1877* (New York: Harper & Row, 1988); Franklin Johnson, *Development of State Legislation Concerning the Free Negro,* 1919 (Reprint, Westport: Greenwood Press, 1979); Myrdal, 1 *An American Dilemma, supra,* note 47, chs. 28–31; Howard N. Rabinowitz, *Race Relations in the Urban South* 329–39 (New York: Oxford University Press, 1978).

134. Charles L. Black, *The Lawfulness of the Segregation Decision,* 69 Yale L.J. 421, 422 n. 8 (1960).

135. Robert J. Harris, *The Quest for Equality* 101 (Baton Rouge: Louisiana State University Press, 1960).

136. *United States v. Buntin,* 10 F. 730 (C.C.S.D. Ohio, 1882). See note on public school segregation following this case. *Id.* at 737.

137. Leon F. Litwack, *The Trouble in Mind: Black Southerners in the Age of Jim Crow* (New York: Alfred A. Knopf, 1998); Myrdal, *American Dilemma, supra,* note 47; John Dollard, *Caste and Class in a Southern Town* (New Haven: Yale University Press, 1937); E. Franklin Frazier, *The Negro Family in the United States* (Chicago: University of Chicago Press, 1939).

138. Weinberg, *A Chance to Learn, supra,* note 49; Henry Bullock, *A History of Negro Education in the South* (Cambridge: Harvard University Press, 1967); Louis Harlan, *Separate and Unequal* (Chapel Hill: University of North Carolina Press, 1958); Horace Bond, *The Education of the Negro in the American Social Order* (Englewood Cliffs, N.J.: Prentice Hall, 1934).

139. 59 Mass. (5 Cush.) 198 (1850). See Levy and Jones, Jim Crow Education; Origins of the "Separate But Equal" Doctrine, in Leonard Levy, *Judgments: Essays on American Constitutional History* 316–41 (Chicago: Quadrangle Books, 1972); Roderick T. Baltimore and Robert F. Williams, *The State Constitutional Roots of the "Separate But Equal" Doctrine: Roberts v. City of Boston,* 17 Rutgers L.J. 537 (1986).

140. 59 Mass. (5 Cush.) at 200.

141. Mass. Declaration of Rights, art. 1. (1780). See Perry and Cooper, *Sources of Our Liberties, supra,* note 30 at 374.

142. 59 Mass. (5 Cush.) at 206–7. The later assertion of Chief Justice Taft that the Mas-

sachusetts constitutional injunction was the same as the Equal Protection Clause of the Fourteenth Amendment was in error. *Gong Lum v. Rice*, 275 U.S. 78, 86 (1927).

143. 59 Mass. (5 Cush.) at 201. See Charles Sumner, 3 *Works*, 51–100 (Boston: Lee and Shepard, 1909).

144. Mass. St. 1855, ch. 256 sec. 1; Mass. Gen. Stat., ch. 41, sec. 9 (1860).

145. Alfred Kelly, *The Congressional Controversy Over School Segregation*, 64 Am. Hist. Rev. 537, 540 (1959).

146. *Id.*

147. *Id.* at 542–44.

148. Michael W. McConnell, *Originalism and the Desegregation Decisions*, 81 Virginia L. Rev. 947, 987–1086 (1995).

149. 175 U.S. 528 (1899).

150. *Id.* at 543.

151. *Id.* at 532.

152. *Id.* at 542.

153. *Id.* at 534.

154. *Id.* at 545.

155. 211 U.S. 45 (1908).

156. 1904 Ky. Acts 181.

157. *Id.* at 54.

158. *Id.*

159. *Id.* at 67.

160. Kluger, *Simple Justice, supra*, note 47 at 88.

161. 275 U.S. 78 (1927).

162. *Id.* at 84.

163. *Id.* at 86.

164. *Missouri ex rel. Gaines v. Canada*, 305 U.S. 337 (1938).

165. *Sipuel v. Board of Regents*, 332 U.S. 631 (1948). See Fisher, Ada. *A Matter of Black and White: Autobiography of Ada Lois Sipuel Fisher*, (Norman, Ok.: University of Oklahoma Press, 1996).

166. *Fisher v. Hurst*, 333 U.S. 147, 150 (1948). Justices Murphy and Rutledge dissented.

167. 339 U.S. 629 (1950).

168. *Id.* at 636.

169. 339 U.S. 637 (1950).

170. *Id.* at 642. See Note, *The Fall of An Unconstitutional Fiction—The "Separate but Equal" Doctrine*, 30 Nebraska L. Rev. 69, 76–78 (1950).

171. 339 U.S. 816 (1950).

172. 54 Stat. 898, 902, 49 U.S.C.A. § 3(1) (1940).

173. *Sweatt v. Painter* and *McLaurin v. Oklahoma S. Regents, Memorandum for the United States as Amicus Curiae*.

174. 100 U.S. 303 (1880).

175. *Sweatt* and *McLaurin Memorandum* 9–10; *Henderson v. United States, Brief for the United States* 38–40. See Philip Elman, *The Solicitor General's Office, Justice Frankfurter, and Civil Rights Litigation 1946–1960*, 100 Harvard L. Rev. 817, 820–22 (1987).

176. *Carr v. Corning*, 182 F. 2d 14 (D.C. Cir. 1950).

177. *Carter v. School Board of Arlington County, Va.*, 182 F. 2d 231 (4th Cir. 1950); *Corbin v. County School Board of Pulaski County* 177 F. 2d 924 (4th Cir. 1949).

178. 347 U.S. 483 (1954).

179. 98 F. Supp. 797 (D. Kan 1951).

180. See Kluger, *Simple Justice, supra,* note 47 at 424, reprinting Finding VIII.

181. 98 F. Supp. 529 (E.D.S.C. 1951).

182. *Id.* at 531.

183. *Id.* at 538.

184. *Briggs v. Elliot,* 342 U.S. 350 (1952).

185. *Briggs v. Elliot,* 103 F. Supp. 920 (E.D.S.C. 1952). For opinion upon reversal, see *Briggs v. Elliot,* 132 F. Supp. 776 (E.D.S.C. 1955).

186. 103 F. Supp. 337 (E.D.Va. 1952).

187. *Id.* at 340–41.

188. 32 Del. Ch. 343, 87 A.2d 862 (1952); *aff'd, Gebhart v. Belton,* 33 Del. Ch. 144, 91 A. 2d 137 (1953); *aff'd sub nom. Brown v. Board of Education,* 349 U.S. 254, 301 (1954).

189. 87 A. 2d at 871, *aff'd,* 91A.2d 137, 152.

190. 347 U.S. 483 (1954).

191. See Kluger, *Simple Justice, supra,* note 47 at 589–613, for a detailed report of the conference.

192. Dennis J. Hutchinson, *Unanimity and Desegregation: Decisionmaking in the Supreme Court, 1948–1958,* 68 Georgetown L.J. 1, 91 (1979), quoting Justice Clark's notes.

193. Elman, *The Solicitor General's Office, supra,* note 175, at 822–24.

194. See Kluger, *Simple Justice, supra,* note 47 at 614–15.

195. *Id.* at 634–47.

196. *Bailey v. Alabama,* 219 U.S. 219 (1911); *United States v. Reynolds,* 235 U.S. 133 (1914); *Taylor v. Georgia,* 315 U.S. 25 (1942); *Pollock v. Williams,* 322 U.S. 4 (1944). See Alexander M. Bickel and Benno C. Schmidt, Jr., *The Judiciary and Responsible Government, 1910–21,* vol. 9, *History of the Supreme Court of the United States,* 820–907 (New York: Macmillan Publishing, 1984).

197. Kluger, *Simple Justice, supra,* note 47 at 656.

198. *Id.* at 678.

199. *Id.* at 681.

200. See Alexander Bickel, *The Original Understanding and the Segregation Decision,* 69 Harv. L. Rev. 1 (1955).

201. Kluger, *Simple Justice, supra,* note 47 at 691–93.

202. *Id.* at 698. On racial segregation as an embarrassment to United States foreign policy, see Mary L. Dudziak, *Desegregation as a Cold War Imperative,* 41 Stan. L. Rev. 61 (1988).

203. See note 2, *supra.*

204. See note 11 to 45, *supra,* and accompanying text.

205. *Plessy,* 163 U.S. at 544.

206. *Brown* 347 U.S. at 492–93.

207. *Id.* at 489.

208. Alexander M. Bickel, *The Least Dangerous Branch* 102 (Indianapolis: Bobbs-Merrill, 1962). See same view in Terrance Sandalow, *Constitutional Interpretation,* 79 Mich. L. Rev. 1033, 1036 (1981).

209. *Brown,* 347 U.S. at 490.

210. The evidence is summarized and quoted in Kluger, *Simple Justice, supra,* note 47, chs. 13–18. See Kenneth B. Clark, *Dark Ghetto: Dilemmas of Social Power* 111–153 (New York: Harper & Row, 1965).

211. See Erving Goffman, *Stigma: Notes on the Management of Spoiled Identity* (Englewood Cliffs, N.J.: Prentice Hall, 1963); Karst, *Belonging to America, supra,* note 8 at 21–27.

212. *Brown,* 347 U.S. at 494.

213. *Brown v. Board of Education of Topeka,* 98 F. Supp. 797 (D. Kan. 1951); *Belton v. Gebhart,* 32 Del. Ch. 343, 87 A. 2d 862 (1952).

214. *Briggs v. Elliot,* 98 F. Supp. 529, 538 (E.D.S.C. 1951).

215. *Brown,* 347 U.S. at 495.

216. 352 U.S. 903 (1956) (*per curiam*), aff'g, *Browder v. Gayle,* 142 F. Supp. 707 (M.D.Ala. 1956). "We think that Plessy *v.* Ferguson has been impliedly, though not explicitly, overruled, and that, under the later decisions, there is now no rational basis upon which the separate but equal doctrine can be validly applied to public carrier transportation." *Id.* at 717.

217. *Baltimore v. Dawson,* 350 U.S. 877 (1955) (segregated beaches); *Holmes v. Atlanta,* 350 U.S. 879 (1955) (golf courses); *New Orleans Parks Ass'n v. Detiege,* 358 U.S. 54 (1958) (parks).

218. 347 U.S. 497 (1954). As to the humiliation of African-American students in the federally enforced public school segregation in Washington, D.C., see the dissent of Judge Henry Edgerton in *Carr v. Corning,* 182 F. 2d 14, 30 (D.C. Cir. 1950). See Kluger, *Simple Justice, supra,* note 47, at 517.

219. See Hans A. Linde, *Judges, Critics, and the Realist Tradition,* 82 Yale L.J. 227, 233–34 (1972).

220. 347 U.S. at 499, citing *Korematsu v. United States,* 323 U.S. 214 (1944); *Hirabayashi v. United States,* 320 U.S. 81 (1943).

221. 347 U.S. at 500.

222. See notes 28 to 32, *supra,* and accompanying text.

223. See Pole, *The Pursuit of Equality, supra,* note 16.

4

# Misconstruction of the Commerce Clause and the Sherman Act: The Baseball Antitrust Cases

In Article I, Section 8, of the Constitution of the United States, Congress is delegated power to regulate "commerce among the several states." In the Sherman Antitrust Act of 1890, Congress adopted this same language for the jurisdiction clause.[1] The language is *in pari materia*. Consequently, Sherman Act jurisdiction was as broad as that of the Commerce Clause. Starting in 1869 and continuing to 1937, the Supreme Court reduced the scope of the Commerce Clause to a fraction of its original meaning.[2] From a plenary power to regulate all transactions in the United States, the federal power was reduced to the regulation of the transport of goods and persons between states. Since the Supreme Court was never delegated the power to reduce the scope of the constitutional clauses, this was both violation of the established common-law rules of documentary interpretation and a usurpation of the amending power.

The Sherman Act became law twenty years after the Supreme Court commenced its radical reduction of the scope of the Commerce Clause; it is not surprising that the clause in the statute was for some time very narrowly construed.[3] A combine of the manufacturers of 90 percent of the sugar in the United States was held not to violate the Sherman Act even though most of the output was eventually shipped by common carrier to other states.[4] Given this judicially narrowed scope of the

Sherman Act, it is also not surprising that a combine of owners of major league baseball clubs in different states to impose a career option reserve clause on baseball players' employment contracts was held not to violate section 1 of the Sherman Act.[5] The large economic rents created by outstanding ballplayers as they attracted patrons to purchase tickets to baseball games were mostly captured by the owners of the baseball clubs through monopsonistic (buyers) combine.

In 1937 and thereafter, when the Supreme Court realized the great errors of the earlier court in reducing the scope of the Commerce Clause, it overruled key erroneous decisions and returned to a broad construction of the clause.[6] Overruling, an express rejection of precedent, is an accepted methodology to correct earlier errors in constitutional construction because only the Constitution is basic and superior law ratified by the peoples' representatives in the states.[7] The Court refused to overrule its holding that professional baseball clubs were not in interstate commerce because this was the construction of a statute, and the methodology to construe statutes is a strict application of *stare decisis*.[8] The usual view is that Congress must act to amend federal statutes if the majority of representatives feel that the statutes have been misconstrued by the Supreme Court. Nonaction by Congress is in some classes of circumstances taken as implied approval of Supreme Court interpretations.

The thesis of this study is that the Supreme Court's refusal to overrule its erroneous holding that major league baseball clubs were not in commerce among the several states was a mistaken application of *stare decisis*. The view here is that the strict application of *stare decisis* to statutes must not be followed blindly and must have some carefully reasoned exceptions. One exception is when statutory language has been deliberately borrowed from a constitutional clause. Since the clauses are *in pari materia*, the reasonable expectation of the bar and the public is that, under constitutional supremacy, the statute must be construed the same way that the Constitution is construed. If the Supreme Court has corrected a series of major misconstructions of a constitutional clause by overrulings, it is not within sound reason for the Court to refuse to correct the same errors in construction of a statute derived from the specific language of the Constitution. In a legal system with a written constitution, statutes must conform to the constitution. From this premise, sound reason would indicate that statutory construction must conform to judicial construction of the same language in the U.S. Constitution.

## ECONOMICS OF PROFESSIONAL BASEBALL

The key characteristic of the firms that engage in major league baseball and other professional sports is that on the output side of the productive process, they are not economically competitive rivals.[9] The economics of location and the need for cooperative efforts of two teams at each game to produce a compound product preclude the possibility of economic competition in the sale of tickets to viewers of games. The New York Yankees and the Chicago White Sox do not compete for the same home customers. The location barrier to competition results from the fact that in any major league sport, the optimum size of stadium or playing field makes it uneconomic to have more than two teams in any metropolitan area, and the cost structure of operation results in only one team operating for a single sport at a single time. Thus the Chicago White Sox and the Chicago Cubs do not schedule home games at the same time. This is not an agreement in restraint of trade but a recognition that costs of operation would make it unprofitable for the two teams to play at home at the same time.

The necessary joint activity of the baseball clubs in planning a complex schedule of sporting events and then combining the various teams with various rivals to execute the games causes the economist to treat the entire set of major leagues as if it were a single firm for purposes of analyzing the output side of the productive process.[10] Ball clubs that share the earnings from each event are together a single firm or a joint venture in economics. Since the playing partners are continuously changing over the year, all of them together are best viewed as a single firm or a joint venture. Furthermore, the quality of baseball games as a salable service cannot be determined by any one club alone. Customers will buy tickets only if teams are fairly well balanced so that a true contest takes place. Thus each club has an interest in seeing that rival clubs in their league have some strong players who will attract large audiences to games.

The Congress was convinced of the compound productive character of the output market of professional sports when, in 1961, it enacted the exemption from the antitrust laws of agreements covering the telecasting of professional sports contests of football, baseball, basketball, and hockey.[11] The purpose of the legislation was to enable the member clubs of these professional sports to pool their separate rights in sponsored telecasting of their games and permit the league to sell the pooled rights to a television network. The legislation was needed to overrule the effect of a 1953 decision by a U.S. district court that held such joint bargaining for sale of television rights to violate the Sherman Act.[12] One primary objective of the leagues was to bargain with the networks to televise the games of all teams, not just the ones with winning records. The long-run survival of the leagues was tied to helping the weaker teams share television income and attract new players so that the games did not become so one-sided that the public would lose interest.

The input markets of the baseball clubs, particularly the market for players, are totally different from the output market. The market for players is one in which active competition by the clubs is feasible and has no significant differences from other labor markets for very highly skilled workers. The market for major league players is most closely analogous to other fields where the most skilled receive great public acclaim such as renowned surgeons, trial lawyers, actors, opera singers, musicians, and television newscasters. In a free, competitive market, persons in these fields who have received great public acclaim command large economic rents as compared to others with average or moderate skills in the same fields. In none of these fields are the employers given immunity from the antitrust laws so that they can combine not to compete for the highly skilled labor and thereby capture the economic rents of unique employees.

Executives of the baseball clubs combined to draft the reserve clauses that gave each club options on the services of players they employed for the person's entire playing career. A key asserted justification for reserve clauses was based on "deep pockets," that if players were free to change clubs yearly, the wealthy clubs would acquire all the best players.[13] This is fallacious. All owners know that there must be some strong players on each club so that games will be true sports contests. Monopolization of all the best players by one or two clubs would cause ticket sales to drop dramatically. The modern era of free agency has demonstrated that stability of employment could be achieved by free bargaining and that career-long reserve options in the clubs were unnecessary. The owners' argument that lifetime clauses in players' contracts were necessary for the survival of professional baseball was totally false.

There are many contractual alternatives to reserve clauses that would enable owners to recover the training costs of players.[14] Rookies could be hired under contracts of employment for four or five years with options in the club to release them if their batting averages or pitching averages were below certain levels. Major leagues players could also be hired under contracts of four or more years with conditions for reduction in case of illness or reduced ability, as shown by batting averages or pitching averages.

Club owners argued that reserve clauses extending over entire professional careers were necessary to recoup the costs of training rookies in minor league affiliate teams that were operated at net losses. This view is contrary to the operation of labor markets in a free society. Large numbers of firms in manufacturing, marketing, and finance lose money on trainees. The firms expect to retain a majority of those they train successfully by paying market wages and maintaining good industrial relations. No firms other than baseball clubs expected long-term control of employees at wages below the market value of the individual.

The other main aspect of the players' contract that is enforced by the combine of the clubs is to force players to consent to assignment of their employment contracts so that players may be sold or traded. The common-law presumption against assignment of service contracts is reinforced by the Thirteenth Amendment prohibition on involuntary servitude. The fact that the common-law presumption may be rebutted by express contract was presumed by the courts to occur in a free labor market. In a monopolized market, where all employers in a trade or profession combine to impose assignment contracts on employees, the consent is not voluntary. Thus, the players argued that their sale or trade was part of peonage that was enforced by a blacklist and a collective boycott enforced by Major League Rule 3(g), the no-tampering rule.[15] The player's choice was to submit to peonage or leave baseball.

The economic impact of the reserve clause plus a new player draft favoring the weaker teams was debated in the economic literature.[16] The theorists demonstrated that the existence of the reserve system should not influence the allocation of playing talent among teams.[17] This is not to suggest that the teams will tend toward an equilibrium of exactly equal playing power. Because of population density in largest cities, the demand for seats at ballparks in those cities is much larger than it is in smaller cities. The larger derived demand for players in leagues where the team size is fixed expresses itself in terms of high bids for some free agents in New York and other large cities.

The effect of the reserve clause in transferring economic rents from players whose popularity created the income to club owners has been the subject of economic studies. Economists have constructed models to estimate the marginal revenue products of batters and pitchers of different demonstrated levels of ability. The marginal revenue product is the amount that the player is estimated to add to team income by his performance. One model combines equations based on team win percentages with measures of team hitting and pitching performances.[18] The model develops gross marginal revenue products, from which average player development costs are subtracted in order to estimate net marginal revenue products. In 1976, average and star hitters received between 13 and 34 percent of their net marginal revenue products. Below-average hitters received compensation in excess of their net marginal revenue products, as did below-average pitchers. In 1976, star and average pitchers received from 16 to 56 percent of their net marginal revenue products.

## ANTITRUST IMMUNITY FOR BASEBALL

*Federal Baseball Club of Baltimore v. National League*[19] brought the issue of the application of antitrust to major league baseball to the Supreme Court. The Baltimore Club was a member of the Federal League, organized in 1913. In 1915 the Federal League was dissolved as a result of an agreement between all of the clubs in the league except Baltimore to merge with the National and American Leagues. Being left with no team with which to compete, the Baltimore club was forced out of business. Baltimore then brought a treble-damage action under section 7 of the Sherman Act against the other leagues and the National Commission, a combine of the two leagues. At trial, the plaintiff was awarded a verdict of $80,000, which was trebled under section 7.

A key violation charged under sections 1 and 2 of the Sherman Act was the National Agreement between the two major leagues to employ players under reserve clauses that controlled their employment throughout their playing careers. One of the jury instructions was that defendants "attempted to monopolize, and did monopolize, a part of commerce, principally through what is called the 'reserve clause' and ineligible list features of certain agreements."[20] The jury found that this monopolization caused the failure of the Federal League. The ineligible list was the result of a horizontal agreement of club owners to boycott players who attempted to change employment.

The Court of Appeals reversed the judgment for plaintiffs on the ground that the business of major league baseball was not in interstate commerce as defined by the Supreme Court in that era.[21] The Court adopted the narrowest dictionary definition of commerce as exchange of goods. The service industry of selling admission to baseball games was held not to be commerce.[22] While the service industry of transporting players and equipment between states was recognized as interstate commerce, this interstate transportation was merely incidental to the main function of presenting baseball games. The reserve clauses of the players' employment contracts, the center of monopolization in this case, were found to have only an indirect effect on the interstate transport of players and were thus not illegal.

The Supreme Court affirmed the Court of Appeals.[23] Justice Oliver Wendell Holmes, who had dissented in *Hammer v. Dagenhart*[24] and argued there for broad application of the Commerce Clause, here wrote an opinion adopting the narrowest interpretation of the same language in the jurisdiction clause of the Sherman Act. For a unanimous Court, he disposed of the law of the case in one paragraph.[25] He first held that the business of giving exhibitions of baseball was purely local. He then adopted the reasoning of the court of appeals that the continuous interstate travel of players was merely incidental to the local games. The numerous interstate business transactions between club owners as they divided income from road games were not mentioned. The fact that the reserve clause, which was in the employment contracts of players who were almost constantly traveling to other states to perform, was the key antitrust issue was sidestepped. Holmes cited only *Hooper v. California*,[26] a case concerning an interstate contract for marine insurance, a holding based on the erroneous rule of *Paul v. Virginia*[27] that such interstate insurance contracts were not interstate commerce subject to federal regulation.

Twenty-seven years after *Federal Baseball* and four years before the Supreme Court was to reaffirm the antitrust exemption of baseball, the court of appeals in the Second Circuit met the issue in *Gardella v. Chandler*.[28] Gardella was a New York Giants player who violated the reserve clause of his employment contract to play in the Mexican league. As a result, the major league instituted a group boycott to bar Gardella for five years when he attempted to return. Gardella filed a treble damage action against the leagues and their key officers. The district court dismissed the action solely on the ground that it lacked jurisdiction under the rule of *Federal Baseball*.[29] The court of appeals reversed by a 2-to-1 vote, the two voting to reverse and to allow Gardella to prove the interstate commercial character of major league baseball being the leading American jurists Learned Hand and Jerome Frank.

Judge Hand held that the allegations of interstate commerce in the league's sale of national broadcasting and television rights stated a factual circumstance not existing in 1922 when *Federal Baseball* was decided, so that Gordella should be allowed a trial to distinguish the changing commercial circumstances.[30] Judge Frank's opinion went much further.[31] He noted that the Supreme Court's recent decisions, giving a very broad interpretation to "commerce among the several states," had "completely destroyed the vitality of *Federal Baseball*" and left that case "but an impotent zombi."[32] Frank stated that the allegations concerning the reserve clause that the combine of the clubs and leagues imposed on all players resembled peonage and that the blacklisting, if proved, violated the Sherman Act.[33]

The defendant leagues must have feared the possible outcome of appealing this decision and entered a money settlement with Gardella.[34] The leagues also settled on an antitrust suit by two other players who had left in 1946 to play in the Mexican leagues, and these two were restored to employment with the St. Louis Cardinals.[35]

By 1953, when the Supreme Court next heard a baseball antitrust case, the Court had corrected its earlier great errors that had reduced the Commerce Clause to a fraction of its original meaning. The key case applying broad commerce regulation to service industries was *United States v. South-Eastern Underwriters Association*.[36] In overruling the 1868 decision that had held insurance contracts not to be commerce, Justice Black noted that holding had given the words of the Constitution "a meaning more narrow than one which they had in common parlance of the times in which the Constitution was written."[37]

In *Toolson v. New York Yankees*,[38] the Court in a *per curiam* opinion adopted the strict application of *stare decisis* to statutes in following the decision in *Federal Baseball Club of Baltimore*. The Court refused to reexamine the underlying issues. Baseball was not within the scope of the federal antitrust laws. Congress had the earlier ruling under consideration and could not assemble a majority to act. The Court felt that after thirty years of congressional inaction, it was not the place for the judiciary to intervene. The nonaction of Congress had created an antitrust immunity for baseball. Justices Harold Burton and Stanley Reed dissented.[39] They pointed to the greatly changed facts of the baseball industry in thirty years. The facts assembled by counsel and included in the opinion left no doubt that interstate commerce was the character of the relations. Burton concluded that in the absence of an express grant of immunity by Congress, interstate baseball had to be subject to the Sherman Act.[40]

Shortly after *Toolson*, the Supreme Court refused to recognize antitrust exemption in other sports and theater activities. In *United States v. International Boxing Club*,[41] immunity was denied to professional boxing. Chief Justice Earl Warren noted that 25 percent of the revenue from championship boxing was derived from radio, television, and motion picture rights. *Toolson* was limited to baseball. Other sports had to be reviewed on their facts. The rejection by Congress of bills to exempt other sports carried the implication that those sports should be subject to the antitrust laws.[42]

In *United States v. Shubert*,[43] decided on the same day as *International Boxing*, Chief Justice Warren for a unanimous Court held the producing, booking, and presentation of legitimate theatrical attractions on a multistate basis to be subject to the federal antitrust laws. Theater performances had the same local character as individual baseball games, but, as in baseball, the organization was nationwide. The district court's dismissal of the complaint on the precedent of *Toolson* was error because *Toolson* was a narrow immunity only for baseball.

In 1957, the Court refused to grant antitrust immunity to professional football in *Radovich v. National Football League*.[44] Radovich had left the Detroit Lions and played in another league. When he tried to return to the National League, he was blacklisted. His action for treble damages was dismissed, and the court of appeals affirmed on the basis of *Federal Baseball Club* and *Toolson*. In reversing, the Supreme Court held *Toolson* limited to baseball. The volume of interstate business in professional football brought it under federal jurisdiction. "If this ruling is unrealistic, or illogical, it is sufficient to answer, aside from the distinctions between businesses, that were we considering baseball for the first time upon a clean slate we would have no doubts."[45] It was the duty of Congress to correct *Toolson*.

In the years following *Radovich*, the courts have denied antitrust exemption to other sports, including basketball,[46] hockey,[47] golf,[48] and tennis.[49] Nevertheless, all lower courts are bound to follow the inconsistency of antitrust exemption for baseball. A key example is *Salerno v. American League* in 1970, in which an antitrust action by two discharged umpires was dismissed for lack of subject-matter jurisdiction. When the dismissal was affirmed, Judge Henry J. Friendly was openly critical of *Toolson*. He wrote of the "unrealistic," "inconsistent," and "illogical" distinction between baseball and other professional sports and commented that "we should not fall out of our chairs with surprise at the news that *Federal Baseball* and *Toolson* had been overruled."[50] Judge Friendly was soon to be disappointed.

In 1969, three years before the Supreme Court again upheld the antitrust immunity of baseball, the key agency of the executive branch concerned with labor relations, the National Labor Relations Board (NLRB), held that baseball was in commerce among the several states.[51] The NLRB took jurisdiction and recognized the Major League Baseball Players Association (MLBPA) as a labor organization within the meaning of the National Labor Relations Act and as exclusive bargaining agent for all members of MLBPA.[52] The NLRB rejected the argument that inaction by Congress to overrule *Federal Baseball* and *Toolson* constituted approval of baseball's system of self-government, in which the Commissioner of Baseball was final arbitrator of all disputes. "The system appears to have been designed almost entirely by employers and owners, and the final arbiter of internal disputes does not appear to be a neutral third party freely chosen by both sides, but rather an individual appointed solely by the member club owners themselves."[53] There is no report of any judicial appeal or challenge to this jurisdictional finding of the executive branch, which was directly contrary to *Federal Baseball* and *Toolson*.

In *Flood v. Kuhn*[54] in 1972, the Court majority reaffirmed the antitrust immunity of baseball. Flood, who had played outstanding baseball for the St. Louis Cardinals for twelve years, was traded against his wishes in 1969 to the Philadelphia Phillies. Flood complained to the Commissioner of Baseball and asked that he be made a free agent. Upon denial, Flood brought an antitrust action against the leagues and twenty-four major league clubs in 1970 and refused to play for Philadelphia, rejecting an offer of $100,000. The District Court dismissed the action under the rule of *Federal Baseball* and *Toolson* and the Court of Appeals affirmed.[55] The Supreme Court in a 5-to-3 decision affirmed the antitrust exemption. Justice

Harry Blackmun for the Court held that professional baseball was a business engaged in interstate commerce, that antitrust exemption for the reserve system was an anomaly, and that *Federal Baseball* and *Toolson* had become an aberration confined to baseball.[56] Nonetheless, honoring strict application of *stare decisis* to statutes, he adhered to the *Toolson* rule that congressional inaction had created antitrust immunity for baseball. Noting that boxing and football were subject to antitrust, he concluded, "If there is an inconsistency or illogic in all this, it is an inconsistency and illogic of long standing that is to be remedied by the Congress and not by this Court."[57]

Justice William Douglas and Justice Thurgood Marshall wrote dissents in which Justice William Brennan concurred. Douglas labeled *Federal Baseball* a judicial derelict based on a view of commerce that had long been overruled.[58] He expressly regretted his vote in *Toolson* and here wished to correct what he believed was its fundamental error. The blacklist used to enforced reserve clauses was group boycott. In any other industry, this was illegal.[59] Congressional inaction to correct *Federal Baseball* and congressional refusal to pass bills exempting other professional sports from antitrust were inconsistent and should not have been a basis for judicial refusal to correct judicial error.[60]

## FREE AGENCY THROUGH COLLECTIVE BARGAINING

Even before the *Flood* case, the players began at least to weaken the reserve clause through collective bargaining. The first discussions were at the time of the initial collective bargaining agreement of 1968 that established the grievance procedures that continued through the 1973 Agreement.[61] Recognition of the Major League Baseball Players Association by the NLRB occurred in 1969. In the 1970 collective bargaining agreement, both parties agreed to abstain from concerted action over the reserve clause until after the final appeal of *Flood v. Kuhn* in 1972.[62]

The 1973 collective bargaining agreement first stated that it did not deal with the reserve clause, but then it incorporated by reference the Uniform Player's Contract, which contained reserve clauses.[63] This inconsistency was sure to lead to grievances relating to the reserve clause. The grievance-arbitration procedure of the 1973 collective bargaining contract enabled players to challenge the reserve system and secure a binding decision of an arbitrator.

The first arbitration decision leading to free agency was the case of James "Catfish" Hunter.[64] Hunter's employment contract with Athletics owner-manager Charles O. Finley provided a total salary of $100,000, with $50,000 paid in cash and the other $50,000 in any manner Hunter chose. Hunter requested Finley to purchase a nontaxable annuity from a specific life insurance company for Hunter's benefit. This would allow Hunter to defer federal income tax until he withdrew the money during his lower-income years after leaving the major leagues. When Finley found out that the club would have to pay taxes on the annuity and be denied use of the money, he balked and refused to act. Counsel for the players' association notified Finley that Hunter was terminating his contract under section 7(a) of the uniform contract, which provided such right after default by the club and failure to remedy the default within 10 days.[65]

Hunter could have filed a grievance to collect his compensation. Instead he elected to frame his grievance on material breach of contract and resort to arbitration in order to become a free agent.[66] Arbitrator Peter Seitz ruled that the Oakland Club owed Hunter $50,000 and declared him a free agent. The club petitioned a California court to vacate the award and lost. On appeal this was affirmed, the Court noting that, under California statutes, grounds for vacating of an arbitration award are strictly limited.[67] Here, as long as notice was given to the Internal Revenue Service, there was no aspect that was illegal or against public policy. Numerous clubs bid for Hunter's services, and he finally signed with the New York Yankees on a five-year contract with salary and benefits estimated to value $3.75 million.[68]

The key arbitration that led to modification of the reserve clauses concerned Andy Messersmith of the Los Angeles Dodgers and Dave McNally of the Montreal Expos.[69] Both refused to sign their 1975 playing contracts because their respective clubs would not include a clause giving them the right to approve or disapprove any trade of their contracts to another team. Their clubs exercised the option in the reserve clause, and they played in 1975 without signing. At the end of the playing season, the Major League Baseball Players Association filed grievances on their behalf and asserted that the two pitchers were free agents because, in their view, the option clause could not be perpetual and apply to nonsigners beyond one year.

Before arbitration could begin, the clubs filed an action for declaratory judgment and injunction with a plea that the reserve clause was not subject to arbitration. At a pretrial conference it was agreed that the arbitration should go forward, with the initial determination of the panel being its own jurisdiction and an agreement that the issue would later be presented to the district court on the basis of the record compiled in arbitration.[70] After an arbitration decision by neutral member Peter Seitz upholding jurisdiction and ruling in favor of free agency for Messersmith and McNally, the district court ruled that the arbitration panel correctly took jurisdiction of the issue of reserve clauses and ordered enforcement of the award.[71] Upon appeal, this decision was affirmed.[72] Article 10 of the 1973 Collective Bargaining Agreement defined grievance as any dispute that concerned "the interpretation of, or compliance with, the provision of any agreement between the Association and the Clubs."[73] The Uniform Players Contract was such an agreement, and the reserve clause and the tampering or blacklisting clause were in the contract.

On the merits of the case, judicial review was limited to whether the award "draws its essence from the collective bargaining agreement."[74] Where the collective bargaining agreement and the uniform contract incorporated therein by reference were ambiguous and even in apparent conflict, the decision by arbitrator Seitz for the players met the stated criterion. The agreement contained no express provision that the reserve system enabled a club to control a player perpetually. While the reserve system seemed to operate in that manner, the MBPA officials had argued for some years that the system allowed a player to become a free agent by playing as a nonsigner under an option renewed for one year. The conclusion was that the arbitration award did not change the reserve system, but merely interpreted various elements thereof under circumstances that had not previously arisen.[75]

Messersmith, who had played the 1975 season for the Dodgers for a salary of $115,000, signed a multiyear contract with the Atlanta Braves with an estimated value of $1.75 million.[76] McNally played part of the 1975 season for Montreal and retired from baseball.

The defeat of the perpetual reserve clause in the arbitration award to Messersmith and McNally led to intense pressure by the players' association during the 1976 contract negotiations to limit reserve clauses. The club owners responded with a seventeen-day lockout during spring training. In July 1976, a new basic agreement was signed.[77]

The compromise four-year contract gave early free agency to existing players but delayed free agency to players hired thereafter. All players who had signed Uniform Players Contracts before August 9, 1976, were bound by renewal options of their clubs for one year after existing contracts expired.[78] After playing the additional year, these players became free agents. They became eligible for the reentry draft in which up to fourteen of the twenty-six clubs could negotiate with any individual player. The object of the draft was to give the weakest teams of the previous season first chance to negotiate with free agents in order to promote competitive balance in games and thereby maintain or increase customer interest in attending games. Any club acquiring a free agent who had previously played on another team had to compensate the former team by assigning one draft choice in baseball's June Amateur Player Draft.

Players who signed contracts on or after August 9, 1976, were subject to reserve clauses by their teams for six years of major league service.[79] Since major league service before 1976 counted in the total, not all signers after August 9 were subject to reserve for six future years, as new players would be. The contract provided minimum wages for each of the four years and a $1,000 increase each year. The six-year reserve clause was also contained in the 1980 agreement.[80]

The impact of free agency is shown in the increase in average salaries of major league players.[81] While the minimum 1976 salary was unchanged in 1977, the average salary rose from $51,501 in 1976 to $76,066 in 1977, an increase of 47.7 percent, in spite of the fact that there were only twenty-five free agents. In 1978, the average salary increased to $99,876, or a 94 percent increase in just two years. By 1989, the minimum salary had increased to $68,500, or 3.6 times the 1976 minimum salary. But, in 1989, the average major league player's salary was $512,804, or 9.8 times the 1976 average. It was clear that free agency was working to allow highly skilled players to receive the economic rents that their specialized skills contributed to the games. This is not to argue that all the effects of antitrust exemption of club owners have disappeared. The prolonged midseason professional baseball strike of 1981 caused members of Congress to reconsider the power remaining in the club owner's exemption and whether to remove it.[82]

While the most severe aspects of player oppression had been relieved through collective bargaining, the market for players was far from competitive. The Commissioner of Baseball, acting for the club owners as a group, still had great power to control interteam relations. Under an extremely vague standard in the Major League Agreement, "not in the best interests of baseball," the Commissioner could disapprove any transfer of players between teams and disapprove an undefined group of other activities.[83] A club owner might be suspended from any activities of his team for a year merely for indicating before league rules permit that he wishes to negotiate with a player on another team.[84] This prohibition on "tampering" was a direct attempt to impede a free market for free agent players. Even disputes over franchises in the minor leagues were subject to control of the commissioner and exempt from antitrust remedies.[85]

## MISUSE OF STARE DECISIS

The primary thesis of this study has been that "among the several states," the jurisdiction clause of the Sherman Act that is derived from the Commerce Clause of the Constitution must be governed by constitutional rules of construction. Constitutional methodology in the Supreme Court is based on the fact that only the Constitution was ratified by the people and therefore includes overruling of past erroneous decisions. In contrast, statutory construction generally requires strict application of *stare decisis*. None of the baseball antitrust opinions even mentioned the fundamental issue of the origin of the jurisdiction clause in the Sherman Act, let alone comparing constitutional and statutory interpretive methodologies. Absent appeals briefs that raised and argued these foundation issues of legal methodology, no member of the Supreme Court had sufficient insight to recognize the issues.

Even the application of *stare decisis* to statutes by the Supreme Court, the method adopted in the *Toolson* and *Flood* cases, was treated superficially. There was no penetrating analysis of the complex reasons for the strict application of *stare decisis* to statutes in the majority of cases. The constitutional separation of powers that mandates judicial respect for legislative enactments and leaves revision to the legislature is only a starting point.[86] Judicial statutory interpretation followed by legislative inaction does not by itself imply legislative approval.[87] If a Supreme Court is convinced that an earlier statutory interpretation was erroneous, justice to later litigants of the issue requires a thorough investigation of why no legislative remedy is forthcoming and to what extent there were reasonable reliances on the erroneous opinion.

Congressional silence in the sense that no bills to remedy an erroneous Supreme Court statutory interpretation achieve majority support in the Congress is not automatic ratification of judicial error. The complexities of political bargaining in a legislature prevent the enactment of much socially useful legislation. The most-often quoted argument against a general rule that congressional silence constitute ratification of judicial interpretation was made in 1940 by Justice Felix Frankfurter for the Court in *Helvering v. Hallock*.[88]

> It would require very persuasive circumstances enveloping Congressional silence to debar this court from re-examining its own doctrines. To explain the cause of nonaction by Congress when Congress itself sheds no light is to venture into speculative unrealities. . . Various considerations of parliamentary tactics and strategy might be suggested as reasons for the inaction . . . of Congress, but they would only be sufficient to indicate that we walk on quicksand when we try to find in the absence of corrective legislation a controlling legal principle.[89]

This view that congressional inaction is not ratification was reiterated for the Court majority in *Girouard v. United States*[90] by Justice Douglas: "it is at best treacherous to find in Congressional silence alone the adoption of a controlling rule of law."[91]

Just two years before *Flood*, in *Boys Markets, Inc. v. Retail Clerks Union*,[92] Justice Brennan for the Court quoted the *Hallock* and *Girouard* opinions in holding that congressional silence did not ratify an unprincipled earlier opinion.

There is great inconsistency in the behavior of Supreme Court justices on the meaning of congressional inaction in response to judicial interpretations. Justice Frankfurter, whose opinion in *Hallock* is the most noted on the topic, seemed to reject his own methodology in some later cases. Frankfurter dissented in *International Boxing*[93] and in *Radovich*,[94] calling for the application of *stare decisis* and adherence to *Federal Baseball* and *Toolson*. In the 1950s, after voting to restore the Commerce Clause to its original breadth, he rightfully saw no differences between the national professional sports in relation to the Sherman Act. His vote for compounding the judicial error of *Federal Baseball* rather than overruling it is clearly inconsistent with his methodological views as stated in *Hallock*.

The *Hallock* rule states a rebuttable presumption against congressional silence as implied approval of highest-court construction of a statute. Considerations in addition to legislative silence are needed to support total judicial deferences to the legislature to reverse statutory interpretations. This requires the court to do a complete functional analysis of the statute. If the scope of the statute is narrow and detailed and often revised, such as the Internal Revenue Code, the Supreme Court may view its first interpretation of one narrow section as clear and unambiguous. In such case congressional inaction may be more likely to be viewed as implied approval. On the other hand, if the statute is broad, controls many types of activities, and is seldom revised by Congress, judicial interpretation of one single application followed by congressional inaction may only mean that a majority cannot be assembled in Congress that agrees on the scope or direction of amendment.[95] The Sherman Antitrust Act, for example, as a charter of freedom for markets, is almost of constitutional breadth and stature.[96] Misconstruction of one minor application, such as the exemption in *Federal Baseball*, may not provoke many

Congresspersons to action. They may not want to amend a great charter to append a mandate for application to a single industry. Minute policing of a broad statute is not a usual legislative function.

If the first interpretation of a statute in the Supreme Court gives a comprehensive interpretation of the language in the statute, relating it to the social objectives found in the legislative hearings and reports or elsewhere, subsequent congressional silence is more likely to be taken as implied approval. On the other hand, if the first opinion has little or no historical-linguistic analysis and merely decides whether a narrow set of facts fall under the law or not, there is much less reason to argue that congressional silence is implied ratification of the opinion. *Federal Baseball* falls in the latter group. Justice Holmes made no comprehensive interpretation of the original meaning of the jurisdiction clause of the Sherman Act. Had he done so, he would have noted that the phrase "among the several states" was borrowed from the Commerce Clause of the Constitution. This would have provoked him to analyze the original meaning of the Commerce Clause. The multistate integrated operations of the baseball leagues based on revenue sharing by home teams and road teams and constant travel by salaried players were clearly a part of commerce. Instead we see Justice Holmes displaying the same bias against the antitrust laws that he displayed in *Northern Securities Co. v. United States.*[97]

The most important issue concerning highest-court reinterpretation of a statute is the extent to which the public has acted in reliance on the first interpretation. The extreme case is where substantial investments have been made in reliance on the existence of the first interpretation by a significant segment of the public. On the other hand, if those who have relied on the first interpretation are a very small group, overruling such erroneous interpretation will have small impact. In the case of professional baseball, the only persons allegedly relying on the decision in *Federal Baseball* were the few persons who owned baseball clubs. The modern era of free agency has proved that the owners' representations that they relied on reserve clauses to invest in training players has been proven false. In the present freer market for players created by collective bargaining, the owners pay large bonuses to gifted young players to sign employment contracts and then send them to affiliated minor league teams for training. The earlier judges and justices, being baseball fans, were deceived by the misrepresentations of the owners that reserve clauses were necessary for the existence of organized baseball. This is but one example of those with vested interests that result in monopoly income fighting to maintain the status quo.

The issue must be kept in perspective. There are only a few rare instances in which highest appeals courts, federal or state, have become convinced that their first interpretation of a statute was totally in error and should be overruled in a later similar case. These few instances are much different from the usual situation, where courts are urged to make slight changes in statutory interpretations from case to case. In this latter situation the courts are urged to ignore the separation of governmental powers and to revise the meaning of statutes from case to case over time, a clear usurpation of the amending power.

In the few cases where highest-appeals courts are urged to overrule their first interpretation of a statute, when legislative overruling is denied or unfeasible for some reason, the courts should give careful consideration to the public policy issues. It is important to change bad law quickly, before members of the public act in reliance on it. Statutes that have been wrongfully interpreted and have created unfairness or oppression, while not raising constitutional issues, must be corrected. If there is legislative inertia, courts should consider overruling themselves. Justices must remember that legislatures are just as able to reverse a court's second, overruling interpretation as they are the first interpretation. If there is legislative inertia to reverse the first interpretation, perhaps because of great lobbying by those with vested interests and monetary gain from the first rule, then judicial overruling is most appropriate. The legislature is free to review and to amend the statutory overruling at any session.

## CONGRESSIONAL OVERRULING

There had not been a collective-bargaining agreement between major league baseball owners and the players' union without a work stoppage since 1970.[98] From 1972 to 1997, there were eight contract negotiations between the players and owners, and each of these resulted in a work stoppage, either a strike or a lockout.[99] The 1990 agreement expired in December 1993, and the subsequent strike suspended portions of the 1994 and 1995 seasons, including the 1994 World Series.[100] The owners of major league teams, exempt from the antitrust laws, acted in combination to try to impose terms and conditions of employment on the players. The players, faced with terms designed to reduce union power and curtail players' free agency, had no choice but to strike. As a result, major league baseball had endured more work stoppages than all other professional sports combined.

Numerous bills to end the baseball antitrust exemption have been proposed in the Senate Judiciary Committee, especially since 1990, but opposition came not only from the owners of the teams but also from senators who feared this would result in losing their home teams to another city or the end of Major League financial support for Minor League teams.[101] After the protracted strike of 1994 and 1995, the pressure in Congress by the players' association to end the baseball antitrust exemption increased. The players made this issue a key element of the negotiations of the new Basic Agreement with owners that was finally signed in March 1997. Article 28 of the agreement indicated that the owners and the players' union would jointly request Congress to amend the antitrust laws to give major league players the same rights as other professional athletes.[102] Labeled in the Senate as the Curt Flood Act, the law was designed to create a judicial remedy for owner combinations that were prohibited by the 1997 labor agreement. Under the agreement, players were to have recourse against owners who engaged in collusion on the terms of player contracts and could recover treble damages through a process of binding arbitration. The proposed statute was enacted into law on October 27, 1998.[103]

The Curt Flood Act of 1998 is codified as Section 27 of the Clayton Act and provides that employment relations in major league baseball shall be subject to the antitrust laws to the same extent as other professional sports business affecting interstate commerce.[104] This is followed by a proviso that the rule for major league baseball shall not provide the basis for any negative inference regarding the caselaw concerning the applicability of the antitrust laws to minor league baseball. The senators were concerned about the future of minor league baseball because the major league teams subsidized the minor league teams and each minor league player's employment contract was with a major league employer and contained a long-term reserve clause. While this statute does not apply to minor league baseball, its effect is surely to overrule *Federal Baseball Club* of 1922, *Toolson* of 1953, and *Flood* of 1972. This surely leaves the major league combination that controls reserve clause rules for minor league players in a questionable legal position.

Section 27 specifically states that it shall not change the applicability of the antitrust laws to the amateur draft and reserve clause of minor league baseball or the relationships between major league and minor league baseball. But it is highly likely that the organization of minor league baseball will have to change if the reserve clauses of minor league players are successfully attacked under the antitrust laws. The amateur draft is resented by young players who are sent to minor league teams far from their homes and paid very low wages.[105] A player may be drafted by a team that already has skilled players in his area of skill so that he will not get to play enough in the minor league to prove his abilities.

One final issue that was not resolved by the 1998 statute was whether the players' union could demand that each owner of a team negotiate with the union separately. The Supreme Court has held in a football case that the federal labor laws imply a "nonstatutory" antitrust exemption where needed to make the collective-bargaining process work.[106] In that case the collective bargaining agreement between the owners and the players' association had expired, and the combine of owners set wages to hire squads of substitute players. Since no labor agreement was in effect, one would assume that the Sherman Act would apply to collusive behavior of the owners. The Supreme Court held the implied antitrust exemption was still effective.

## NOTES

1. "Every contract, combination in the form of trust or otherwise, or conspiracy, in restraint of trade or commerce among the several states, or with foreign nations, is hereby declared to be illegal." 26 Stat. 209 (1890), 15 U.S.C.A.1 (1973).
2. See Michael Conant, *The Constitution and the Economy: Objective Theory and Critical Commentary*, 100–105 (Norman: University of Oklahoma Press, 1991).

3. William Letwin, *Law and Economic Policy in America*, 121–42 (New York: Random House, 1965).

4. *United States v. E.C. Knight Co*, 156 U.S. 1 (1895). See implied overruling in *Mandeville Island Farms v. Sugar Co.*, 334 U.S. 219 (1948).

5. *Federal Baseball Club of Baltimore v. National League*, 259 U.S. 200 (1922).

6. See, e.g., *United States v. Darby*, 312 U.S. 100 (1941), overruling *Hammer v. Dagenhart*, 247 U.S. 251 (1918); *United States v. South-Eastern Underwriters Ass'n*, 322 U.S. 533 (1944), overruling *Paul v. Virginia*, 75 U.S. (8 Wall.) 168 (1869).

7. See Edward H. Levi, *Introduction to Legal Reasoning*, 57–60 (Chicago: University of Chicago Press, 1961); Note, *The Power That Shall Be Vested in a Precedent: Stare Decisis, the Constitution and the Supreme Court*, 66 B.U.L. Rev. 345, 370 (1986). See authorities cited in William N. Eskeridge, Jr., *Overruling Statutory Precedents*, 76 Geo.L.J. 1361, 1380–83 (1988).

8. *Toolson v. New York Yankees, Inc.*, 346 U.S. 356 (1953).

9. See Jesse v. Markham and Paul V. Teplitz, *Baseball Economics and Public Policy* 19–25 (Lexington, Mass.: D.C. Heath, 1981), H. Ward Classen, *Three Strikes and You're Out: An Investigation of Professional Baseball's Antitrust Exemption*, 21 Akron L. Rev. 369, 370–76 (1988).

10. See Walter C. Neale, *The Peculiar Economics of Professional Sports*, 78 Quart. J. of Econ. 1 (1964).

11. 75 Stat. 732 (1961), 15 U.S.C.A. §1291 (1982). See John P. Morris, *In the Wake of the Flood*, 38 L. & Contemp. Problems 85, 92–96 (1973).

12. *United States v. National Football League*, 116 F. Supp. 319, 323–24 (E.D. Pa. 1953).

13. See Michael Canes, *The Social Benefits of Restrictions on Team Quality, in Government and the Sports Business* 82–86, Roger Noll. ed. (Washington, D.C.: Brookings Institution, 1974).

14. See Roger G. Noll, Alternatives in Sports Policy, in *Government and the Sports Business, supra,* note 13, at 415–17.

15. See *Flood v. Kuhn*, 407 U.S. 258, 259 n. 1 (1972); James B. Dworkin, *Owners versus Players: Baseball and Collective Bargaining* 77 (Boston, Auburn House, 1981).

16. George Daly and William J. Moore, *Externalities, Property Rights and the Allocation of Resources in Major League Baseball*, 19 Economic Inquiry 77 (1981).

17. The classic study is Simon Rottenberg, *The Baseball Players' Labor Market*, 64 J. Pol. Econ. 242 (1956).

18. James R. Hill, *The Threat of Free Agency and Exploitation in Professional Baseball: 1976–1979*, 25 Quart. Rev. of Econ. and Bus. 68 (1985).

19. 259 U.S. 200 (1922).

20. *National League, Etc. v. Federal Baseball Club*, 269 F. 681, 684 (D.C. Cir. 1920).

21. *Id.*

22. "A game of baseball is not susceptible of being transferred." *Id.* Under the narrow definition of commerce as only sale of goods, Chief Justice Marshall would have erred in holding sale of transportation services to be a class of commerce in *Gibbons v. Ogden*, 22 U.S. (Wheat.) 1 (1824).

23. 259 U.S. 200 (1922).

24. 247 U.S. 251 (1918).

25. *Federal Baseball*, 259 U.S. at 208–09. The antitrust exemption created by this case is limited to the reserve system. *Piazza v. Major League Baseball* 831 F. Supp. 420, 438 (E.D.Pa. 1993).

26. 155 U.S. 648 (1895).

27. 75 U.S. (8 Wall.) 168 (1869), overruled, *United States v. South-Eastern Underwriters Ass'n*, 322 U.S. 533 (1944).

28. 172 F. 2d 402 (2d Cir. 1949).

29. *Gardella v. Chandler*, 79 F. Supp. 260 (S.D.N.Y. 1948).

30. 172 F.2d at 407.

31. *Id.* at 408.

32. *Id.* at 409.

33. See *Fashion Originators Guild of America v. FTC*, 312 U.S. 457 (1941). For restatement of rule, see *Klor's Inc. v. Broadway-Hale Stores, Inc.*, 359 U.S. 207 (1959).

34. H.R. Rep. 2002, 82d cong., 2d Sess. 84 (1952); *New York Times*, June 16, 1950, p. 32, col. 3. The $300,000 claim was reportedly settled for $65,000. *New York Times*, Jan. 4, 1970, Sec. V, p. 5, col. 2. A. B. Chandler, former Commissioner of Baseball, testified, "I do not think the lawyers thought we could win the Gardella case." Hearings, Subcomm. on Monopoly Power, Comm. on Judiciary, House of Rep., Serial 1, Part 6, 82d Cong., 1st Sess., 290 (1952).

35. *Martin v. National League Baseball Club*, 174 F. 2d 917 (2d Cir. 1949); New York Times, July 9, 1949, p. 16, col. 6.

36. 322 U.S. 533 (1944).

37. *Id.* at 539.

38. 346 U.S. 356 (1953).

39. *Id.* at 357–65.

40. *Id.* at 364.

41. 348 U.S. 236 (1955).

42. *Id.* at 243–44.

43. 348 U.S. 222 (1955).

44. 352 U.S. 445 (1957). See Gary Roberts, *Sports League Restraints on the Labor Market: The Failure of Stare Decisis*, 47 U. Pitt. L. Rev. 337, 353–57 (1986).

45. 352 U.S. at 452.

46. *Haywood v. Nat'l Basketball Ass'n*, 401 U.S. 1204 (1971).

47. *Philadelphia World Hockey Ass'n v. Philadelphia Hockey Club*, 351 F. Supp. 462 (E.D. Pa. 1972).

48. *Deesen v. Professional Golfers Ass'n.*, 358 F. 2d 165 (9th Cir. 1966), *cert. denied* 385 U.S. 846 (1966).

49. *Gunter Hartz Sports, Inc. v. United States Tennis Ass'n.*, 65 F.2d 222 (8th Cir. 1981).

50. 429 F.2d 1003 (2d Cir. 1970), *cert. denied*, 400 U.S. 1001 (1971).

51. 429 F. 2d at 1005.

52. *American League of Professional Baseball Clubs*, 180 N.L.R.B. 190, 192–93 (1969).

53. *Id.* at 191.

54. 407 U.S. 258 (1972). See Curt Flood, *The Way It Is* (New York: Trident Press, 1971).

55. *Flood v. Kuhn*, 316 F. Supp. 271 (S.D.N.Y. 1970), *affirmed*, 443 F.22 264 (2d Cir. 1971).

56. 407 U.S. at 282.

57. *Id.* at 284.

58. *Id.* at 286–88.

59. *Klor's Inc. v. Broadway-Hale Stores, Inc.*, 359 U.S. 207 (1959).

60. 407 U.S. at 292 (Marshall, J., dissenting).

61. Basic Agreement Between the American League of Professional Baseball Clubs and

the National League of Professional Baseball Clubs and Major League Baseball Players Association, Art. XIV (Jan. 1, 1970), cited in *Kansas City Royals v. Major League Baseball Players*, 532 F. 2d 615, 623 (8th Cir. 1976).

62. Basic Agreement Between the American League of Professional Baseball Clubs and the National League of Professional Baseball Clubs and the Major League Baseball Players Association, Art. XV (Jan. 1, 1973), cited in *Kansas City Royals v. Major League Baseball Players*, 532 F.2d 615, 618–19 (8th Cir. 1976).

63. *Id.* at 627.

64. *American and National Leagues of Professional Baseball Clubs v. Major League Baseball Players Association*, Decision No. 23 (1974) (Seitz, Chairman), cited in Mark L. Goldstein, *Arbitration of Grievance and Salary Disputes in Professional Baseball: Evolution of a System of Private Law*, 60 Cornell L. Rev. 1049, 1064 (1975).

65. Uniform Players Contract, §7(a), reprinted in Dworkin, *Owners versus Players, supra* note 15, at 220.

66. *Id.* at 72.

67. *American & N.L. of P. Base. Cl. v. Major L. Base. Pl. Ass'n.*, 59 Cal. App. 3d 493, 130 Cal. Rptr. 626 (1976).

68. Dworkin, *Owners versus Players, supra,* note 15, at 72.

69. *Id.* at 72–82; Roger I. Abrams, *Legal Bases: Baseball and the Law* 117–33 (Philadelphia: Temple University Press, 1998).

70. *Kansas City Royals v. Major League Baseball Players*, 532 F.2d 615, 619 (8th Cir. 1976).

71. *Kansas City Royals v. Major League Baseball Players*, 409 F. Supp. 233 (W.D. Mo. 1976).

72. *Kansas City Royals v. Major League Baseball Players*, 532 F.2d. 615 (8th Cir. 1976).

73. *Id.* at 618.

74. *United Steelworkers of America v. Enterprise Wheel & Car Corp.*, 363 U.S. 593, 597 (1960).

75. 532 F.2d at 631.

76. Kenneth M. Jennings, *Balls and Strikes: The Money Game in Professional Baseball* 189 (New York: Praeger Publishers, 1990).

77. Dworkin, *Owners versus Players, supra,* note 15, at 34.

78. *Id.* at 83.

79. James R. Hill and William Spellman, *Professional Baseball: The Reserve Clause and Salary Structure*, 22 Industrial Relations 1, 3 (1983).

80. For a summary of free agent negotiations in the 1980s, see Jennings, *Balls and Strikes, supra,* note 76, at 190–99.

81. *Id.* at 213.

82. See Robert G. Berger, *After the Strikes: A Reexamination of Professional Baseball's Exemption from the Antitrust Laws*, 45 U. Pitt. L. Rev. 209 (1983).

83. *Charles O. Finley & Co., Inc. v. Kuhn*, 569 F. 2d. 527 (7th cir. 1978), *cert. denied* 439 U.S. 876 (1978). See Bowie Kuhn, *Hardball: The Education of a Baseball Commissioner* 173–187 (New York: Times Books, 1987).

84. *Atlanta Nat. League Baseball Club v. Kuhn*, 432 F. Supp. 1213 (N.D. Ga. 1977). See Kuhn, *Hardball, supra*, note 83, at 259–64.

85. *Professional Baseball Schools & Clubs, Inc. v. Kuhn*, 693 F. 2d 1085 (11th Cir. 1982).

86. "Considerations of stare decisis have special force in the area of statutory interpretation, for here, unlike in the context of constitutional interpretation, the legislative

power is implicated, and Congress remains free to alter what we have done." *Patterson v. McLean Credit Union*, 491 U.S. 164, 172–73 (1989).

87. Levi, *Introduction to Legal Reasoning, supra,* note 7, at 32; Eskridge, *Overruling Statutory Precedents, supra,* note 7, at 1364–76.

88. 309 U.S. 106 (1940), overruling *Klein v. United States*, 283 U.S. 231 (1931); *Helvering v. St. Louis Union Trust Co.*, 296 U.S. 39 (1935); *Becker v. St. Louis Union Trust Co.*, 296 U.S. 48 (1935). See Menitove, *Baseball's Antitrust Exemption: The Limits of Stare Decisis*, 13 B.C. Ind. & Com. L. Rev. 737, 742 (1971); C. Paul Rogers, *Judicial Reinterpretation of Statutes: The Example of Baseball and the Antitrust Laws*, 14 Houston L. Rev. 611, 622 (1977).

89. 309 U.S. at 119–21.

90. 328 U.S. 61 (1946), overruling *United States v. Schwimmer*, 279 U.S. 644 (1929); *United States v. Macintosh*, 283 U.S. 605 (1931); *United States v. Bland*, 283 U.S. 636 (1931). See Frank E. Horack, *Congressional Silence: A Tool of Judicial Supremacy*, 25 Tex. L. Rev. 247, 253–59 (1947).

91. 328 U.S. at 69–70.

92. 398 U.S. 235 (1970), overruling *Sinclair Refining Co. v. Atkinson*, 370 U.S. 195 (1962).

93. *United States v. International Boxing Club*, 348 U.S. 236, 248–253 (1955).

94. *Radovich v. National Football League*, 352 U.S. 445, 455 (1957).

95. See Henry Friendly, *The Gap in Lawmaking—Judges Who Can't and Legislators Who Won't*, 63 Colum. L. Rev. 787, 792 (1963).

96. See, e.g., *Northern Pac. Ry. v. United States*, 356 U.S. 1, 4 (1958), where Justice Black notes: "The Sherman Act was designed to be a comprehensive charter of economic liberty aimed at preserving free and unfettered competition as the rule of trade. It rests on the premise that the unrestrained inter-action of competitive forces will yield the best allocation of our economic resources, the lowest prices, the highest quality and the greatest material progress, while at the same time providing an environment conducive to the preservation of our democratic and social institutions." See *Appalachian Coals, Inc. v. United States*, 288 U.S. 344, 359–60 (1933); Hans B. Thorelli, *The Federal Antitrust Policy* 608 (Baltimore: Johns Hopkins University Press, 1954); Walton Hamilton & Irene Till, *Antitrust in Action* 119 (TNEC Monograph No. 16, 1940).

97. *Northern Securities Co. v. United States*, 193 U.S. 197, 400 (1904) (Holmes, J., dissenting).

98. See Kathleen L. Thurland, *Major League Baseball and Antitrust: Bottom of the Ninth, Bases Loaded, Two Outs, Full Count and Congress Takes a Swing*, 45 Syracuse L. Rev. 1328, 1346–48 (1995).

99. *Major League Baseball Antitrust Reform*, Hearing before Senate Committee on the Judiciary, 105th Cong., 1st Sess. 7–13 (1997) (Statement of Donald A. Fehr)

100. The 1995 baseball season began only after a federal judge issued an injunction restoring terms of the prior agreement. *Silverman v. Major League Baseball Player Relations Comm.*, 880 F. Supp. 246 (S.D.N.Y. 1995) (National Labor Relations Board had reasonable cause to believe that the owners' unilateral actions constituted an unfair labor practice), *aff'd*, 67 F. 3d 1054 (2d Cir. 1995). See Abrams, *Legal Bases, supra,* note 69 at 189–200.

101. See Thurland, *Major League Baseball and Antitrust, supra,* note 98 at 1361–67.

102. *Curt Flood Act of 1997*, Senate Rep. 105–118, 105th Cong., 1st Sess., Judiciary Comm. 3 (1997).

103. Public Law 105–297 (approved October 27, 1998). See *Congressional Record* H9942–9946 (October 7, 1988), reporting the final approval in the House of Representatives.

104. 15 U.S.C. §27 (1998).

105. *Major League Baseball Antitrust Reform, supra,* note 99 at 13–16 (Statement of Dan Peltier).

106. *Brown v. Pro Football, Inc.*, 518 U.S. 231 (1996).

5

# Federalism under the Commerce Clause: *United States v. Lopez*

In spite of the alarmed response of some commentators, the future of federalism was not at stake in *United States v. Lopez*.[1] The highly unusual issue of federalism in *Lopez* was whether noncommercial activity, the mere possession of gun near a school, could be subject to national criminal regulation under the enumerated power in Congress to regulate commerce among the several states. Any careful student of constitutional law would first note that the mass of Supreme Court decisions from *Gibbons v. Ogden*[2] to date that concerned statutes regulating commercial transactions would shed no light on the narrow issue of *Lopez*. Legal historians of the original meaning of the Commerce Clause and the most recent decisions of the Court assert that the commerce power, like the others enumerated in Article I, Section 8, is plenary.[3] National transactions and local transactions when aggregated form an integrated whole subject to national regulation.

From this viewpoint, the justices mistakenly treated the history of the opinions on the scope of the commerce power as a primary issue. The resulting six opinions cover many pages of redundant reviews of the opinions of the Court on the regulation of commercial transactions, which are not relevant to the noncommercial events in *Lopez*. Chief Justice Rehnquist, for example, asserts that the major cases after 1937 "expanded congressional power under the Commerce Clause."[4] But the broad commerce power, as Chief Justice Marshall told us in *Gibbons*, was delegated to Congress in 1789 by ratification of the people. The Court was not delegated the power to contract the Commerce Clause, as it did from 1869 to 1936, so that the decisions in 1937 and thereafter were not an expansion but a restoration. It is clear that all this fuzzy history was not relevant to the noncommercial events of *Lopez.*

The Court failed to recognize that the federalism issue in *Lopez* still existed even when one accepted the view that the commerce power in Congress is plenary. Since mere gun possession is not commerce and there was neither a commerce jurisdiction clause nor legislative findings of effects on commerce for the courts to weigh, the case turned on arguments of counsel about effects on commerce. The result was unsettled law when five justices found the effects on commerce too remote and four justices found them substantial. This is strong evidence that the justices on both sides of the decision adopted the wrong standard. While no justice defined the word "substantial" in estimating effects on commerce, it seems that the standard itself is fallacious. Even if there was some effect on the commerce of the nation because of gun possession near schools, this was not ground to subsume noncommercial activity under the Commerce Clause. Rehnquist, for the majority, was correct in asserting that the issue is whether under constitutional structure a set of enumerated powers can have limits that protect the residual powers in the states.[5]

## COURT OPINIONS

The Gun-Free School Zones Act of 1990 made it a crime for "any individual knowingly to possess a firearm at a place that the individual knows, or has reasonable cause to believe, is a school zone."[6] A school zone was defined as the area "within a distance of 1,000 feet from the grounds of a public, parochial or private school."[7] Lopez was a senior at a San Antonio high school carrying a concealed handgun and five bullets. He was originally charged under a Texas statute, clearly the correct law to punish a local criminal act defined in terms of the property law concept of "possession."[8] The state charges were dismissed when Lopez was charged under the federal act. Counsel for Lopez moved the district court to dismiss his indictment on the ground that the federal act was unconstitutional, as beyond the power of Congress to regulate local public schools. The motion was denied, the district court holding that the act "is a constitutional exercise of Congress' well-defined power to regulate activities in and affecting commerce, and the 'business' of elementary, middle and high schools . . . affects interstate commerce."[9] Lopez was tried and convicted.

The court of appeals reversed the conviction and held the federal act as beyond the power of Congress under the Commerce Clause.[10] The lack of findings in the legislation was held crucial. "Where Congress has made findings, formal or informal, that regulated activity substantially affects interstate commerce, the courts must defer 'if there is any rational basis for' the findings. . . . Practically speaking, such findings almost always end the matter."[11] Since neither the legislative history nor the statute itself suggested a nexus to the Commerce Clause, the

Court could not properly perform its duty to determine if there was a rational basis for such a nexus.

The Supreme Court, by a vote of 5 to 4, affirmed the court of appeals.[12] Chief Justice William Rehnquist wrote the majority opinion. His first paragraph explicates the principle of federalism that the national government is one of delegated, enumerated powers with all residual powers reserved to the states. Federalism, like the separation of powers, is designed to ensure protection of our fundamental liberties and thus reduce the risk of tyranny. Rehnquist notes that the act "neither regulates a commercial activity nor contains a requirement that the possession be connected in any way to interstate commerce."[13] He then proceeds to spend some pages reviewing the history of leading Commerce Clause cases, all of which concerned regulation of transactions in commerce. He finally returns to the test for a noncommercial activity: "an analysis of whether the regulated activity 'substantially affects' interstate commerce."[14] He notes that the act "contains no jurisdictional element which would ensure, though case-by-case inquiry, that the firearm possession in question affects interstate commerce."[15] Furthermore he reports that the government concedes that "[n]either the statute nor its legislative history contain[s] express congressional findings regarding the effects upon interstate commerce of gun possession in a school zone."[16] All of these defects could have been remedied if the trial had proved that in this case the gun had moved in commerce, but there was no such proof.

The brief of the United States argued that firearms in schools could result in violent crime that could affect interstate commerce in at least three ways.[17] First, the aggregate costs of violent crime raise insurance rates and, through insurance, these costs are spread throughout the population. There was no estimate of whether school gun crimes were statistically significant in raising insurance rates. Second, violent crimes in aggregate reduce the willingness of individuals to travel to the areas of the country that are perceived to be unsafe. There were no statistical estimates of the geographical distribution of school gun crimes. Third, guns in schools threaten the learning environment. This could handicap educational processes and lower the productivity of the workforce. Rehnquist's response to these arguments was that they support federal government power to regulate all violent crime and all activities that might lead to violent crime, regardless of how tenuously they related to interstate commerce. Under this argument, Congress would have a general police power to regulate any acts related to economic productivity, even family law.[18] "To uphold the Government's contentions here, we would have to pile inference upon inference in a manner that would bid fair to convert congressional authority under the Commerce Clause to a general police power of the sort retained by the states."[19]

Rehnquist is correct that the government's arguments would in effect destroy the concept of enumerated powers. The Congress has a plenary power to regulate transactions in commerce. But noncommercial intrastate crimes are twice remote from an estimable substantial affect upon commerce. In fact the entire concept of "substantial affect" is open to question.[20] Neither the Court nor the Congress has defined "substantial" as applied to effects on commerce. The fact that the Court has consistently deferred to the published assertions of Congress, both in formal findings in the legislation itself and inferences from committees reports and testimony in committees hearings, that the effects are "substantial" is not proof. Mere statutory assertions or anecdotal testimony does not establish truth. Separating out the effects of one cause out of may joint causes, such as separating guns in school from all other guns, may be impossible even with the use of modern statistical techniques.

The alternative method to convert noncommercial local crimes into federal crimes and thereby effect the federal commerce power is to add a jurisdictional clause to the statute. This was the method in the Omnibus Crime Control and Safe Streets Act of 1968.[21] This statute made it a crime for a convicted felon to receive, possess or transport "in commerce or affecting commerce . . . any firearm."[22] In *Scarborough v. United States*,[23] defendant was in legal possession of four firearms in his home before and at the time he was convicted of a state felony narcotics offense. He was subsequently charged with receipt and possession of the arms in violation of the federal act. Evidence at his jury trial proved that the firearms had at some time traveled in interstate commerce. The Court held that this was sufficient nexus with commerce to turn mere local possession into a crime. The conviction was affirmed on the basis of statutory interpretation without treating the constitutional issue of the scope of the Commerce Clause. Justice Stewart dissented, arguing that under the time-honored rule of lenity, the ambiguous federal statute should apply only to receipt, possession, and transport of guns after the defendant is convicted of a felony.

The logic of converting noncommercial, local crimes into federal ones by a jurisdictional clause is highly questionable.[24] Some sets of facts rest on remoteness. A person who purchases a gun locally and legally without knowledge that others in a chain of ownerships in the past brought it from another state has no substantial relationship to interstate commerce. A prior owner who transported the gun from another state as part of changing residence and without intent to sell the gun would not have transported it in interstate commerce. The subsequent decision to sell does not retroactively turn the transport of the gun into interstate commerce. In *Brooks v. United States*,[25] the case upholding the constitutionality of the National Motor Vehicle Theft Act,[26] the Supreme Court not only emphasized the jurisdictional clause of transporting a motor vehicle in interstate commerce knowing it to be stolen but also emphasized the substantive commercial objective, the jury finding that the purpose was profiting from the subsequent transaction in stolen goods. Contrast the destitute person who steals a car to drive to a town across the state line to see his sick mother and leaves the car near the police station in the destination town. Competent counsel could argue that this was interstate transport with no commercial objective and hence outside the scope of the statute.[27]

Justice Anthony Kennedy, joined by Justice Sandra Day O'Connor, concurred. His opinion, like that of Chief Justice Rehnquist, contains many pages reviewing past Supreme Court cases under the Commerce Clause that concerned regulation of commercial transactions and were thus not in point to mere gun possession.[28] At the end of his eighth page, he finally turns to federalism and quotes Madison in *Federalist* No. 51 that the national and state governments "will control each other, at the same time that each will be controlled by itself." On his thirteenth page, he finally gets to *Lopez*. He notes that education is a traditional concern of the states and tells us that each state or municipality must determine how harsh criminal sanctions are necessary and wise to deter students from carrying guns on school premises. "The statute now before us forecloses the States from experimenting and exercising their own judgment in an area in which States lay claim by right of history and expertise, and it does so by regulating an activity beyond the realm of commerce in the ordinary and usual sense of that term."[29]

Justice Clarence Thomas wrote a concurring opinion in which he argued that Congress could not regulate many matters that affect commerce.[30] He rejected Rehnquist's test of substantial effects on commerce and argued that certain activities are not subject to national regulation regardless of the level of effects on interstate commerce. He reached this conclusion by misinterpreting the *obiter dictum* of Chief Justice John Marshall in *Gibbons v. Ogden*[31] that the commerce power does not extend to local commerce that does not affect other states. He cites with favor the totally repudiated decisions in *United States v. E.C. Knight Co.*[32] and *Carter v. Carter Coal Co.*,[33] in which the Court had failed to recognize that the issues concerned transactions, commerce in the sugar refining and mining industries. Thus, his conclusion about the limited original meaning of the Commerce Clause is contrary to that of the leading historians of the clause.[34]

Justice Stephen Breyer wrote the main dissenting opinion, in which Justices John Stevens, David Souter and Ruth Bader Ginsberg joined. He first asserted three basic principles of Commerce Clause-interpretation: (1) the power to "regulate commerce . . . among the several states" encompasses the power to regulate local activities insofar as they significantly affect interstate commerce; (2) in determining whether a local activity will likely have a significant effect upon interstate commerce, a court must consider the cumulative effect of all similar instances; and (3) the Constitution requires us to judge the connection between a regulated activity and interstate commerce, not directly, but at one remove, that is, whether Congress could have had a rational basis for so concluding.[35] Statutory findings by Congress of significant effect on commerce would leave the Court less leeway to find the contrary. In *Lopez*, there was no such finding by Congress.

Breyer found the Gun-Free School Zone Act "well within the scope of the commerce power."[36] He cited a large literature that makes it clear that the problem of guns in and around schools is widespread and extremely serious. Consequently, Congress could have found, given the effect of education upon interstate and foreign commerce, that gun-related violence in and around schools is a commercial problem.[37] The difficulty with this reasoning is that it destroys the concept of national enumerated powers. Many branches of local law result in judgments that could have a significant effect on commerce. Rehnquist had pointed to family law, where decrease for alimony and child support, when cumulated, surely affect commerce. Rehnquist also had argued that regulating guns in and near schools because they affect education, which affects commerce, means that Congress may preempt all state and local education law with national statutes. Breyer's response to this was that the school gun problem was a particularly acute threat to the educational process.

Justice Breyer asserted three serious legal problems with the majority opinion: (1) it was inconsistent with precedent, (2) it relied on the critical distinction between commercial and noncommercial activities, and (3) it fostered legal uncertainty in an area of law that seemed reasonably well settled.[38] All the alleged precedents that Breyer cites concerned regulations of commercial transactions and were thus subject to the plenary power in Congress to regulate commerce. The Gun-Free School Zones Act is distinguished by its failure to mention commerce or the Commerce Clause. Furthermore, the federalism issue is constitutional, and the Supreme Court is not bound by precedent when making a constitutional decision.[39] The commerce-noncommerce distinction is the essence of dealing with this enumerated power. The remoteness of mere possession of a handgun to significant affect upon interstate commerce is first and foremost distinguishable from statutes regulating economic activity. As to increasing uncertainty where there was settled law, this was one of very few statues without a jurisdictional clause and without commercial subject matter. Its precedential scope is very narrow and limited.

Even if one argues against judicial review of congressional powers delegated and enumerated in Article I, Section 8, the argument for departmental review, *Lopez* would still be subject to judicial review. The issue of federalism would still be contestable even under departmental review. The Congress would have final say for the scope of all statutes regulating commercial transactions. But attempts of Congress to subsume noncommercial regulations under the Commerce Clause would raise the federalism issue of whether Congress had exceeded its enumerated powers. Breyer asserts in *Lopez* that he is not arguing an end to the distinction between what is national and what is local.[40] But his dissent presents no practical limit to national regulation of any activity merely by labeling it as having a significant effect on interstate commerce.

## AMENDED STATUTE

Six months before the Supreme Court decision in *Lopez*, the Congress had amended the Gun-Free School Zones Act to add nine findings to justify the statute.[41] At the oral argument in the Supreme Court, counsel for the United States did not rely on these subsequent findings as a substitute for the absence of such factual findings in the trial court.[42] After the Supreme Court decision, the Congress added a jurisdictional clause to the statute, which became law in September 1996. It reads: "It shall be unlawful for any individual knowingly to posses a firearm that has moved in or that otherwise affects interstate or foreign commerce at a place that the individual knows, or has reasonable cause to believe, is a school zone."[43] This requirement of proof of a tie to interstate or foreign commerce is the same that has been upheld as valid in other sections of Article 18. The findings are as follows:

922 (q)(1) The congress finds and declares that—

(A) crime, particularly crime involving drugs and guns, is a pervasive, nationwide problem;

(B) crime at the local level is exacerbated by the interstate movement of drugs, guns, and criminal gangs;

(C) firearms and ammunition move easily in interstate commerce and have been found in increasing numbers in and around schools, as documented in numerous hearings in both the Committee on the Judiciary of the House of Representatives and the Committee on the Judiciary of the Senate;

(D) in fact, even before the sale of a firearm, the gun, its component parts, ammunition, and the raw materials from which they are made have considerably moved in interstate commerce;

(E) while criminals freely move from State to State, ordinary citizens and foreign visitors may fear to travel to or through certain parts of the country due to concern about violent crime and gun violence, and parents may decline to send their children to school for the same reason;

(F) the occurrence of violent crime in school zones has resulted in a decline in the quality of education in our country;

(G) this decline in the quality of education has an adverse impact on interstate commerce and the foreign commerce of the United States;

(H) States, localities, and school systems find it almost impossible to handle gun-related crime by themselves—even States, localities, and school systems that have made strong efforts to prevent, detect, and punish gun-related crime find their efforts unavailing due in part to the failure or inability of other States or localities to take strong measures; and

(I) the Congress has the power, under the interstate Commerce Clause and other provisions of the Constitution, to enact measures to ensure the integrity and safety of the Nation's schools by enactment of this subsection.[44]

Congressional findings A, B, C, and D would apply to all use of guns in crimes and do not even mention schools. The severity of the crime problem in the United States and the movement of guns and gun parts in commerce are appropriate findings for national control of the possession of all guns. No one questions the power of the Congress to criminalize the interstate movement of guns and gun parts, but this is not part of local school regulation.

Finding E is concerned with the impact on persons of gun crimes and is a rationale for general gun control and increased numbers of police. It is not the existence of guns but the inadequate numbers of police at schools that may cause parents to keep children home from school. It is the states, not the national government, that must police the school zones and school entrances. There is no excuse for the few states that have failed to enact special laws to punish guns at schools.

Findings F and G are about violent crimes and schools generally. It does not indicate that gun crimes are a significant proportion of this total violence. The impact on commerce is asserted, but when applied to guns in schools, the impact may be too small to estimate.

Finding H asserts that the states have been unsuccessful in controlling guns at schools. There is no evidence of the extent to which this is true. It is difficult to assume that a federal statute duplicating state statutes criminalizing guns in school will help. Lopez had been charged under a Texas statute, and the charges were dropped after the federal indictment against Lopez. There is no reason to assume that a Texas prosecution would have been inadequate.

Even if federal resources would improve local enforcement, there is no apparent reason for duplicate statutes. Federal subsidies to state agencies would surely be more effective in increasing police presence in school zones.

## IMPACT OF *LOPEZ*

The impact of the *Lopez* opinion has provoked challenges to federal regulation of many types of local crimes. Most of the federal statutes have jurisdiction clauses requiring that some aspect of the local crime move in or affect interstate commerce, and the courts of appeal have generally upheld the constitutionality of these statutes. Since they require proof of the nexus of the local activity to interstate commerce, their language clearly conforms to the requirements of federalism. The 1996 amendments to the Gun-Free School Zones Act puts it in this category and isolates *Lopez* as a historical anomaly.

The Drug-Free School Zones Act,[45] while analogous to the Gun-Free School Zone Act, can be distinguished. The statute makes it illegal to distribute or to possess with intent to distribute a controlled substance within 1,000 feet of a school. "Distribute" means a sale, which is commerce. In *United States v. Jackson*,[46] defendant was convicted of possessing with intent to distribute cocaine base within 1,000 feet of a school. Even though the statute did not have a jurisdiction clause prescribing use of or effects on interstate commerce, the statute was upheld under the Commerce Clause. Cocaine arrives in the United States by foreign commerce, and local sale is part of the aggregate demand that affects commerce.

One of the key federal criminal statutes without a jurisdiction clause relating to interstate commerce is the one that makes it unlawful for a person to transfer or possess a machine gun.[47] In a number of recent cases, persons convicted of possessing machine guns have challenged the federal jurisdiction under the rule of *Lopez* as not concerning commerce, and the challenges have failed. In *United States v. Wright*,[48] the Court held that neither a jurisdictional statement in the statute nor formal legislative findings connecting the regulated activity to interstate commerce were necessary. Where all transfer of machine guns is banned, mere possession becomes part of the ban because possession is found usually to precede sale, and most sales are in interstate commerce. "In our view, the connection between the elimination of the lawful demand for machineguns and the manufacture, importation, and interstate transfer of these products is obvious and direct. We therefore hold that Congress had a rational basis to determine that a total ban on machineguns would have a substantial effect on interstate commerce."[49]

The Comprehensive Environmental Response, Compensation, and Liability Act (CERCLA)[50] is a key example in which Congress failed to include a commerce jurisdictional clause or legislative findings of the impact on commerce. Under CERCLA, the government may bring civil actions to order firms to clean properties of hazardous waste that poses a threat to environment. In *United States v. Olin Corp.*,[51] such action was brought against defendant concerning one chemical plant in Alabama where all the contamination was within the property of Olin. The district court dismissed the action on the basis of *Lopez,* and the court of appeals reversed. Hazardous waste disposal is a costly economic activity. The question was whether such economic activities, viewed in the aggregate, substantially affected interstate commerce. The issue here was whether on-site waste disposal affected interstate commerce.[52] The legislative history, as shown by a key Senate report, demonstrated the nexus between improper waste disposal and interstate commerce.[53] A national policy to protect water and air, the largest part of which will affect interstate commerce, may be applied to the local instance where no interstate impact is proved.

In 1994, Congress passed the statute entitled "Freedom of Access to Clinic Entrances"[54] in response to increasing incidents of violence and obstruction at abortion clinics. In *Cheffer v. Reno,*[55] the Court rejected an argument under *Lopez* that the statute concerned only local activity unrelated to commerce. The statute did not contain a jurisdiction clause requiring proof of a relation to commerce, but Congress had made several findings to that effect. Congress found that doctors and patients often travel across state lines to provide and receive services.[56] In addition, clinics received supplies in interstate commerce.[57] Congress concluded that past violence and obstruction of clinic entrances threatened interstate commerce in the provision of reproductive health services.[58] In contrast to the noncommercial character of the gun possession in *Lopez,* the sale of medical services was commerce and much of it was interstate. The Court concluded that the findings of Congress were plausible and provided a rational basis for concluding that the Access Act regulates activity that substantially affects interstate commerce.[59]

The Interstate Domestic Violence statute of 1994[60] was challenged under the rule of *Lopez* even though it had an interstate jurisdictional clause because the acts of domestic violence were noncommercial. The statute criminalized the crossing of a state line with intent to injure, harass, or intimidate a spouse or intimate partner or to so travel and cause bodily harm. It also covers one who causes a spouse or intimate partner to cross a state line by force, coercion, duress, or fraud and thereby causes bodily injury. In *United States v. Bailey,*[61] the Court affirmed a conviction under the Interstate Domestic Violence statute for the defendant's kidnapping of his wife. The Court found it unnecessary to review *Lopez* or to distinguish it as being under a statute without an interstate jurisdiction clause. Instead it relied on two noncommercial precedents under the "other immoral purposes" section of the Mann Act.[62] Immorality is not sexual commerce. The mere crossing of a state line does not establish interstate commerce jurisdiction and the substantive act of domestic violence is not commercial. Under the rule of *Lopez*, the separate count for domestic violence in *Bailey* should have been dismissed.

In contrast to the Interstate Domestic Violence Statute, the 1999 case of *Brzonkala v. Virginia Polytechnic Institute*[63] was brought under the Violence Against Women Act, which has no interstate jurisdiction clause. The Fourth Circuit Court majority affirmed dismissal of a rape case brought under the section of the act which created a private cause of action against any person who committed a crime of violence motivated by gender. The act was held not to regulate activity that would have a substantial effect on interstate commerce. This is a judicial rather than a legislative question. Not only was rape noncommercial activity but there was no allegation in the complaint of commercial motive of defendants. "Because Section 13981 neither regulates an economic activity nor includes a jurisdictional element, it cannot be upheld on the authority of *Lopez* or any other Supreme Court holding demarcating the outer limits of Congress' power under the substantially affects test."[64] The court rejected congressional findings of effects on interstate commerce as meeting the test of substantial impact. The costs to society of all violent crimes are second order effects on commerce, but if these costs were allowed to satisfy the substantial effects test, federalism would be terminated as the national government would have authority to take over all criminal law historically reserved to the states. The court also ruled that wholly private acts of gender-motivated violence are not state action and can never violate the Equal Protection Clause of the Fourteenth Amendment.

The Court in *Lopez* noted that the absence of a federal jurisdictional clause in the Gun-Free School Zones Act prevented determination, through case-by-case inquiry, that the firearm possession in question affected interstate commerce.[65] Hence, one would expect that statutes containing a commerce jurisdictional clause would not be challenged under the *Lopez* precedent. Such expectation would be in error, because many such federal statutes have been challenged, though unsuccessfully, under the *Lopez* ruling.

Even the earlier Supreme Court decision in *Scarborough v. United States*,[66] that conviction of a felon for possession of a firearm that previously had traveled in interstate commerce was valid, was challenged under the *Lopez* ruling. In *United States v. McAllister*,[67] the *Scarborough* holding that the interstate commerce element was met by demonstrating a "minimal nexus" was followed. Defendant's *Lopez* challenge was rejected, and his conviction as a felon in possession of a gun was affirmed. There was proof in this case, as in *Scarborough*, that the gun had traveled in interstate commerce. The jurisdiction clause in the statute distinguished it from the Gun-Free School Zones Act in *Lopez*.[68]

In *United States v. Trupin*,[69] defendant was convicted of possessing a stolen painting by Chagall in violation of the federal statute making the receiving, possession, or selling of stolen goods of the value of $5,000 or more, knowing them to be stolen, a felony if the goods have crossed a state or United States boundary after being stolen.[70] In 1986, the jurisdiction language was changed from "moving in interstate commerce" to "have crossed a state or United States boundary."[71] The purpose was to expand jurisdiction to make it a felony knowingly to possess stolen goods that many years before had moved in interstate commerce. The history of the statutes demonstrated that their purpose was the prosecution of persons who knew that goods were stolen whether the person were sellers, buyers, or mere receivers. Unlike *Lopez*, possession in the statute is closely related to transactions in commerce.

*United States v. Bongiorno*[72] was one of a number of cases that failed in a challenge to the Child Support Recovery Act of 1992 on the basis of the *Lopez* opinion. The statute makes willful failure "to pay a past due support obligation with respect to a child who resides in another state" a federal crime.[73] The courts held this a judicially imposed obligation to pay money in interstate commerce. The Court in *Bongiorno* noted that "commerce" in the Commerce Clause context is a term of art that includes transactions that might strike lay persons as noncommercial.[74] Using the mails or any other type of carrier to send money to another state satisfies the jurisdiction requirement. In requiring interstate child support, the statute creates a legal obligation to complete such interstate movement of funds.

The Auto Theft Act of 1992, known as the carjacking statute, which contains a jurisdiction clause of "transported, shipped, or received in interstate or foreign commerce," was also challenged under the rule of *Lopez*.[75] The statute proscribes the taking of a motor vehicle with intent to cause death or serious bodily harm. In *United States v. Coleman*,[76] defendant was convicted of a carjacking in which the owner was shot and killed. The 1992 law became part of the Anti-Car Theft Act, which had criminalized interstate trafficking in stolen automobiles. Congressional hearings before the enactment resulted in findings that auto theft was a national problem because stolen cars and parts were transported in interstate and foreign commerce. The Court held that Congress could rationally believe that auto theft had a substantial effect on interstate commerce. The carjacking statute had none of the deficiencies of the *Lopez* statute, as theft was usually succeeded by sale of cars and there was both a jurisdictional clause in the statute and congressional findings of effects on interstate commerce.[77]

The national anti-arson statute punishes malicious damage or destruction of building, vehicle, or other property used in interstate or foreign commerce.[78] The Supreme Court had held in 1985 that the statute constitutionally applied to a rented apartment building.[79] Both the express terms of the statute and the legislative history indicated Congress created at statute to protect all business property, including rental property. After *Lopez*, the constitutionality was again challenged when applied to housing, and again the statute was upheld. In *United States v. Gaydos*,[80] the Court followed a number of other circuits in holding that the commerce jurisdictional clause in the statute distinguished it from *Lopez*. In this case, however, the facts showed that the house was vacant and uninhabitable and that defendant did not intend to return it to the stream of commerce as rental property. Consequently, the facts here did not show a nexus with commerce.[81]

This array of cases in the courts of appeal demonstrate that there has been very little impact of the *Lopez* case on federalism. It has been distinguished in federal criminal cases whether the statutes do or do not contain commerce jurisdiction clauses. And *Lopez* has been distinguished whether the statutes do or do not have express findings that the criminal acts substantially affect commerce. In those cases where the criminal act involves the sale of goods or services, the Supreme Court has no incentive to grant certiorari merely to affirm the broad scope of the commerce power. In most cases like *Lopez*, where the criminal act has been noncommercial, the Supreme Court has also refused certiorari. *Brzonkala* was the exceptional case in this group where the district court and the appeals court both rejected congressional findings of effects on commerce as being insubstantial, and the Supreme Court affirmed.

## RATIONALITY AND OTHER RATIONALES

Only theoretical economists and Supreme Court justices seem to have an irrational passion for dispassionate rationality.[82] In *Lopez*, Rehnquist cites three of the leading post-1937 cases of economic regulation that applied to local transactions, noting the Congress may regulate intrastate economic activity that substantially affects interstate economic activity.[83] He concludes that since 1937, "the Court has heeded that warning and undertaken to decide whether a rational basis existed for concluding that a regulated activity sufficiently affected interstate commerce."[84] But, for economic activity, a rational-basis test tested nothing. In a highly integrated national economy, local economic activity necessarily affects national economic activity. Whether it is local motels serving interstate travelers,[85] local restaurants serving meat shipped in interstate commerce,[86] or local loan sharks tied to interstate crime mobs who lend at illegal rates and use threats of violence,[87] no rational-basis test is needed to observe local transactions affecting commerce. This demonstrates that precedents relating to local commerce have no bearing on noncommercial activities such as the gun possession in *Lopez*.

Justice Breyer, in dissent, also indicates that justices must second-guess the rationality of congressmen when the real issue is scope of the federal structure as defined in the Constitution. Breyer asserts that "we must ask whether Congress could have had a rational basis for finding a significant (or substantial) connection between gun-related school violence and interstate commerce."[88] When the statute was passed, no relation to commerce was indicated, and many congressmen could have given no thought to which enumerated power was the basis of the enactment. When the statute was amended in 1994, Congress voted a set of findings relating school guns to commerce, but there is no evidence that the amendment received serious debate in Congress. While the findings are based on reason and are therefore rational, they are no test of whether the effects are remote or substantial. Not only were they *ex post facto* to *Lopez*, they miss the true issue of federalism. Just as the total of local common-law tort damages or the total of local alimony and child support payments may have an effect on commerce, the federal structure bars federal preemption of local tort law or family law.

The entire approach to the Commerce Clause, that "among the several states" was a synonym for "interstate commerce," is the underlying fallacy of *Lopez*. The most important historical truth is that the word "state" in the late eighteenth century was not used to mean a territory.[89] The two main uses of state were as a synonym for government or as a group of people with a common government. The context of the Commerce Clause, concerning regulation of behavior of persons and firms, means that the latter of the two definitions was being used. Since commerce among the several groups of peoples who formed the thirteen states was all their commerce, the Commerce Clause was plenary, just like the other powers in Article I, Section 8, unless expressly limited.

There is a more fundamental reason for the courts to question and reexamine congressional findings of fact relating statutes to an enumerated power. Despite much gospel to the contrary, a legislature does not assemble the staff to use scientific methods to gather facts. Legislative committees have no duty to distinguish anecdotal evidence from systematic evaluation. Members of a legislature may have greatly different views of the social problems that a bill is designed to remedy. They may disagree on the severity of the social problems the majority recognize, and they may feel that the compromise language in a statute is wholly inadequate as a remedy. As it seems in *Lopez*, the majority in Congress may not have reflected on which constitutional power underlies the legislation.

The federal structure of the national government was recently reviewed in *Gregory v. Ashcroft*.[90] The federal Age Discrimination in Employment Act of 1967 (ADEA) was held not to override the clause of the Missouri constitution that required judges other than municipal judges to retire at the age of seventy years. The decision was one of statutory interpretation. The ADEA exempted state officials on the policymaking level. Judges were exempted under the exception in the absence of a clear statement in ADEA that judges were to be included. The Court in *Lopez* did not expressly apply the clear statement rule, but it did quote the obiter dictum in *Gregory* concerning the protection against tyranny afforded by the balance of powers between the nation and the states. The absence in *Lopez* of a commerce jurisdiction clause or findings of impact on commerce by Congress is analogous to an application of the clear statement rule. Noncommercial activity is presumptively not subject to regulation under the Commerce Clause. A clear statement that specific noncommercial activity substantially affected commerce would not bind the judiciary but would make a presumption that it did.

## NOTES

1. 514 U.S. 549 (1995). See *Symposium: The New Federalism after United States v. Lopez*, 46 Case West. Res. L. Rev. 643-959 (1996); Lino A. Graglia, *United States v. Lopez: Judicial Review Under the Commerce Clause*, 74 Texas L. Rev. 719 (1996); Lawrence Lessig, *Translating Federalism: United States v. Lopez*, 1995 Sup. Ct. Rev. 125.
2. 22 U.S. (9 Wheat.) 1 (1824).

3. William W. Crosskey, 1 *Politics and the Constitution in the History of the United States* 3-186 (Chicago: University of Chicago Press, 1953); *E.E.O.C. v. Wyoming,* 460 U.S. 226, 248-49 (1983).

4. *Lopez,* 514 U.S. at 556.

5. *Id.* at 567.

6. 18 U.S.C. §922 (q)(2)(A) (1990).

7. 18 U.S.C. §921 (a)(25)(B).

8. *Lopez,* 514 U.S. at 551.

9. *Id.*

10. *United States v. Lopez,* 2 F. 3d 1342 (5th Cir. 1993).

11. *Id.* at 1363.

12. *United States v. Lopez,* 514 U.S. 549 (1995).

13. *Id.* at 551.

14. *Id.* at 559.

15. *Id.* at 561.

16. *Id.* at 562.

17. *Id.* at 563-64.

18. *Id.* at 564.

19. *Id.* at 567.

20. See *United States v. Lopez,* 2 F. 3d 1342, 1362 (5th Cir. 1993)

21. Pub. L. No. 90-351, 82 Stat. 236 (codified as amended in 18 U.S.C. §922 (1994).

22. 18 U.S.C. §1202 (a)(1), recodified and amended at 18 U.S.C. §922 (g)(1) (1994).

23. 431 U.S. 563 (1977).

24. Henry J. Friendly, *Federal Jurisdiction: A General View* 56-61 (New York: Columbia University Press, 1973).

25. 267 U.S. 432 (1925).

26. 41 Stat. 324 (1919), amended 106 Stat. 3385, 18 U.S.C. 2312 (1992).

27. See *Mortensen v. United States,* 322 U.S. 369 (1944) (Brothel proprietors gave prostitutes a free auto ride for an interstate vacation; the return trip was not transport in interstate commerce for the purpose of prostitution though the prostitutes resumed their trade.) Compare *Cleveland v. United States,* 329 U.S. 14 (1946) (Mormon's transport of plural wives across state lines in family auto was held interstate commerce).

28. *Lopez* at 514 U.S. 567-83.

29. *Id.* at 583.

30. *Id.* at 595.

31. 22 U.S. (9 Wheat.) 1 (1824).

32. 156 U.S. 1 (1895), *overruled, Swift & Co. v. United States,* 196 U.S. 375 (1905). The *Knight* case was a statutory interpretation in which the Court failed to recognize the financial agreements between sugar refiners (in commerce) to create a national monopoly to control the price of sugar sold in commerce.

33. 298 U.S. 238 (1936). The commerce aspect of this case was in effect overruled in *National Labor Relations Board v. Jones & Laughlin Steel Corp.,* 301 U.S. 1 (1937).

34. See *Gibbons,* 22 U.S. (9 Wheat.) at 227 (Johnson, J., concurring) (observing that Congress was delegated a plenary power to regulate commerce); Robert L. Stern, *That Commerce That Concerns More States Than One,* 47 Harv. L. Rev. 1335 (1934); Crosskey, *Politics and the Constitution in the History of the United States, supra,* note 3 at 17-186.

35. *Lopez,* 514 U.S. at 616.

36. *Id.* at 624

37. *Id.* at 620.

38. *Id.* at 625-30.

39. As Justice Frankfurter noted, "The ultimate touchstone of constitutionality is the Constitution itself and not what we have said about it." *Graves v. New York*, 306 U.S. 466, 491-92 (1939).

40. *Lopez*, 514 U.S. at 624.

41. Violent Crime Control and Law Enforcement Act, Pub. L. 103-322, 108 Stat. 1796, 2125-26 (1994), 18 U.S.C. §922 (q)(1)-(4) (1997). This was highly unusual congressional response to a court of appeals opinion.

42. *United States v. Lopez*, Trans. of Oral Arg. 25.

43. 18 U.S.C. §922 (q)(1).

44. 110 Stat. 3009, 18 U.S.C. §922 (q)(2)(A) (1997).

45. Comprehensive Drug Abuse Protection and Control Act of 1970, §419 (a) as amended, 21 U.S.CA. §860 (a) (1997).

46. 111 F. 3d 101 (11th Cir. 1997), *cert. denied* 522 U.S. 878 (1997). The Court cites seven other appeals cases with similar holdings, including *United States v. McKinney*, 98 F. 3d 974 (7th Cir. 1996), *cert. denied*, 520 U.S. 1110 (1997). See *United States v. Henson*, 123 F. 3d 1226 (9th Cir. 1997).

47. Pub. L. No. 99-308, §110C, 100 Stat. 449, 461 (1986), 18 U.S.C. §922 (o) (1997).

48. 117 F. 3d 1265 (11th Cir. 1977), *cert. denied*, 522 U.S. 1007 (1997). See *Wright* at 1270 n.9, citing cases to demonstrate that every federal court of appeals to entertain a Commerce Clause challenge to 18 U.S.C. §922 (o) has upheld its constitutionality.

49. *Wright* at 1270 (footnotes omitted).

50. 42 USCA §9606 (a) (1997).

51. 107 F. 3d 1506 (11th Cir. 1997).

52. *Id.* at 1510.

53. *Id.* at 1511.

54. 108 Stat. 694, as amended in 108 Stat. 2150 (1994), 18 U.S.C.A. §248 (1997).

55. 55 F. 3d 1517 (11th Cir. 1995).

56. *American Life League, Inc. v. Reno*, 47 F. 3d 642, 647 (4th Cir. 1995), *cert. denied*, 516 U.S. 809 (1995).

57. *Id.*

58. *Id.*

59. *Cheffer*, 55 F. 3d at 1520-21.

60. 108 Stat. 1926, 18 U.S.C.A. §2261 (1997).

61. 112 F. 3d 758 (4th Cir. 1997), *cert. denied*, 522 U.S. 896 (1997).

62. *Caminetti v. United States*, 242 U.S. 470 (1917) (transportation of a mistress across state lines held illegal); *Cleveland v. United States*, 329 U.S. 14 (1946), (Mormon transportation of plural wives across state lines held illegal). These are two of the most negatively criticized cases in constitutional law.

63. 169 F. 3d 820 (4th Cir. 1999), *affd sub* nom. *United States v. Morrison*, 120 S. Ct. 1740 (2000). The appeal in the Fourth Circuit was reheard en banc and the district court dismissal was affirmed by a vote of 7-to-4. See 42 U.S.C.A §13981. The Supreme Court opinion became available too late to be analyzed for this publication.

64. 169 F. 3D at 836.

65. *Lopez*, 514 U.S. at 561.

66. 431 U.S. 563 (1977).

67. 77 F. 3d 387 (11th Cir. 1996), *cert. denied*, 519 U.S. 905 (1996).

68. 18 U.S.C.A. §922 (g)(1) (1997 Supp.), recodified from former 18 U.S.C. §1202 (a)(1).

69. 117 F. 3d 678 (2nd Cir. 1997), *cert. denied* 522 U.S. 1051 (1998).

70. 100 Stat. 3618, 18 U.S.C. §2315 (1997).

71. *Trupin*, 117 F. 3d at 682.

72. 106 F. 3d 1027 (1st Cir. 1997). See *United States v. Parker*, 108 F. 3d 28 (3rd Cir. 1997) *cert. denied*, 522 U.S. 837; *United States v. Hampshire*, 95 F. 3d 999 (10th Cir. 1996), *cert. denied*, 519 U.S. 1084 (1997); *United States v. Mussari*, 95 F. 3d 787 (9th Cir. 1996); *United States v. Sage*, 92 F. 3d 101 (2d Cir. 1996), *cert. denied*, 519 U.S. 1099 (1997).

73. 18 U.S.C. §228 (a) (1997).

74. *Bongiorno*, 106 F. 3d at 1031.

75. 106 Stat. 3384 (1992), 18 U.S.C. §2119 (1997).

76. 78 F. 3d 154 (5th Cir. 1996), *cert. denied*, 519 U.S. 891 (1996). See *United States v. Bishop*, 66 F 3d 569 (3rd Cir. 1995), *cert. denied*, 516 U.S. 1032 §1066 (1995); *United States v. Cobb*, 144 F. 3d 319 (4th Cir. 1998).

77. *Coleman*, 78 F. 3d at 159.

78. 18 U.S.C. §844 (i).

79. *Russell v. United States*, 471 U.S. 858 (1985).

80. 108 F. 3d 505 (3rd Cir. 1997). See *United States v. Grimes*, 142 F. 3d 1342, 1346 (11th Cir. 1998), *cert. denied*, 525 U.S. 1088 (1999).

81. *United States v. Papadopalous*, 64 F. 3d 522 (9th Cir. 1995) (Arson to defendants' private residence not subject to federal prosecution when only tie to interstate commerce was receipt of natural gas from out-of-state sources). See *U.S. v. McGuire*, 178 F. 3d 203 (3rd Cir. 1999).

82. See Robert F. Nagel, *Constitutional Cultures: The Mentality and Consequences of Judicial Review* 84-120 (Berkeley: University of California Press, 1989).

83. *NLRB v. Jones & Laughlin Steel Corp.*, 301 U.S. 1 (1937); *United States v. Darby*, 312 U.S. 100 (1941); *Wickard v. Filburn*, 317 U.S. 111 (1942).

84. *Lopez*, 514 U.S. at 557.

85. *Heart of Atlanta Motel, Inc. v. United States* 379 U.S. 241 (1964).

86. *Katzenbach v. McClung*, 379 U.S. 294 (1964).

87. *Perez v. United States*, 402 U.S. 146 (1971).

88. *Lopez*, 514 U.S. at 618.

89. Crosskey, 1 *Politics and the Constitution in the History of the United States, supra,* note 3, at 50-83.

90. 501 U.S. 452 (1991).

# 6

# State Police Power Limited by the Bill of Rights: The Flag Salute Cases

The relationship of state police powers to the Bill of Rights is a subset of the relationships of legislative and executive powers to express constitutional limitations. Presented on the level of potentially conflicting general principles, where statutory language appears to be an express violation of the Bill of Rights, the presumption of constitutionality of the statute ceases. The legal presumption then favors the express constitutional limitation, though this may be rebutted by showing harm to the society or specific individuals. It is elementary that the function of constitutional limitations is to protect the civil rights of persons against abusive official actions in any branch of government. The thesis here is that the structure and purposes of constitutional limitations should be pleaded and argued in terms of underlying presumptions in cases where civil rights are in contest.

The illustrative example here is the flag salute cases, the argument of Jehovah's Witnesses that their children had a constitutional right based on the free exercise of religion to be exempt from compulsory flag salutes and pledges of allegiance enforced by school boards.[1] The Supreme Court in 1940 held by a vote of eight to one in *Minersville School District v. Gobitis*[2] that it was constitutional for the school board to expel those children who disobeyed the order to salute the flag. In 1943, the Court overruled *Gobitis* in *West Virginia State Board of Education v.*

*Barnette*[3] and held, by a vote of six to three, that expulsion of Witness children for failure to salute the flag and pledge allegiance violated both the free speech and the free exercise of religion clauses in the First Amendment as incorporated in the Fourteenth Amendment. In neither of these landmark opinions did the justices review the structure and purposes of the Bill of Rights in setting presumptions in favor of the Witness children. This study is designed to explain why resort to basic constitutional doctrine can be a powerful tool in the solution of hard cases.

One thesis of these studies is that the structure and one key purpose of the Fourteenth Amendment were to make the Bill of Rights effective against the state governments through the Privileges-or-Immunities Clause.[4] Any lawyer or historian who has reviewed the pressures from the states and the final passage and ratification of the Bill of Rights knows that these civil rights are all fundamental privileges or immunities of citizens of the United States.[5] Decades before *Gobitis*, it should have been standing law that the First Amendment in all its parts was effective against the states. Instead, the Supreme Court in the *Slaughter-House Cases*,[6] in a highly contested 5-to-4 decision concerning governmental grants of monopoly in the ordinary trades, held the Privileges-or-Immunities Clause to be without significant effect. This opinion should have been overruled by the Court at an early date or at least distinguished as inapplicable to the Bill of Rights. Instead, it was treated as controlling law in the federal system. It was only in 1925 in *Gitlow v. New York*[7] that the Court first held that the free speech and free press protection of the First Amendment had been incorporated in the Fourteenth. But this was done by holding speech and press to be "liberties" protected by the Due Process Clause. Thus the highly questionable substantive due process concept was substituted for the Privileges-or-Immunities Clause. Only two weeks before the *Gobitis* opinion, the Court held that the religion protections of the First Amendment were incorporated into the Fourteenth,[8] but *Gobitis* was litigated on the argument of liberty under the Due Process Clause.


## HISTORICAL PRIORITY OF CIVIL RIGHTS

The historical evidence of the ideological origins of the American Revolution and of American constitutionalism in the rights of Englishmen presents a foundation argument for the presumptive superiority of the established civil rights of persons over governmental legislative powers.[9] This involved two transitions in thinking. The first was from the English emphasis in constitutional law to the American. While most colonial charters recited the colonists' rights to the "liberties of Englishmen,"[10] the English emphasis in constitutional law was on the structure of government, with the civil rights of persons as a secondary aspect. The American Revolution rejected the English governmental structure of king, nobility, and commons, and the Declaration of Independence emphasized the rights of persons.

The second transition in thinking was from the natural law emphasis of the

Declaration of Independence to the positive law character of the Constitution. Just as the new structure of government had to be based on positive law, so the rights of persons could be enforced only if found in positive law. The existing positive rights of persons was the rights of Englishmen against government found in the charters, statutes, and key judicial opinions that by the conventions of English law were considered constitutional.[11] The civil rights of Englishmen had required hundreds of years of conflict with the Crown in order to become established law. Immunity from taxation without representation was the most prominent of these.

The rights of Englishmen were only against the Crown because the long conflict to establish these rights replaced executive supremacy with legislative supremacy in the Bill of Rights of 1689.[12] This created an anomaly. While the conventions of English law held that Parliament would never repeal a statute that the nation considered a constitutional civil right, legislative supremacy meant that Parliament had the constitutional power to repeal any law.[13] At the American constitutional convention, it was clear that the separation of governmental powers would not permit executive or legislative supremacy. In the First Congress, Madison proposed the national Bill of Rights and noted the great difference between the English and U.S. constitutions. He observed that "it may not be thought necessary to provide limits for the legislative power in that country, yet a different opinion prevails in the United States. The people of many States have thought it necessary to raise barriers against power in all forms and departments of Government. . . . It therefore must be leveled against the legislative, for it is most powerful, and most likely to be abused, because it is under the least control."[14]

The rebuttable presumption that the Bill of Rights and other constitutional limitations take a higher status than legislative or executive powers was emphasized by the Supreme Court in 1938 in the *obiter dicta* of footnote 4 of *United States v. Carolene Products Co.*[15] The facts of the case concerned a substantive due process challenge to the federal Filled Milk Act, which the Court majority rejected, following the rationale of its overruling of economic due process in *West Coast Hotel Co. v. Parrish.*[16] Justice Harlan Stone wrote the famous footnote 4 to warn the lower courts and the bar that the judicial repudiation of the constitutionally fallacious substantive due process was narrowly confined and was not a general attempt to weaken the Bill of Rights and other constitutional limitations. The footnote, excluding citations, reads as follows:

There may be narrower scope for operation of the presumption of constitutionality when legislation appears on its face to be within a specific prohibition of the Constitution, such as those of the first ten amendments, which are deemed equally specific when held to be embraced within the Fourteenth.

It is unnecessary to consider now whether legislation which restricts those political processes which can ordinarily be expected to bring about repeal of undesirable legislation, is to be subjected to more exacting judicial scrutiny under the general prohibitions of the Fourteenth Amendment than are most other types of legislation.

Nor need we enquire whether similar considerations enter into the review of statutes directed at particular religious, or national, or racial minority: whether prejudice against discrete and insular minorities may be a special condition, which tends seriously to curtail the operation of those political processes ordinarily to be relied upon to protect minorities, and which may call for a correspondingly more searching judicial inquiry.[17]

This footnote is now considered a primary source of "strict scrutiny" judicial review of statutes that are challenged as invading the civil rights of persons. But the true issue is not one of scrutiny but of the presumptions implied by constitutional structure. In fact, the first paragraph of the footnote was not in the original draft. It was Chief Justice Charles Evans Hughes's comment to Justice Stone that changed the emphasis of the footnote by the addition of the first paragraph. Hughes wrote Stone, "Are the 'considerations' different or does the difference lie not in the *test* but in the nature of the right invoked?"[18] Stone responded, "You are quite right in saying that the specific prohibitions of the first ten amendments and the same prohibitions when adopted by the Fourteenth Amendment leave no opportunity for presumptions of constitutionality where statutes on their face violate the prohibition."[19] Stone recognized that the express specification of constitutional limitations is a structural factor of precedence, commanding judicial review to protect citizens from abuse or injury by officials exercising the power of government. In the flag salute cases, it will be shown that even if a statute on its face is valid for most persons or situations, proof that its application to a specific class of persons invades a clause of the Bill of Rights creates a legal presumption in favor of exemption for the special class.

## *GOBITIS* CASE

The legal background to the *Gobitis* case was a series of state cases in which the courts upheld the compulsory flag salute statutes as secular regulations. The courts thus rejected the claims of the plaintiffs, who sued to reenter schools from which they were expelled, that there was a religious significance to their refusal to salute the flag. *Nicholls v. Mayor and School Committee of Lynn*[20] is exemplary. The Massachusetts court recognized the constitutional importance of religion as defined by the dictates of one's own conscience. The court concluded, however, that "the flag salute and pledge of allegiance here in question do not in any just sense relate to religion."[21] Similar holdings were made by the highest courts of a number of states.[22]

The Supreme Court record prior to the *Gobitis* case was one in which the Witnesses' similar flag salute appeals from state courts had been dismissed *per curiam* for want of jurisdiction.[23] And *Johnson v. Deerfield*,[24] the one case in the Supreme Court from a U.S. district court holding that the flag salute requirement was merely a secular regulation, was in 1939 affirmed *per curiam*. This judicial background made it especially difficult for appellants in later actions to convince the Supreme Court that the acts of religious conscience had occurred in order to create a narrow exception to a valid secular regulation.

*Gobitis v. Minersville School District*[25] concerned children in a Pennsylvania town who refused to salute the flag and were expelled from school in November 1935. The action in the federal court was for an injunction to restrain the school board from enforcing the regulation against these two children. The allegation was not that the statute was unconstitutional but, as to these children, the enforcement violated the Fourteenth Amendment to the Constitution of the United States.

In 1937, District Judge Albert B. Maris denied defendant's motion to dismiss the complaint.[26] Since this was three years before the Supreme Court was to hold that the Fourteenth Amendment incorporated the religion clauses of the First Amendment as effective against the states, the issue pleaded by counsel was one of substantive due process: Did the complaint describe a violation of "liberty" under the Fourteenth Amendment? This was in Pennsylvania, a state whose initial founding was by persons who in England were religious dissidents, and Judge Maris was a Quaker.[27] He found the complaint to describe a violation of the Pennsylvania constitution's protection of the "indefeasible right to worship Almighty God according to the dictates of their own consciences."[28] This in turn would describe an invasion of liberty under the Fourteenth Amendment.

After the trial in 1938, Judge Maris granted the injunction.[29] The findings of fact by the court were crucial to the case because they were contrary to the earlier cases that found the flag salute requirement to be secular and without religious significance. Judge Maris found that each of the plaintiffs sincerely and honestly believed that the act of saluting the flag contravened the law of God as stated in the twentieth chapter of Exodus.[30] Two additional findings in his opinion were as follows:

> I think it is also clear from the evidence that the refusal of these two earnest Christian children to salute the flag cannot even remotely prejudice or imperil the safety, health, morals, property or personal rights of their fellows. . . . Our Country's safety surely does not depend upon the totalitarian idea of forcing all citizens into one common mold of thinking and acting or requiring them to render a lip service of loyalty in a manner which conflicts with their sincere religious convictions.[31]

The remedy for the Gobitis children was affirmed by the court of appeals in 1939.[32] Judge William Clark stated the issue: "These little children ('suffer them') are asking us to afford them the protection of the First Amendment (Bill of Rights) to the Constitution and to permit them the 'free exercise' of their 'religion.'"[33] The court rejected the argument of counsel for the appellant "that religion is an objective matter" and that "no one could conceivably appraise non-flag saluting in theological terms."[34] Noting the minimum definition of religion as one's views of his relations to his Creator and the obligations they impose, the court held that Jehovah's Witnesses clearly came within the definition. "It is the very thoroughness of their belief in the supernatural that has gotten them into trouble."[35]

Judge Clark noted that the police power of the state would prevail over an argument based on conscience in only three types of situations: "(a) wherever its mental or physical health is affected, (b) wherever a violation of its sense of reverence makes a breach of the peace reasonably foreseeable, and (c) wherever the 'defense of the realm' is imperiled."[36] The court held that none of these special situations applied to the compulsion to salute the flag. Furthermore, forcing members of this tiny minority to salute the flag was senseless. "There is a psychological futility in compelling a child to salute the flag when that impinges upon his or her religious tenets; such compulsion generates resentment, and is calculated to produce a precisely antithetical result to that which was planned by the authors of the flag-saluting ceremony."[37]

The decision of the court of appeals in *Gobitis* was contrary to earlier flag salute appeals to the Supreme Court that were dismissed for lack of jurisdiction because the trial courts had held that there was no issue of violation of the free exercise of religion. The Supreme Court granted *certiorari* and the opinion was handed down in 1940.[38] Justice Felix Frankfurter wrote the opinion reversing the court of appeals, to which only Justice Harlan Stone dissented.

A key factor leading to the reversal of the lower court had to be the defective brief in the Supreme Court written by counsel for the Jehovah's Witnesses, Joseph F. Rutherford. Instead of arguing for a religious exception to the Minersville regulation, based on the action for injunction and the lower court ruling, Rutherford made primarily religious arguments that the entire Minersville regulation was invalid.[39] In pressing the viewpoint of a religious fanatic, he stated the issue as follows: "The arbitrary totalitarian rule of the state versus full devotion to the THEOCRATIC GOVERNMENT or Kingdom of Jehovah God under Christ Jesus His anointed King."[40] The brief of twenty-five pages contained references to sixty-one biblical passages, while only fifteen judicial opinions were cited.[41] The law of God was not presented as a First Amendment argument but as a supervening natural law to be recognized as "liberty" under the Fourteenth Amendment.

The confusion created by the overwhelming religious arguments, including seven legal citations that the United States was a Christian nation, left the *Gobitis* brief without significant rigorous legal argument. The same was true of Rutherford's oral argument.[42] As a consequence, at the justices' conference to review the *Gobitis* case, Chief Justice Charles E. Hughes could treat this case summarily as an analog to the earlier flag salute cases that had been dismissed.[43] He reiterated the established doctrine that public school boards could require a flag salute as part of teaching loyalty to the nation. The accepted view that the flag salute was not religious was not opposed at conference, and it was only after Justice Frankfurter's draft opinion was circulated that Justice Stone indicated that he would dissent.[44] Justice Frankfurter was astounded at this news and wrote Justice Stone a five-page letter in order to elaborate the consideration he had given this "tragic issue."[45]

Given the findings of the trial court on the religious character of the children's refusal to salute the flag, Frankfurter could not follow earlier courts that had held that there was no religious aspect to the flag salute. He began with this admission: "We must decide whether the requirement of participation in such a ceremony, extracted from a child who refuses upon sincere religious grounds, infringes without due process of law the liberty guaranteed by the Fourteenth Amendment."[46] The anomalous background to the *Gobitis* opinion was the unanimous decision of the Court by Justice Owen Roberts in *Cantwell v. Connecticut*,[47] upholding the right of a Jehovah's Witness to sell religious literature without procuring a license. The Court had held in *Cantwell* two weeks before *Gobitis* that the Fourteenth Amendment incorporated the clause of the First Amendment protecting the free exercise of religion. But Justice Frankfurter followed the briefs of counsel and limited his analysis to the substantive due process concept of "liberty." Since substantive due process had been totally repudiated in the economic field in 1937,[48] it had been proven a vague and unreliable standard.[49]

After reviewing the importance of the freedom to follow one's conscience and even citing *Cantwell* as authority, Frankfurter stated the controversy: "Our present task then, as so often the case with courts, is to reconcile two rights in order to prevent either from destroying the other."[50] One must assume he means the right of the school board to enforce a valid general state regulation, not recognizing that the narrow issue here of immunity for members of a tiny, politically powerless religious minority who claim exception would not destroy the general regulation. Ignoring the findings of fact in the trial court about the nonexistence of negative impact on fellow students, Frankfurter concludes that "the question remains whether school children, like the Gobitis children, must be excused from conduct required of all the other children in the promotion of national cohesion."[51]

Frankfurter then devoted some pages to defending the validity of flag salute statutes, even though he had previously noted that this action only claimed a rare constitutional exception to valid law. "The precise issue, then, for us to decide is whether the legislatures of the various states and the authorities in a thousand countries and school districts of this country are barred from determining the appropriateness of various means to evoke that unifying sentiment without which there can ultimately be no liberties, civil or religious."[52]

Frankfurter ended his opinion with an argument for judicial restraint in deference to the legislature. He argued that for the Court to affirm constitutional immunity for the religious dissidents was "to maintain that there is no basis for a legislative judgment that such an exemption might introduce elements of difficulty into the school discipline, might cast doubts in the minds of the other children which would themselves weaken the effect of the exercise."[53] But there was no evidence at the trial that any legislator had given thought to possible dissidents, and there was a clear finding of fact that the religious exception would not affect other children.

This opinion of Frankfurter shows no recognition of the principles of constitutional structure and purposes that were argued here for a principled solution. While the brief of counsel for the Gobitis children centered on the vague concept of "liberty" under the due process under the Fourteenth Amendment,[54] Frankfurter had two weeks earlier joined the unanimous opinion in *Cantwell v. Connecticut* holding that the First Amendment was incorporated into the Fourteenth. He could have recognized that the issue here was the Bill of Rights as constraint on state police power. The *amicus curiae* brief of the American Bar Association's Committee on the Bill of Rights was written primarily by its chairman, Grenville Clark, one of the most noted lawyers in the nation. Clark emphasized the place of freedom of religion in the American constitutional structure and the narrow limits on governmental limits on religious practices such as harm to persons or to the defense of the nation.[55]

Justice Stone's dissenting opinion utilized the principles in the first and third paragraphs of the *Carolene Products* footnote and emphasized the First Amendment as effective against the states by the Fourteenth Amendment.[56] He viewed the compulsion to salute the flag and pledge allegiance thereto as violating both freedom of speech and free exercise of religion as guaranteed by the Bill of Rights. He recognized that these freedoms were limited by practices inimical to public safety, health, and good order. But disciplining children to compel public affirmations that violate their religious consciences could not be justified as preventing public harm.

Justice Stone stressed the underlying functions of the First Amendment as "guaranties of freedom of the human mind and spirit and of reasonable freedom and opportunity to express them."[57] These freedoms guarantee that one will not be compelled to bear false witness to one's religion. History, he noted, teaches us that infringements of personal liberty are usually justified in the name of public good and usually directed against politically helpless minorities. The Constitution does not command expressions of loyalty to the government. "The very terms of the Bill of Rights preclude . . . any reconciliation of such compulsions with the constitutional guaranties by a legislative declaration that they are more important to public welfare than the Bill of Rights."[58]

## EFFECTS OF *GOBITIS*

Historians record a wave of anti-Witness persecution following the 1940 *Gobitis* decision in the Supreme Court.[59] For at least two years, there were significant physical violence and arbitrary arrests of Witnesses. There were 843 recorded incidents of alleged persecution. This was a period of rising emotions of nationalism as the war in Europe led to preparations for war by the United States. Hence, it is impossible to determine how much of the persecution of Jehovah's Witnesses could be a feedback from publicity of the *Gobitis* case and the Supreme Court decision against the Witnesses. It is argued that this wave of persecutions was ended when the Civil Rights Section of the Department of Justice in May 1942 prompted U.S. attorneys across the nation to warn local officials of possible prosecution under the United State Criminal Code.[60]

Two key events encouraged the lawyers for the Jehovah's Witnesses to initiate another challenge to the absolute enforcement of state school flag salute statutes. The first was the *Cantwell* opinion, which had informed them that a First Amendment argument could be the prime element of their brief.[61] The dissent of Justice

Stone in *Gobitis* reinforced this view. In fact, this approach had been tried in the state courts since the *Gobitis* opinion, and three state courts had repudiated that case as precedent.[62]

The second key event was the *Jones v. Opelika* cases.[63] Jehovah's Witnesses were convicted of selling books and pamphlets without paying a license tax as required by a municipal ordinance. In a 5-to-4 decision, Justice Stanley Reed affirmed the conviction, ruling that selling religious books was more of a commercial transaction than a religious or educational act. Justice Stone dissented, noting that the Witnesses were engaged in a nonprofit activity of disseminating religious ideas.[64] Justices Black, Douglas, and Murphy, who joined in the dissent, added a public recantation of their earlier vote to join Frankfurter's opinion in the *Gobitis* case.[65] They emphasized the function of the Bill of Rights in the structure of democratic government. "Certainly our democratic form of government functioning under the historic Bill of Rights has a high responsibility to accommodate itself to the religious views of minorities however unpopular and unorthodox those views may be. The First amendment does not put the right freely to exercise religion in a subordinate position."[66]

The appointment of Wiley Rutledge to the Court in early 1943 assured a fifth vote on the side of the First Amendment. The Court granted rehearing in the *Opelika* case and three months later reversed the earlier judgment.[67] At that time, the Court majority also upheld the Jehovah's Witnesses in two other cases where they failed to procure licenses required by statute.[68]

## *BARNETTE* CASE

The Witnesses made their challenge to the *Gobitis* opinion in what became *West Virginia State Board of Ed. v. Barnette*.[69] This was a class action filed in August 1942 for an injunction restraining the State Board of Education from enforcing the requirement of flag salute against the children of Jehovah's Witnesses. A motion to dismiss on the basis of the Supreme Court's decision in the *Gobitis* case was denied.[70] Judge John J. Parker for the three-person court noted that in the rehearing of *Jones v. Opelika*[71] four members of the Supreme Court indicated that the *Gobitis* decision was unsound and that the majority in *Opelika* chose to distinguish *Gobitis* rather than rely on it. Noting that religious belief was a matter of individual conscience, the Court was without power to determine the reasonableness of the belief. "The religious freedom guaranteed by the 1st and 14th Amendments means that he shall have the right to do this, whether his belief is reasonable or not, without interference from anyone, so long as his action or refusal to act is not directly harmful to the society of which he forms a part."[72]

Having found the refusal of the Witness children to salute the flag was based on religious conscience and that no harm to the public ensued, the injunction was granted. Judge Parker noted that religious freedom was no less sacred than freedom of speech.[73] Since speech advocating overthrow of the government but not constituting a clear and present danger may not be forbidden, conscientious scruples against flag salute need not give way to educational policy when there is not direct harm to public safety. It was clearly a judicial function to enforce freedom of religion against the "petty tyranny" of the School Board.[74] The purpose of constitutional limitations was to protect individuals or helpless minorities against the tyranny of majorities.

The Supreme Court affirmed the district court in the *Barnette* case, with Justices Reed and Roberts noting dissent and Justice Frankfurter writing a long dissenting opinion.[75] The Court overruled the *Gobitis* case and the earlier *per curiam* opinions in flag salute cases that preceded it. Justice Robert Jackson, for the Court, specifically explained why the *Gobitis* opinion was wrong.

In contrast to the substantive due process reasoning of the *Gobitis* case, the *Barnette* opinion was based on the First Amendment as incorporated by the Fourteenth Amendment. Justice Jackson noted that the detailed standards of the First Amendment were much more definite than the term "liberty" in the Fourteenth Amendment, as construed by Frankfurter in *Gobitis*. "Much of the vagueness of the Due Process Clause disappears when specific prohibitions of the First [Amendment] become its standard."[76] Furthermore, Jackson demonstrated that the flag salute and the oral pledge of allegiance violated both the free exercise of religion and freedom of speech. Freedom not to speak against one's conscience is surely part of free speech. Following the argument of the brief for the Witnesses, Jackson put the emphasis on freedom of speech and the test developed by Justice Oliver Wendell Holmes in earlier cases of clear and present danger to the society. Under this test, it was elementary that a few children with extreme religious views could be excused from the flag salute and pledge of allegiance without the slightest chance of a clear and present danger to fellow students or to the nation. "The freedom asserted by these appellees does not bring them into collision with rights asserted by any other individual. . . . The sole conflict is between authority and rights of the individual."[77]

Justice Jackson explained that the Gobitis opinion posed the wrong issues. The strength or the weakness of the government was not at issue when courts excuse a few children from saluting the flag because of religious conscience. This narrow exception based on the First Amendment would not materially interfere with the authority of educational officers across the nation or make the Court "the school board for the country."[78] The question of whether to create an exception based on the Bill of Rights was not primarily a legislative function. "The very purpose of a Bill of Rights was to withdraw certain subjects from the vicissitudes of political controversy, to place them beyond reach of majorities and officials and to establish them as legal principles to be applied by the courts."[79] The idea that legislative or executive officials have an absolute right to select appropriate means to enforce national unity as the basis of national security is fallacious. The Bill of Rights does not allow compulsion that violates free religion and free speech as a permissible means. "Those who begin coercive elimination of dissent soon find themselves exterminating dissenters. Compulsory unification of opinion achieves only the unanimity of the graveyard."[80]

The findings of fact in the trial court made Justice Jackson's majority holding in this case for the First Amendment over state regulation inevitable. But in Jackson's eloquent opinion he admits that he has not applied structural constitutional principles. He asserts that "the task of translating the majestic generalities of the Bill of Rights, conceived as part of the pattern of liberal government in the eighteenth century, into concrete restraints on officials dealing with the problems of the twentieth century, is one to disturb self-confidence."[81] He follows this with a statement that is arguably contrary to the ideological origins of the American Revolution. "These principles grew in soil which also produced a philosophy that the individual was the center of the society, that his liberty was attainable through mere absence of governmental restraints, and that government should be entrusted with few controls and only the mildest supervision over men's affairs."[82] Jackson confuses the social preference for a free market economy with a political system that ranks all constitutional limitations on government as absolutely fundamental.

## CONCLUSION

Part of the fault for the unfortunate opinion in *Gobitis* must be charged to Rutherford, attorney for the Witness children. He mistakenly argued that the entire flag salute statute was unconstitutional when he should have been arguing for a narrow exception to a presumptively valid statute. Rutherford was secondly at fault for focusing his entire constitutional argument on the concept of "liberty" in the Due Process Clause and failing to argue the Religion Clause in the First Amendment. The briefs in the concurrent *Cantwell* litigation named Rutherford as co-counsel. As the counsel for *Gobitis*, he could easily have prepared an additional count under the First Amendment as incorporated into the Fourteenth, but he failed to do so.

The dominant fault for the *Gobitis* opinion must fall on its author, Justice Frankfurter. He did not have to limit his opinion to the deficient arguments of the attorney for the Gobitis family that rested on "liberty" under substantive due process. The *amicus curiae* brief of the American Bar Association and the dissent of Justice Stone emphasized religious liberty, and these correctly posed the true structural issue of state police power versus the Bill of Rights.

Justice Frankfurter's largest error was his violation of the established rule of judicial deference and respect, that findings of fact in a trial court will not be reversed on appeal unless they are against the manifest weight of the evidence. In *Gobitis*, Frankfurter ignored the findings of the trial court that the failure of the Witness children to salute the flag and pledge allegiance would have no negative impact on fellow students. Instead, Frankfurter asserted just the opposite. This raises a fundamental question concerning appeal briefs. Does counsel only have to emphasize the key findings of fact of the trial court, or does he or she also have to brief the precedents that those facts may not be reversed on appeal unless they are against the manifest weight of the evidence?

The *Barnette* case was decided after *Cantwell* clearly had demonstrated that the Religion Clause of the First Amendment was incorporated by the Fourteenth Amendment as effective against the states. Thus *Barnette* expressly met one conflict between state police power and the First Amendment. The arguments were radically different from the "liberty" argument of due process under *Gobitis*. It is bewildering to observe Justice Frankfurter's long dissent in *Barnette,* when the issues had been reframed from *Gobitis* by Justice Jackson to center on the Bill of Rights. From the advantage of hindsight, the observer of today can only conclude that Justice Frankfurter had lost his perspective.

The purpose here is to emphasize constitutional structure and the decision process based on structural analysis. This requires courts to explain constitutional conflicts on a level of generalization that reveals the presumptive priorities of different types of constitutional clauses. If the justices in *Gobitis* and *Barnette* had begun their analyses with a review of the basic relation of state police power to the Bill of Rights, they would have found the resolution of the key issue as a mere subset of their more general analysis.


## NOTES

1. See David R. Manwaring, *Render unto Caesar: The Flag-Salute Controversy* (Chicago: University of Chicago Press, 1962); Richard Danzig, *Justice Frankfurter's Opinions in the Flag Salute Cases: Blending Logic and Psychologic in Constitutional Decisionmaking*, 36 Stanford L. Rev. 675 (1984).
2. 310 U.S. 586 (1940).
3. 319 U.S. 624 (1943).
4. *Supra*, chapter 3, note 13. See Michael Kent Curtis, *No State Shall Abridge: The Fourteenth Amendment and the Bill of Rights* (Durham, N.C.: Duke University Press, 1986).
5. See Robert A. Rutland, *The Birth of the Bill of Rights 1776–1791* (Chapel Hill: University of North Carolina Press, 1955).
6. 83 U.S. (16 Wall.) 36 (1873).
7. 268 U.S. 652 (1925). This view was followed in *Near v. Minnesota*, 283 U.S. 697 (1931), and *Schneider v. Irvington*, 308 U.S. 147 (1939).
8. *Cantwell v. Connecticut*, 310 U.S. 296 (1940).
9. See Bernard Bailyn, *The Ideological Origins of the American Revolution* 175–98 (Cambridge: Harvard University Press, rev. ed., 1992).
10. See A. E. Dick Howard, *The Road from Runnymede: Magna Carta and Constitutionalism in America* 14–34 (Charlottesville: University of Virginia Press, 1968)
11. See Forrest McDonald, *Novus Ordo Seclorum: The Intellectual Origins of the Constitution* 9–55 (Lawrence: University of Kansas Press, 1985); Gordon Wood, *The Creation of the American Republic, 1776–1787*, 10–17 (New York: W. W. Norton, 1972).
12. 1 Will. and Mary, sess. 2, c. 2 (1689).
13. See A. V. Dicey, *Introduction to the Study of the Law of the Constitution* 413–68 (London: Macmillan and Co., 7th ed. 1908).
14. 1 *Annals of Congress* 457 (1834). See Zechariah Chafee, *How Human Rights Got into the Constitution* 19–21 (Boston: Boston University Press, 1952).
15. 304 U.S. 144 (1938). See Robert M. Cover, *The Origins of Judicial Activism in the Protection of Minorities*, 91 Yale L.J. 1287 (1982).

16. 300 U.S. 379 (1937).

17. Carolene Products, 304 U.S. at 152 n.4.

18. Louis Lusky, *Footnote Redux: A Carolene Products Reminiscence*, 82 Colum. L.R. 1093,1097 (1982).

19. *Id.* at 1098.

20. 297 Mass. 65, 7 N.E. 2d. 577 (1937).

21. *Id.* at 580

22. *Hering v. State Board of Education*, 117 N.J.L. 455, 189A. 629 (1937*), affirmed per curiam*, 118 N.J.L. 566, 194 A. 177 (1937), *appeal dismissed*, 303 U.S. 624 (1938); *Leoles v. Landers*, 184 Ga. 580, 192 S.E. 218 (1937), *appeal dismissed*, 302 U.S. 656 (1937); *Gabrielli v. Knickerbocker*, 12 Cal. 2d 85, 82 P. 2d 391 (1938), *appeal dismissed*, 306 U.S. 621 (1939); *People ex rel. Fish v. Sandstrom*, 279 N.Y. 523, 18 N.E. 2d 840 (1939); *Johnson v. Deerfield*, 25 F. Supp. 918 (D. Mass. 1939), *affirmed per curiam*, 306 U.S. 621 (1939).

23. See note 22 above.

24. 306 U.S. 621 (1939).

25. 310 U.S. 586 (1940).

26. *Gobitis v. Minersville School Dist.*, 21 F. Supp. 581 (E.D. Pa. 1937).

27. *Manwaring, supra*, note 1, at 91.

28. 21 F. Supp. at 584

29. *Gobitis v. Minerville School Dist.*, 24 F. Supp. 271 (E.D. Pa. 1938).

30. *Id.* at 274.

31. *Id.* at 275.

32. *Minersville School Dist. v. Gobitis*, 108 F. 2d 683 (3d Cir. 1939).

33. *Id.* at 684.

34. *Id.* at 685.

35. *Id.*

36. *Id.* at 689.

37. *Id.* at 691.

38. *Minersville School Dist. v. Gobitis*, 310 U.S. 586 (1940).

39. *Gobitis*, Respondents' Brief, reprinted in 37 *Landmark Briefs and Arguments of the Supreme Court of the United States: Constitutional Law* 367–412, Philip B. Kurland and Gerhard Casper, eds. (Washington, D.C.: University Publications of America, 1975).

40. *Gobitis*, Respondents' Brief at 9 (381 in *Landmark Briefs*).

41. *Gobitis*, Respondents' Brief.

42. See reprint of Rutherford's oral argument in Jehovah's Witness publication, *Consolation*, May 29, 1940 at 19.

43. See Merlo J. Pusey, 2 *Charles Evans Hughes* 728–29 (New York: Macmillan Co., 1951).

44. *Id.* at 729.

45. Alpheus T. Mason, *Harlan Fiske Stone: Pillar of the Law* 526 (New York: Viking Press, 1956).

46. *Minersville*, 310 U.S. at 592–93.

47. 310 U.S. 296 (1940).

48. *West Coast Hotel Co. v. Parrish*, 300 U.S. 379 (1937), *overruling, Adkins v. Children's Hospital*, 261 U.S. 525 (1923). See the 1923 losing brief of Professor Frankfurter, counsel for Adkins et al., the Minimum Wage Board, in which he failed to treat the original procedural meaning of due process of law.

49. *Ferguson v. Skrupa*, 372 U.S. 726, 730–32(1963). See John H. Ely, *Democracy and Distrust: A Theory of Judicial Review* 18 (Cambridge: Harvard University Press, 1980), demonstrating that "process" in 1791 was and today is a synonym for "procedure" and that substantive due process is an oxymoron.

50. 310 U.S. at 594.

51. *Id.* at 595.

52. *Id.* at 597.

53. *Id.* at 600.

54. *Meyer v. Nebraska*, 262 U.S. 390 (1923); *Pierce v. Society of Sisters*, 268 U.S. 510 (1925).

55. *Gobitis*, Brief of the Committee on the Bill of Rights of the American Bar Association, as Friends of the Court, reprinted in 37 *Landmark Briefs and Arguments of the Supreme Court of the United States: Constitutional Law* 453–504.

56. 310 U.S. at 601. See note 45, *supra,* and accompanying text.

57. 310 U.S. at 604.

58. *Id.* at 605.

59. See Manwaring, *Render unto Caesar, supra,* note 1 at 163–86.

60. *Id.* at 185.

61. *Cantwell,* 310 U.S. 296 (1940).

62. *Brown v. Skustad*, St. Louis, Minn. Dist. Ct. (unreported), noted in Manwaring, *Render unto Ceasar, supra,* note 1, at 193; *State v. Smith*, 155 Kan. 588, 127 P. 2d 518 (1942); *Bolling v. Superior Court,* 16 Wash. 2d 373, 133 P. 2d 803 (1943).

63. 316 U.S. 584 (1942).

64. *Id.* at 598, 608.

65. *Id.* at 623–24.

66. *Id.* at 624.

67. *Jones v. Opelika*, 319 U.S. 103 (1943).

68. *Murdock v. Pennsylvania,* 319 U.S. 105 (1943); *Martin v. Struthers*, 319 U.S. 141 (1943).

69. 319 U.S. 624 (1943).

70. *Barnette v. West Virginia State Board of Ed.,* 47 F. Supp. 251 (S.D. W. Va. 1942).

71. 319 U.S. 103 (1943).

72. 47 F. Supp. at 253.

73. *Id.* at 254.

74. *Id.* at 255.

75. 319 U.S. 624 (1943)

76. *Id.* at 639.

77. *Id.* at 630.

78. *Id.* at 637.

79. *Id.* at 638.

80. *Id.* at 641.

81. *Id.* at 639.

82. *Id.* at 639–40.

# 7

# Defining Freedom of Speech: The Flag Desecration Cases

The First Amendment prohibits Congress from "abridging freedom of speech, or of the press."[1] The Supreme Court has held that the Fourteenth Amendment incorporates these immunities against infringement by the state legislatures.[2] The definitions of speech and press in this constitutional context are technical legal definitions. The meaning of the phrases "freedom of speech" and "freedom of the press" must be determined as of 1791, because the changing use of English language over time is not a constitutionally approved method of amending the Constitution.[3] The key issue that the Supreme Court has avoided is the definition of "freedom of speech" as used in the First Congress.

The issue treated here is the judicial creation of symbolic speech from communicative physical conduct.[4] The Supreme Court in two 5-to-4 decisions in 1989 and 1990 held that the physical act of flag burning as a political protest is symbolic speech protected by the First Amendment.[5] The Court failed to treat the issue of whether flag burning is *sui generis* or one of a large class of communicative physical acts. In 1992, the Court held that the burning of a fiery cross in the yard of an African-American family was protected speech.[6] If symbolic speech includes a specific class of acts, the Court failed in these cases to explain the scope and characteristics of the class. The conclusion here returns to original meanings: that the protection of physical conduct was not part of freedom of speech as ratified in the Bill of Rights. But one must take care to recognize that other elements of the First Amendment do protect physical conduct, such as publishing, assembly of persons, and carrying on organized religion.

Speech is only one type of communication or expression; since it is a subset, speech should not be used as a synonym for the words "communication" or "expression." The First Amendment denotes speech and press as the two specific types of communication subject to restraint on Congress. This does not preclude technologies that utilize speech or new types of printing. Speech by radio or accompanying motion pictures or television is still speech.[7] Motion picture and video films are printed on tape for publication and are also protected under freedom of the press.

Language as a subset of communication is composed of signs and symbols that denote specific words, phrases, and sentences. Symbolic speech should denote only those symbols that serve as virtually exact linguistic equivalents. Thus Braille and Morse code and other methods of communication that have a one-to-one correlation with a letter, word, or phrase are symbolic speech or press.[8]

Freedom of speech as a legal term is much more limited than the layman's use of speech as a synonym for speaking. Freedom of speech is concerned with protecting a civil right to oral linguistic expression on all the issues that could come into controversy in a society.[9] While the primary concern of the First Congress was to protect political speech,[10] the concept must include all social, economic, scientific, mechanical, and artistic issues.[11] Controversies over the meaning of a play by Shakespeare or of a sculpture by Rodin may be of more importance to some persons than are the contests for elective office or whether Congress should enact a tariff.

The protection of the First Amendment applies only to the content of speech, the substantive expression of a viewpoint.[12] In contrast, the time, place, and manner of delivering a speech must be subject to reasonable regulation. No person may trespass on another's property in order to make a speech. No unelected citizen, for example, has the right to make a speech on the floor of Congress. As to time, public parks reserved for speeches may be closed at sundown. As to manner, public streets and parks reserved for quiet may be subject to valid public regulations barring sound-amplifying equipment.[13]

The historical context of the First Amendment reveals a set of absolute prohibitions on Congress.[14] Thus, the bar to abridging the content of speech makes it clear that "speech" in the legal sense did not include oral communication of criminal or civil wrongs. Perjury, solicitation to crime, inciting to riot, slander, fraud, oral noise found to constitute a nuisance, and pornographic expressions were not part of speech in its legal sense.[15] As Justice Oliver Wendell Holmes commented,

> the 1st Amendment, while prohibiting legislation against free speech as such, cannot have been, and obviously was not, intended to give immunity for every possible use of language. . . . We venture to believe that neither Hamilton or Madison, nor any other competent person then or later, ever supposed that to make criminal the counseling of murder within the jurisdiction of Congress would be an unconstitutional interference with free speech.[16]

The same principle applies to freedom of the press.

The confusion of some modern courts in labeling oral crimes or torts as a type of "speech" that may be subject to prosecution or civil action means they are using "speech" in a nonlegal sense, a synonym for speaking. This may cause some readers of court opinions mistakenly to believe that the prohibitions of the First Amendment, including freedom of speech, are not absolute concerning issues of content. It may lead courts to believe that they have to balance legal harms against the prohibitions of the First Amendment, as opposed to defining categories of speech and non-speech.[17]

The social context in which the Bill of Rights was adopted was one in which Americans asserted retention of all of their former rights as Englishmen against government and the enhancement of some of them.[18] The First Amendment was designed to bar Congress from abridging civil rights in four areas—speech, press, assembly, and religion. While it left potential regulation of these rights to the states, where most early Americans felt they had firm control on their legislators, the amendment absolutely barred national regulation. In the area of religion, for example, Puritans and Quakers, who had fled persecution in England, demanded that the national government be barred from abridging the free exercise of one's chosen faith.

The freedom of speech that the colonists brought from England was a narrow concept, namely, a parliamentary privilege.[19] The right of members of the House of Commons to speak without fear of retaliation by the Crown had been asserted since the reign of Queen Elizabeth and was incorporated in the Bill of Rights of 1689.[20] But this freedom of comment on the controversial issues of the society had not been extended to ordinary citizens.

The same right of freedom of speech was asserted by colonial legislatures, and after the revolution began, it was enacted in the Bills of Rights of some states.[21] This protection for legislators was adopted in Article I, Section 6, of the Constitution of the United States, which states for Senators and Representatives: "for any speech or debate in either House, they shall not be questioned in any other place."[22] It is thus clear that freedom of speech in the First Amendment was an extended civil right for all persons as against Congress, a great advance over the civil rights of Englishmen against the Crown.

In order to determine the meaning of the phrase "freedom of speech" in eighteenth-century America, one finds the colonists read the works of the English political writers in the Whig tradition.[23] Locke, Bolingbroke, Sidney, and Addison were among the prominent ones. But Gordon and Trenchard's *Cato's Letters* was the most popular, quotable, and esteemed source of political ideas in the colonial period.[24] In *Cato's Letters*, it is clearly explained that freedom of "speech," as there distinguished from freedom of the press, is concerned with verbal linguistic commentary on the controversial issues of the day.[25]

The resolutions and proposals for the Bill of Rights indicate that "speech" was limited to oral linguistic comment. Madison's resolution to the Congress on June 8, 1789, contained the follow proposed addition to Article 1, Section 9: "The people shall not be deprived or abridged of their right to speak, to write, or to publish their sentiments."[26] The House Committee Report of July 28, 1789, proposed the language, "The freedom of speech . . . shall not be infringed," and the House Resolution of August 24 used the same language.[27] On September 4, the Senate agreed to amend the language to "Congress shall make no law abridging freedom of speech."

The leading modern case distinguishing freedom of speech from physical conduct is *Giboney v. Empire Storage and Ice Co.*[28] An association of retail ice peddlers who drove their own trucks and had the legal characteristics of independent contractors formed a union and affiliated with the American Federation of Labor. The union persuaded all ice wholesalers except Empire not to sell ice to nonunion peddlers. Union picketing of Empire caused members of other unions not to cross picket lines, and Empire's business dropped by 85 percent. Empire, claiming the union activities were a violation of the state antitrust law, obtained an injunction against further picketing by the peddler's union. The Supreme Court unanimously affirmed. Justice Hugo Black, for the Court, held that the physical conduct of picketing was more than speech and could be regulated. The purpose of the picketing was to force Empire to become a party to an illegal combination in restraint of trade. The printed signs carried by pickets here did not give them First Amendment immunity from the state antitrust laws. "[I]t has never been deemed an abridgment of freedom of speech or press to make a course of conduct illegal merely because the conduct was in part initiated, evidenced, or carried out by means of language, either spoken, written or printed."[29]

In the two cases appealed under the title *Cox v. Louisiana*,[30] the Court upheld a state statute making it illegal to obstruct public passages or to picket in or near a courthouse. However, a conviction was reversed here, where the demonstrators were on a sidewalk across the street from the courthouse. Justice Arthur Goldberg noted that conduct mixed with speech may be regulated or prohibited.[31] In the case concerning obstructing public passages, he wrote, "We emphatically reject the notion urged by appellant that the First and Fourteenth Amendments afford the same kind of freedom to those who would communicate ideas by conduct such as patrolling, marching, and picketing on streets and highways, as these amendments afford to those who communicate by pure speech."[32] Justice Black, concurring, took a more categorical view that marching or picketing was conduct entirely outside the protection of the First Amendment.

In *Brown v. Louisiana*,[33] one year after *Cox*, the Court held that the conduct of African Americans who remained standing or sitting in a public library after being refused service constituted expression within the protection of the First Amendment:

> As this Court has repeatedly stated, these rights [of freedom of speech, assembly and petition] are not confined to verbal expression. They embrace appropriate types of action which certainly include the right in a peaceable and orderly manner to protest by silent and reproachful presence, in a place where the protestant has every right to be, the unconstitutional segregation of public facilities.[34]

Since the African Americans had been denied equal protection of the laws in violation of the Fourteenth Amendment, their continued presence in the library was merely part of their earlier valid verbal demand for equal service. The Court could have upheld their continued presence in the library as part of their right to equal protection that here overrode the state's breach-of-peace statute, rather than labeling their action symbolic speech under the First Amendment.

Cases combining speech plus physical conduct led to a two-level theory for First Amendment cases. The speech or press activities received the highest level of judicial protection, while the accompanying physical conduct was subjected to regulation.[35] This was followed by the development of the theory that physical acts could be classified as symbolic speech and receive the same protection as speech.[36] The cases relating to flag misuse and similar physical acts of protest are treated in the next section. The most striking recent case, unrelated to flags or protest, illustrates the extent of judicial mislabeling of purely physical conduct as symbolic speech. In *Barnes v. Glen Theatre, Inc.*,[37] the theater company brought an action for injunction to prevent Indiana from enforcing its public indecency law against nude dancers performing in its lounge. A state statute required the dancers to wear minimal cover, known in the theater as "pasties" and "G-strings." Since the statute applied to nudity, and the dancers could legally perform in an almost nude state with pasties and G-strings, the district court denied the injunction on the ground that the addition of nudity to erotic dancing was not "expressive activity protected by the Constitution of the United States."[38]

The court of appeals heard the case en banc and reversed the district court. It held that nonobscene nude dancing performed for entertainment is expression (speech) protected by the First Amendment and that the public indecency statute was an improper infringement because its purpose was to prevent the message of eroticism and sexuality conveyed by the dancers.[39] Ignoring the finding of fact by the trial judge, the majority in the court of appeals found an erotically significant difference between dancing wearing pasties plus G-string and dancing nude.

The Supreme Court reversed the court of appeals by a vote of 5-to-4, but eight of the nine justices held that nudity in dancing for entertainment was expression protected by the First Amendment, namely, symbolic speech. Chief Justice Rehnquist, writing for three members of the majority, held that the application of the Indiana statute to nude dancing had not violated the First Amendment even though such dancing was expressive conduct within the outer perimeters of the First Amendment.[40] The public indecency statute was clearly within the state's constitutional power, and the statute's purpose was to protect societal order and morality. The statute thus furthered a substantial governmental interest and was unrelated to the suppression of free expression.[41] Here the incidental restriction on First Amendment freedom by the minimal statutory requirement of pasties and G-string did not deprive the dance of whatever erotic message it conveyed. Lastly, the restriction was no greater than was essential to the furtherance of the governmental interest to bar nudity.

Only Justice Scalia, concurring in the reversal, found the public indecency statute to be a general law regulating physical conduct and not specifically directed at expression.[42] It was therefore not subject to First Amendment scrutiny at all. Noting the dissent of Judge Frank Easterbrook in the court of appeals, Scalia reiterated the fact that the state statute did not regulate dancing, but only public nudity. The statute was not concerned with messages of eroticism but with public decency, including the physical conduct of public nudity in all public places and circumstances. If the people of Indiana, through the legislative process, chose to adopt a moral bias against nudity into statute, it was not necessary to justify the statute by proving that some persons were offended by nudity. Scalia was the only justice to explore original definitions and note that the First Amendment explicitly protects freedom of speech and of the press—oral and written language—not "expressive conduct."[43] He then went on to try to explain his vote with the majorities in the flag-burning cases, where admittedly communicative physical conduct was held to violate the First Amendment.

## BACKGROUND CASES ON FLAG MISUSE AND PROTEST

One of the earliest sources of confusion over symbolic speech was *Stromberg v. California*.[44] This leading precedent that conduct could be speech concerned facts that should have been tried as an issue of freedom of the press. Defendant director of a Communist youth camp was convicted under California's red-flag law of leading the young campers in pledging allegiance to the red flag.[45] The statute made it a felony to display the red flag as a symbol of opposition to organized government, a stimulus to anarchistic action, or an aid to seditious propaganda. The Supreme Court, by a vote of 7 to 2, correctly reversed the conviction because the statute was vague and indefinite. But the briefs and the opinion of Justice Charles Evans Hughes erroneously center on freedom of speech while the facts relate to freedom of the press.[46] The red flag was a piece of red print cloth or cloth dyed to simulate red print. The closest analogy in the field of communications is the printed one-page handbill. There was no evidence here of incitement to anarchy or sedition. The peaceful political statement of the flag should have been recognized as protected content under freedom of the press. Instead, it is an oft-cited precedent for symbolic speech.[47]

The Supreme Court, without reference to the original technical legal meaning of "freedom of speech," has engaged in an uneven expansion of the concept of symbolic speech to cover communication by physical conduct. In *United States v. O'Brien*,[48] the Court upheld the conviction of the defendant for burning his draft card in violation of a federal statute making the destruction a crime. Chief Justice Earl Warren, for the Court, first held that the statute on its face did not abridge free speech. "We cannot accept the view that an apparently limitless variety of conduct can be labeled 'speech' whenever the person engaging in the conduct intends thereby to express an idea."[49] Having defined the category of this act as nonspeech, Warren equivocated. He stated that even on the assumption that the communicative element in O'Brien's conduct is sufficient to bring into play the First Amendment, it is not in this case protected. "[W]e think it clear that a government regulation is sufficiently justified if it is within the constitutional power of the Government; if it furthers an important or substantial governmental interest; if the governmental interest is unrelated to the suppression of free expression; and if the incidental restriction on alleged First Amendment freedom is not greater than essential to the furtherance of that interest."[50] The finding here was that all these requirements were met. This four-part test was to be adopted in a number of later cases on flag desecration.

Nine months later, the Court held that an act of physical conduct in protest of the Vietnam war was symbolic speech protected by the First Amendment. In *Tinker v. Des Moines Community School District*,[51] students had been suspended from school for wearing black armbands, and an action for injunction by the parents was dismissed by the district court.[52] The Supreme Court reversed the judgment by a vote of 7 to 2. Justice Abe Fortas, for the Court, held that this physical act was symbolic speech, and, absent actual or potential disruptive conduct, was closely akin to "pure speech."[53] Students, who would not be allowed any classroom time to make a verbal antiwar speech, had a constitutional right to engage in symbolic speech in all their classes. Justice Black dissented to this transfer of control of public school pupils from elected state officials to the Supreme Court.[54] Since this was not a regulation of the content of the asserted symbolic speech, the issue was the necessary reasonable regulation of the time, place, and manner of the "speech." Black concluded that the issue of whether this type of nonverbal expression detracted from the assigned learning of other students was one for decision by school officials.

In *Cohen v. California*, the defendant was convicted of disturbing the peace by offensive conduct in wearing a jacket bearing the words "Fuck the Draft" in the corridor of the courthouse.[55] The word "fuck" did not mean sexual intercourse in this context and was not obscenity, but it was found offensive to the public. There is no suggestion that there would have been prosecution if "fuck" had been replaced by "stop," "terminate," "repeal," or "evade." Hence, this was not a prosecution to stop the publication of the content, an antidraft message on a jacket. The brief for the State of California argued that Cohen had engaged in offensive conduct in violation of Section 415 of the California Penal Code and not in speech protected by the First Amendment.[56] Nevertheless, the U.S. Supreme Court reversed the conviction by a vote of 5 to 4.[57] Justice John Harlan, for the majority, held that Cohen's conviction for printing "Fuck" on his jacket, not being obscenity or fighting words, rested squarely upon his exercise of "freedom of speech."[58] The danger of censorship of content provoked the court to protect offensive language even though, in this case, a strong antidraft printing could have been effected without the offensive word.[59] Harlan wrote that the First Amendment also protects the emotive function of speech, including immoderate language. Justice Harry Blackmun, for the dissenters, began, "Cohen's absurd and immature antic, in my view, was mainly conduct and little speech."[60] He cited Justice Frank Murphy's earlier dictum that lewd and obscene words neither contributed to the expression of ideas nor possessed any "social value" in the search for truth.[61] It seems that Justices Harlan and Blackmun both mistakenly treated Cohen's conduct as at least in part "speech" when the only analogy of a printed notice on a jacket is to printed publications, which is questionable.

*Street v. New York,*[62] in 1969, was the first case concerning the illegality of flag burning. A New York law made it a misdemeanor to "publicly mutilate, deface, defile, or defy, trample upon, or cast contempt upon either by words or act" any flag of the United States.[63] Defendant African American heard the news report that James Meredith, the first African American to enroll at the University of Mississippi, had been shot by a sniper. He took his American flag to the street and set it on fire. He told a police officer, "We don't need no damn flag. . . . If they let that happen to Meredith we don't need an American flag."[64] Street was arrested and convicted for his words and conduct. The Supreme Court reversed the conviction by a vote of 5 to 4. Justice Harlan, for the majority, held that since there was no trial court opinion, defendant could have been convicted "merely for speaking defiant or contemptuous words about the American flag."[65] Harlan's opinion makes it a pure speech case and not about the physical conduct of flag burning.

The dissenters indicated that the majority had failed to reach the only issue in contest, the physical act of flag burning. Justice Black wrote: "It passes my belief that anything in the Federal Constitution bars a state from making the deliberate burning of the American flag an offense. It is immaterial to me that words are spoken in connection with the burning. It is the *burning* of the flag that the State has set its face against."[66] Justice Fortas, in dissent, indicated that flag burning was not *sui generis*. A state statute making it a misdemeanor to burn any item on the public street could not be asserted to violate a citizen's constitutional right if violated.[67]

The next year the New York Court of Appeals in *People v. Radich*[68] affirmed the conviction for the display of a sculpture that defiled the U.S. flag. Defendant publicly displayed the flag in the form of the male sexual organ, erect and protruding from the upright member of a cross; also in the form of a human body, hanging from a yellow noose; and again, wrapped around a bundle resting upon a two-wheeled vehicle, a gun caisson.[69] The court of appeals reiterated its view in the *Street* case that the statute was valid in relation to physical desecration of the flag. Regardless of the ideological views of the defendant, a reasonable man would consider the conduct here to dishonor the flag. The objective of the statute is not to limit freedom of speech or of the press to any person who wishes to protest governmental action. On appeal, an equally divided Supreme Court affirmed the judgment without opinion;[70] Justice Douglas took no part in the case

In *Smith v. Goguen,*[71] defendant had been convicted in a Massachusetts trial court for violating a state law that made it illegal to publicly treat the flag contemptuously.[72] His physical conduct was having a small American flag sewn to the seat of his pants. His petition in federal court for a writ of habeas corpus was granted, and this was affirmed in the Supreme Court by a vote of 6 to 3.[73] Justice Lewis Powell, for the majority, held the Massachusetts law invalid on the due process doctrine of vagueness. The legislature failed "to set reasonably clear guidelines for law enforcement officials and triers of fact in order to prevent 'arbitrary and discriminatory enforcement.'"[74] Justice Byron White disagreed on the issue of vagueness, but concurred in the judgment on the basis that a flag sewn to the seat of the pants was symbolic speech protected by the First Amendment.[75] Justice Harry Blackmun dissented on the ground that the state law protected only the physical integrity of the flag and that this conviction was for physical conduct.[76]

*Spence v. Washington*[77] concerned a conviction for violating the state statute that made it illegal to place any figure, mark, picture, or design upon any flag of the United States.[78] Defendant had hung an American flag upside down from his apartment window and attached a peace symbol to the flag in protest of the war in Vietnam and Cambodia. Defendant's conviction was affirmed in the Supreme Court of Washington.[79] The U.S. Supreme Court reversed the judgment by a vote of 6 to 3 on the basis that defendant's conduct was symbolic speech, citing *Stromberg v. California*[80] as a leading authority. The Court listed important factors: (1) the flag was privately owned by Spence, (2) the flag was displayed on private property, (3) there was no evidence of any risk of breach of the peace, and (4) Spence had engaged in a form of communication.[81] The Court held that there was no risk that Spence's acts would mislead viewers into assuming that the government endorsed his viewpoint since the display was a protest. Furthermore, Spence's acts had not significantly impaired any interest which the state might have in preserving the physical integrity of a privately owned flag.[82]

## TEXAS v. JOHNSON

The Supreme Court finally met the issue of physical conduct of burning of the flag in *Texas v. Johnson*.[83] The statute made it illegal for a person intentionally or knowingly to desecrate a public monument, burial place, or a flag. Desecrate was defined as "deface, damage, or otherwise physically mistreat in a way that the actor knows will seriously offend one or more persons likely to observe or discover his action."[84] In protest to the Republican National Convention in Dallas in 1984, Johnson unfurled the American flag, doused it with kerosene, and set it on fire. While the flag burned, his fellow protesters chanted, "America, the red, white, and blue, we spit on you."[85] Johnson was convicted of violating the statute, but his conviction was reversed by the Texas Court of Criminal Appeals on the ground that his conduct was symbolic speech protected by the First Amendment.[86] The Supreme court affirmed the dismissal by a vote of 5 to 4.

The brief for the State of Texas failed to make any argument on the original meaning of "speech" in the First Amendment that would establish that it had included only oral communication. Rather, it noted the recent cases that held nonverbal expression may constitute speech.[87] Thus, it admitted the existence of a balancing test to decide whether expressive conduct must give way to other 'societal interests. The brief then argued the right of the state to preserve the flag as a symbol of nationhood and national unity was a compelling state interest that superseded any First Amendment rights of individuals.[88] It also argued that Texas had a legitimate interest in preventing breaches of the peace that could result from flag desecration.[89]

Justice William Brennan, for the majority, observed that the "First Amendment literally forbids the abridgment only of 'speech.'"[90] But he noted that conduct may be sufficiently imbued with elements of communication to fall within the scope of the First and Fourteenth Amendments.[91] It was clear that the flag burning was expressive conduct of a political nature, and counsel for Texas conceded this fact. Having found that this flag burning was symbolic speech, Brennan held that the Court must decide whether Texas had asserted an interest in support of Johnson's conviction that was unrelated to the suppression of expression. As to the state's interest in preventing breaches of the peace, there had been no evidence at the trial that the protesters or those offended by their behavior breached the peace.[92] As to the state's interest in preserving the flag as a symbol of nationhood and national unity, this is directly related to suppression of free expression as protected by the First Amendment. Johnson's conduct would violate the statute only if it seriously offended others, and this condition demonstrates that the restriction in the statute is content based. Therefore, Brennan held that that the Court must subject the state's asserted interest in preserving the special symbolic character of the flag to the most exacting scruntiny.[93] Brennan cited a long list of past cases to support his conclusion: "If there is a bedrock principle underlying the First Amendment, it is that the government may not prohibit the expression of an idea simply because society finds the idea itself offensive and disagreeable."[94]

Throughout his opinion, Justice Brennan asserted that physical conduct can be symbolic speech. He adopted the previous assertion of this view in *Spence v. Washington,*[95] a case of wrongful display but not one brought under a flag desecration statute. Since the briefs of counsel did not attack the underlying assumption of symbolic speech, this judicial creation was automatically accepted as constitutional law. Brennan makes numerous references to *West Virginia State Board of Ed. v. Barnette,*[96] where Jehovah's Witness children refused to salute the flag and say a pledge of allegiance. Professor Louis Lusky, who helped Grenville Clark write the *amicus curiae* brief in *Barnette,* labels this attempt at analogy as "almost frivolous."[97] In *Barnette,* the children said and did nothing to dishonor the flag. They merely stood silent during the salute and pledge because of their deep religious convictions. Respectful silence is not analogous to flag burning. The *obiter dicta* of Justice Jackson in *Barnette* can not tie nonspeech to the judicial concept of symbolic speech.

Chief Justice William Rehnquist wrote the first dissent. He asserted that the public burning of the flag by Johnson was not an essential part of any exposition of ideas. Johnson was protected by law to make any verbal or printed denunciation of the flag he wanted.[98] Rehnquist quoted Justices Black and Fortas, dissenting in *Street v. New York,*[99] that this one limit on physical conduct is not a limit on speech. He quoted Justice Blackmun that the flag is a national monument subject to the same protection as other monuments.[100] Justice John Stevens, in his separate dissent, adopted the same theme, that expressive physical conduct is not speech. As to Johnson's burning of the flag, Stevens wrote:

> Had he chosen to spray-paint—or perhaps convey with a motion picture projector—his message of dissatisfaction on the facade of the Lincoln Memorial, there would be no question about the power of Government to prohibit his means of expression. The prohibition would be supported by the legitimate interest in preserving the quality of an important national asset. Though the asset at stake in this case is intangible, given its unique value, the same interest supports a prohibition on the desecration of the American flag.[101]

## UNITED STATES v. EICHMAN

The strong negative reaction of the public and in the Congress to the majority decision in *Texas v. Johnson* led to calls for action.[102] President Bush issued a call for constitutional amendment that received support from many members of Congress. Upon reflection, leaders of the House and Senate issued reports favoring a legislative solution.[103] The result was the Flag Protection Act of 1989.[104] Reflecting public sentiment, the final bill passed the Senate by a vote of 91 to 9 and passed the House by a vote of 371 to 43.[105] The key section of the act is an unqualified prohibition on physical flag desecration: "Whoever knowingly mutilates, defaces, physically defiles, burns, maintains on the floor or ground, or tramples upon any flag of the United States shall be fined under this title or imprisoned for not more than one year, or both."[106]

The background to the 1989 act was the fact that the Supreme Court had earlier held a Massachusetts law criminalizing the treatment of the flag contemptuously as invalid for vagueness.[107] Since the Federal Flag Desecration Act of 1968[108] was written in terms of "knowingly casting contempt" on the flag by acts of desecration, the call was for elimination of the limiting term, "casting contempt." In one of the few earlier convictions under the 1968 act, Justice Brennan wrote a dissent to a denial of *certiorari* and noted that "casting contempt" meant "espousing unpopular political views."[109] He viewed this conduct as establishing symbolic speech.

The second background fact was the state law in *Texas v. Johnson* that rested liability on the subjective reaction of the viewers of the desecration. The language of the Texas statute was "the actor knows will seriously offend one or more persons likely to observe or discover his action."[110] It was thus reasonable for Congress to draft a statute that unconditionally protected the physical integrity of the flag, language that avoided requiring contempt by the burner or serious offense by the viewer.

In *United States v. Eichman*,[111] the government appealed two cases under the Flag Protection Act of 1989 in which district courts had held prosecutions to violate the First Amendment. Both district judges found that the flag burnings in their cases were for the purpose of political protest and that they were thus bound to follow the rule of *Texas v. Johnson* and dismissed the prosecutions. The courts rejected the argument that an unqualified statute designed to protect the physical integrity of the flag for everyone's use and no one's destruction distinguished this case from *Johnson*. The finding was that the object was still to preserve the flag as a symbol of the nation and could not be content-neutral. Consequently, burning of the flag for political protest was protected symbolic speech.

The appeal brief for the United States by Solicitor General Kenneth W. Starr, like the brief in *Johnson*, failed to include an argument on the original meaning of "speech" in the First Amendment that would establish that it included only oral communication. Once the brief admits that some expressive conduct is protected speech, it has to argue that the Flag Protection Act is unique in guarding a national symbol.[112] The brief emphasizes Congress's considered legislative judgment that there is a compelling national interest in protecting the flag.[113] The brief misconstrues speech to include speaking civil and criminal wrongs in order to show exceptions to the First Amendment.[114] Slander and perjury are not types of speech, and neither is expressive conduct.

The Supreme Court affirmed the district court judgments by a vote of 5 to 4.[115] Justice Brennan, for the majority, began by noting that the government conceded that defendants' flag burning constituted expressive conduct.[116] As in *Johnson*, he rejected the government's claim that flag burning was in a special class like obscenity or "fighting words" that did not enjoy the full protection of the First Amendment. He also noted but failed to give weight to the fact that the flag was originally adopted as an incident of sovereignty to designate the nationality of ships and not as a symbol of patriotism or national unity.[117] As to the unqualified language of the statute designed to protect the physical integrity of the flag under all circumstances, Brennan concluded that it is nevertheless clear that the government's asserted interest is related to the suppression of free expression.[118] Defendants burned the flag because of its symbolic role. The broader language of the federal statute had the same flaw as the Texas statute in *Johnson*: It suppressed expression out of concern for its likely communicative impact.[119] The astonishing aspect of this case is that the political liberal Brennan was joined by the political conservative Antonin Scalia, who violated his own methodology of originalism in ignoring the 1791 meaning of speech as limited to oral communication.[120] This dramatically illustrates the statement in chapter 1 that 5-to-4 constitutional decisions in the Supreme Court have low epistemic value.

Justice Stevens, in dissent, did not emphasize the fact that flag burning is physical conduct, not speech.[121] Nor did he note that the flag was an incident of sovereignty that Congress had the constitutional power to protect by enacting a statute mandating unconditional respect for its physical integrity. Rather, Stevens emphasized a balancing approach. Was the prohibition unrelated to suppression of the ideas the "speaker" sought to express? Did the prohibition interfere with the "speaker's" ability to express ideas by other means? Was the "speaker's" complete freedom to chose other means less important than the societal interest supporting the prohibition?

Stevens concluded that the government should protect the symbolic value of the flag without regard to the specific content of the flag burner's accompanying speech. The importance of the national symbol to the society outweighs the importance of the individual in preferring flag burning as means of communication.[122]

## CONCLUSION

Rigor in the use of the English language is a first essential of fairness in the American system of separated governmental powers. Citizens act in reasonable reliance that language in the Constitution and in statutes will be interpreted by the judiciary either in its established technical meaning if such exists or, if nontechnical, in generally accepted usage. Freedom of speech, as an absolute prohibition on Congress to regulate the content of oral expressions of fact or opinion on the issues in contest in the society, was new technical language in the law. To the extent that the word "speech" was borrowed from the English parliamentary concept of free speech, it was clearly limited to oral expression. There is no evidence that in 1791 Americans used the word "speech" for any activity other than oral expression.

The judicial protection of symbolic speech in the latter part of the twentieth century and its application to purely physical conduct is a radical change in the meaning of constitutional language. Deficient appeals briefs by the opponents of this conversion of physical acts into "speech" must take part of the blame. Communicative physical conduct can take thousands of different forms. Flag burning, nude dancing, wearing armbands, and wearing yamulkas are only first examples. It is probable that every political and social interest group has a few extremist members who wish to engage in physical acts to attract attention to their causes. Vegetarians, Armenians, or environmentalists may engage in a misdemeanor to tape a black shroud around the Washington Monument at the ten-foot level and pass out handbills explaining their cause. The handbills are protected by freedom of the press. The demonstrators would argue that the black shroud, not damaging to the monument, is symbolic speech protected by the principle expounded by the Court in *Texas v. Johnson* and *United States v. Eichman.*

Nonlawyers are astounded that the Supreme Court labeled the physical act of flag desecration as a type of speech. Only lawyers, living in a world of artificial linguistic constructs, could conceive of such misuse of the English language. Some lawyers are highly paid to engage in word magic in order to win lawsuits. It is no wonder that the ultimate master of the English language, William Shakespeare, expressed a negative view of lawyers.

## NOTES

1. U.S. Const., Amend I.
2. *Gitlow v. New York,* 268 U.S. 652 (1925); *Fiske v. Kansas,* 274 U.S. 380 (1927). See Thomas I. Emerson, *The System of Freedom of Expression* 103 (New York: Random House, 1970).
3. As to the amending procedures, see U.S. Const., Art. V. On the requirement that the

interpretation must be contemporary with the document, see Joseph Story, 1 *Commentaries on the Constitution of the United States*, §405a-§407 (Boston: Hilliard-Gray, 1833).

4. See Thomas I. Emerson, *The System of Freedom of Expression, supra*, note 2 at 292–98; C. Edwin Baker, *Human Liberty and Freedom of Speech* 70–73 (New York: Oxford University Press, 1989).

5. *Texas v. Johnson*, 491 U.S. 397 (1989); *United States v. Eichman*, 496 U.S. 310 (1990).

6. *R.A.V. v. St. Paul*, 505U.S. 377(1992).

7. *Joseph Burstyn, Inc. v. Wilson*, 343 U.S. 495 (1952).

8. See Frederick Schauer, *Free Speech: A Philosophical Inquiry* 96 (Cambridge: Cambridge University Press, 1982).

9. See Hugo L. Black, *A Constitutional Faith* 45–47 (New York: Alfred A. Knopf, 1968); Alexander Meiklejohn, *The First Amendment Is an Absolute*, 1961 Sup. Ct. Rev. 245.

10. "There is practically universal agreement that a major purpose of the [First] Amendment was to protect the free discussion of governmental affairs." *Mills v. Alabama* 384 U.S. 214, 218 (1966). See Harry Wellington, *Freedom of Expression*, 88 Yale L.J. 1105, 1110–16 (1979); Francis Canavan, *Freedom of Speech and Press: For What Purpose?*, 16 Amer. J. Juris. 95 (1971).

11. Meiklejohn, *The First Amendment Is an Absolute, supra,* note 9 at 263 (quoting Harry Kalven Jr., *Metaphysics of the Law of Obscenity*, 1960 Sup. Ct. Rev. 1, 16).

12. See Harry Kalven, Jr., *A Worthy Tradition: Freedom of Speech in America*, 6–19 (New York: Harper & Row, 1988); Geoffrey R. Stone, *Restrictions of Speech Because of Its Content: The Peculiar Case of Subject Matter Restrictions*, 46 Univ. of Chi. L. Rev. 81 (1978).

13. *Kovacs v. Cooper*, 336 U.S. 77 (1949).

14. Meiklejohn, *The First Amendment Is an Absolute, supra,* note 9.

15. *Roth v. United States*, 354 U.S. 476, 483–85 (1957) (obscenity not speech); *Chaplinsky v. New Hampshire*, 315 U.S. 568, 571–72 (1942) ("fighting" words not speech). See Cass Sunstein, *Pornography and the First Amendment*, 1986 Duke L.J. 589, 615, n. 146.

16. *Frohwerk v. United States* , 249 U.S. 204, 206 (1919).

17. See argument for balancing in *Konigsberg v. State Bar*, 366 U.S. 36, 49–56 (1961) (Harlan, J.). See Rodney A. Smolla, *Free Speech in an Open Society* 39–42 (New York: Alfred A. Knopf, 1992); Kathleen M. Sullivan, *Post-Liberal Judging: The Roles of Categorization and Balancing*, 63 Univ. of Col. L. Rev. 293 (1992); Robert F. Nagel, *Liberals and Balancing*, 63 Univ. of Col. L. Rev. 319 (1992); T. Alexander Alienikoff, *Constitutional Law in the Age of Balancing*, 96 Yale L.J. 943 (1987).

18. See Forrest McDonald, *Novus Ordo Seclorum: The Intellectual Origins of the Constitution* 9–55 (Lawrence: University of Kansas Press, 1985).

19. J. E. Neale, The Commons' Privilege of Free Speech in Parliament, in *Tudor Studies* 257–86, ed. R. W. Seton-Watson (London: Longmans, Green & Co., 1924); Harold Hulme, *The Winning of Freedom of Speech by the House of Commons*, 61 Amer. Hist. Rev. 825–53 (1956).

20. 1 Will. and Mary, sess. 2, c.2 (1689).

21. Richard L Perry, ed., *Sources of Our Liberties* 135 , 149, 347, 377, 385 (Chicago: American Bar Foundation, 1952).

22. U.S. Const., Art. 1, Sec. 6 .

23. Clinton Rossiter, *Seedtime of the Republic* 141 (New York: Harcourt, Brace and Co., 1953).

24. *Id.*

25. See quotation in Leonard W. Levy, *Emergence of a Free Press* 110 (New York: Oxford University Press, 1985).

26. *4 Documentary History of the First Federal Congress of the United States 9*, Linda DePauw et al., eds. (Baltimore: Johns Hopkins University Press, 1986). This follows the language of the Constitution of Pennsylvania of August 16, 1776, which read "XII. That the people have a right to freedom of speech, and of writing, and publishing their sentiments." Perry, *Sources of Our Liberties, supra,* note 21 at 330.

27. *4 Documentary History of the First Federal Congress, supra,* note 26, at 28, 36.

28. 336 U.S. 490 (1949).

29. *Id.* at 502.

30. 379 U.S. 536 (1965) and 379 U.S. 559 (1965).

31. 379 U.S. at 563.

32. 379 U.S. 536, 555.

33. 383 U.S. 131 (1966).

34. *Id.* at 141–42.

35. "Picketing is free speech *plus.*" *Walker v. City of Birmingham*, 388 U.S. 307, 316 (1967).

36. See Melville B. Nimmer, *The Meaning of Symbolic Speech Under the First Amendment*, 29 U.C.L.A. L. Rev. 29 (1973); Note, *Symbolic Conduct* , 68 Colum. L. Rev. 1090 (1968).

37. 501 U.S. 560 (1991). See Vincent Blasi, *Six Conservatives in Search of the First Amendment: The Revealing Case of Nude Dancing*, 33 William and Mary L. Rev. 611 (1992). In *City of Erie v. Pap's A.M.*, 120 S. Ct. 1382 (2000), the Supreme Court upheld a similar general ordinance prohibiting public nudity in another case concerning nude dancers.

38. *Glen Theatre, Inc. v. Civil City of South Bend*, 695 F. Supp. 414, 419(N.D. Ind. 1988).

39. *Miller v. Civil City of South Bend*, 904 F. 2d 1081 (7th Cir. 1990).

40. *Schad v. Mount Ephriam*, 452 U.S. 61 (1981) (invalidating a borough ordinance that permitted adult motion picture theaters and bookstores but excluded live nude dancing from area zoned for business).

41. See the four-element test in *United States v. O'Brien*, 391 U.S. 367 (1968), quoted in *Barnes*, 501 U.S. at 567.

42. *Barnes*, 501 U.S. at 572.

43. *Id.* at 576.

44. 283 U.S. 359 (1931).

45. Cal. Penal Code, §403a (1919), reenacted as Cal. Military and Veterans Code §616 (1935) (West 1988).

46. 283 U.S. at 368–69.

47. See *Schneider v. Irvington*, 308 U.S. 147, 160 (1939). Justice Roberts, for the Court, upheld the right to distribute handbills. On one page he refers to "liberty of free speech" (p. 163), and on the next he refers to "freedom of the press" (p. 164).

48. 391 U.S. 367 (1968). See John Hart Ely, *Flag Desecration: A Case Study in the Roles of Categorization and Balancing in First Amendment Analysis*, 88 Harv. L. Rev. 1482 (1975).

49. 391 U. S. at 376.

50. *Id.* at 377.

51. 393 U.S. 503 (1969).

52. *Tinker v. Des Moines Community School Dist.*, 258 F. Supp. 971 (S.D. Iowa 1966).

53. 393 U.S. at 505.

54. *Id.* at 515.

55. The conviction was affirmed in *Cohen v. California*, 1 Cal. App. 3d 94, 81 Cal. Rptr. 503, 1969), citing *Cantwell v. Connecticut*, 310 U.S. 296, 308 (1940): "The offense known as breach of the peace embraces many varieties of conduct destroying or *menacing* public order and tranquility. It includes not only violent acts but acts and words *likely* to produce violence in others" (emphasis added).

56. *Cohen v. California*, 403 U.S. 15 (1971), Brief of Appellee 10, reprinted in 70 *Landmark Briefs and Arguments of the Supreme Court of the United States* 781 (1975).

57. *Cohen v. California*, 403 U.S. 15 (1971)

58. *Id.* at 19. See Kalven, *A Worthy Tradition, supra,* note 12, at 106–110.

59. 403 U.S. at 23–25.

60. *Id.* at 27. See critique of Robert F. Nagel, *Constitutional Cultures: The Mentality and Consequences of Judicial Review* 27–59 (Berkeley: University of California Press, 1989). "If judicial protection, as the chief mechanism for giving effective meaning to the first amendment, continuously creates that meaning by attempting to fit specific facts to grand theory, public sympathy for free speech will be jeopardized." *Id.* at 45–46.

61. *Chaplinsky v. New Hampshire*, 315 U.S. 568, 571–72 (1942). See Kalven, *A Worthy Tradition, supra,* note 12, at 78–80.

62. 394 U.S. 576 (1969).

63. N.Y. Penal Law §369–b (McKinney 1967) (current version in N.Y. Gen. Bus. Law §136) (McKinney 1989).

64. 394 U.S. at 579.

65. *Id.* at 581.

66. *Id.* at 610 (Black, J., dissenting).

67. *Id.* at 616–17 (Fortas, J., dissenting).

68. 26 N.Y. 2d 114, 257 N.E. 2d 30 (1970)

69. *Id.* at 31.

70. *Radich v. New York*, 401 U.S. 531 (1971).

71. 415 U.S. 566 (1974).

72. Mass. Gen. Laws Ann. ch. 264, §5 (West 1974).

73. *Goguen v. Smith*, 343 F. Supp. 161 (D. Mass. 1972), *affirmed*, 471 F.2d 88 (1st Cir. 1972), *affirmed*, 415 U.S. 566 (1974).

74. 415 U.S. at 573.

75. *Id.* at 584–89 (White, J., concurring in the judgment).

76. *Id.* at 591 (Blackmun, J., dissenting).

77. 418 U.S. 405 (1974) (*per curiam*).

78. Wash. Rev. Code Ann. §9.86020 (West 1988). This improper-use statute was separate and distinct from the state's flag desecration statute.

79. *State v. Spence*, 81 Wash. 2d 788, 506 P 2d 293 (1973).

80. 283 U.S. 359 (1931). See *supra,* notes 44 to 46 and accompanying text.

81. 418 U.S. at 408–09.

82. *Id.* at 415.

83. 491 U.S. 397 (1989). See Rodney A. Smolla, *Free Speech in an Open Society, supra,* note 17, at 73–95; Kent Greenwalt, *Fighting Words: Individuals, Communities and Liberties of Speech* 28–46 (Princeton: Princeton University Press, 1995).

84. Texas Penal Code Ann. §42.09 (West 1989).

85. *Johnson*, 491 U.S. at 399.

86. *Johnson v. State*, 755 SW 2d 92 (Tex .Crim. App. 1988).

87. *Texas v. Johnson*, 491 U.S. 397 (1989), Brief for State of Texas 12–19, reprinted in 190 *Landmark Briefs and Arguments of the Supreme Court of the United States* 456–63 (1990).

88. *Id.* at 463–74.

89. *Id.* at 475–81.

90. *Johnson*, 491 U.S. at 404.

91. *Id.* at 406, citing *Spence v. Washington*, 418 U.S. 405 (1974).

92. *Johnson*, 491 U.S. at 407–08.

93. *Id.* at 412.

94. *Id.* at 414.

95. 418 U.S. 405 (1974).

96. 319 U.S. 624.

97. Louis Lusky, *Our Nine Tribunes: The Supreme Court in Modern America* 64 (Westport, Conn.: Praeger, 1993). See dissent of Justice Stevens, 491 U.S. at 437.

98. *Johnson*, 491 U.S. at 430.

99. 394 U.S. 576, 609–17 (1969) (Black, J., White, J., and Fortas, J., dissenting), cited at 491 U.S. 433.

100. *Id.* at 434.

101. *Id.* at 438–39.

102. See, e.g., *A Fight for Old Glory: The Supreme Court Rules That Flag-Burning Is Not a Crime—Sparking Outrage Across the Nation*, Newsweek, July 3, 1989, at 18; Michelle Battle, *Poll: 69% Wanted Flag Protected*, USA Today, June 23, 1989, at 1A.

103. S. Rep. No. 101–152, 101st. Cong., 1st Sess. 4 (1989); H.R. Rep. 101–131, 101st Cong., 1st Sess. 2 (1989). See Charles Tiefer, *The Flag-Burning Controversy of 1989–1990: Congress' Valid Role in Constitutional Dialogue*, 29 Harv. J. on Legislation 357 (1992); Daniel H. Pollitt, *The Flag Burning Controversy: A Chronology*, 70 N.C.L. Rev. 553 (1992).

104. 103 Stat. 777(1989), 18 U.S.C. §700 (1997).

105. 135 Congressional Record 23420 (Senate) and 24180 (House) (1989).

106. 18 U.S.C. §700 (a)(1).

107. *Smith v. Goguen*, 415 U.S. 566 (1974).

108. 82 Stat. 291 (1968), 18 U.S.C. §700 (1976).

109. *Kime v. United States*, 459 U.S. 949, 954 (1982). See Frederick W. Bogdan, *Congressional Prohibition of Contemptuous Flag Burning Suppresses Constitutionally Protected Free Speech*, 40 Washington and Lee L. Rev. 1541 (1983).

110. Texas Penal Code Ann. §42.09 (1989).

111. 496 U.S. 310 (1990), affirming 731 F. Supp. 1123 (D.D.C. 1990) and *U.S. v. Haggerty* 731 F. Supp. 415 (W.D. Wash. 1990).

112. *United States v. Eichman*, 496 U.S. 310 (1990), Brief for the United States 26–27, Reprinted in 194 *Landmark Briefs and Arguments of the Supreme Court of the United States* 411–12 (1991).

113. *Id.* at 413–16.

114. *Id.* at 416–418.

115. *United States v. Eichman*, 496 U.S. 310 (1990).

116. *Id.* at 315.

117. *Id.* at 316. In affirming a conviction under the 1968 federal flag protection law, the court of appeals concluded "that the power to enact such legislation is an incident of sovereignty which inheres in the Government of the United States of America as a nation and which the Constitution recognizes and implements." *Joyce v. United States* 454 F. 2d 971, 985 (D.C. Cir. 1971), *cert. denied*, 405 U.S. 969 (1972).
118. 496 U.S. at 315.
119. *Id.* at 317.
120. See Antonin Scalia, *A Matter of Interpretation: Federal Courts and the Law* 37–47 (Princeton: Princeton University Press, 1997).
121. 496 U.S. at 319.
122. *Id.* at 322.

# Table of Cases

# Index

## ABOUT THE AUTHOR

MICHAEL CONANT is Professor Emeritus of Business Law in the graduate school at the University of California, Berkeley.

CPSIA information can be obtained
at www.ICGtesting.com
Printed in the USA
BVHW07*1052270918
528493BV00011B/63/P

9 780313 316692